THE
Westminster
Pulpit

VOLUME VI

THE
Westminster
Pulpit

VOLUME VI

The Preaching of
G. CAMPBELL MORGAN

WIPF & STOCK · Eugene, Oregon

Wipf and Stock Publishers
199 W 8th Ave, Suite 3
Eugene, OR 97401

The Westminster Pulpit vol. VI
The Preaching of G. Campbell Morgan
By Morgan, G. Campbell
Copyright©1954 by The Morgan Trust
ISBN 13: 978-1-60899-315-4
Publication date 1/15/2011
Previously published by Fleming H. Revell, Co., 1954

CONTENTS

CHAPTER		PAGE
I	THE COMING OF THE WORD	9
II	THE KING AT THE DOOR	23
III	UNDERSTANDING, OR BIT AND BRIDLE	36
IV	THE DIVINE WORKER	48
V	PARDON BY THE CROSS	61
VI	PURITY BY THE CROSS	75
VII	PEACE BY THE CROSS	86
VIII	POWER BY THE CROSS	100
IX	PROMISE AT THE CROSS	113
X	THE HOLY SPIRIT: THROUGH CHRIST, IN THE CHURCH, FOR THE WORLD	127
XI	JUBILATION IN DESOLATION	140
XII	THE FIRST MESSAGE OF JESUS	154
XIII	THE WORK OF FAITH	167
XIV	ETERNAL LIFE	181
XV	THE EXALTED CHRIST	192
XVI	LIFE THROUGH DEATH	206
XVII	FOLLOW ME	220
XVIII	GODLINESS AND GAIN	234
XIX	THE SECRETS OF REST	248
XX	WATCHING FOR SOULS	260
XXI	GOD'S THOUGHT OF THE KING	273

CHAPTER		PAGE
XXII	THE KING'S THOUGHT OF MAN	287
XXIII	THE RIGHTEOUSNESS WHICH EXCEEDS	300
XXIV	ETHICAL PERFECTION	314
XXV	THE SANCTIONS OF ORDINANCES	327
XXVI	PEACE AMONG MEN OF GOD'S PLEASURE	340

THE
Westminster
Pulpit

VOLUME VI

CHAPTER I

THE COMING OF THE WORD

Rejected or Received?

He came unto His own, and they that were His own received Him not. But as many as received Him, to them gave He the right to become children of God, even to them that believe on His name; which were born, not of blood, nor of the will of the flesh, nor of the will of man, but of God.

JOHN 1:11, 13.

PERHAPS ONE OF THE OUTSTANDING CHARACTERISTICS OF Scripture is the simplicity with which the sublimest things are stated. There are times when one wonders whether we have not allowed the simplicity of this statement to rob us of the sense of awe which ought to possess us in the presence of the truth which it declares. In some senses the whole fact of the mission of our Lord by way of incarnation and all related thereto is perfectly and finally declared.

In this paragraph we have the third stage of one declaration; and all that which has preceded it is necessary to the full understanding of the sublimity and grandeur of these words of our text.

This prologue of the gospel of John opens with what I

think I may without irreverence characterize as the most sublime and stupendous statement of the whole of the Divine library, "In the beginning was the Word, and the Word was with God, and the Word was God," a statement suddenly bringing us into the presence of matters that far transcend the possibility of human understanding, or interpretation. I venture to say in regard to this wonderful word at the opening of the gospel that one of the purposes of the Spirit in writing these sentences through John was to remind men that behind the fact of Christ are mysteries too sublime for their comprehension or final explanation, "In the beginning was the Word, and the Word was with God, and the Word was God." That is an eternal fact, and therefore spiritual; and it is forever beyond the perfect comprehension of the finite mind.

Then follows a great parenthesis, in which John describes for us facts growing out of the eternal. In the opening word we have the statement of eternal facts concerning our Lord and Master, and immediately following we have the statement of temporal facts, that is, facts related to time. Time is but a term of human and finite life. There is a sense in which it would be accurate to say that in the being of God time is not. "The same was in the beginning with God," and in those words we are carried far down from the sublime, stupendous height of the first verse; for this beginning is the beginning of Genesis, of creation. Yet we see the same Person present when the morning stars sang together and the sons of God shouted for joy in the presence of the wonder of primal creation.

The apostle continues, and declares that the One Who was there has continued through all the processes of that which He originally created; nothing has been created subsequently, or by any development, or by new intrusion of power, apart from this selfsame Person. Then he inclusively affirms that He is the fountain of all life, in the words "In Him was life." Life in man became light as it is in no other part of the creation. Nothing in creation apart from man has light in that sense. Nothing in creation looks back into the face of the Creator and is capable of knowing the Creator.

Coming still further down in the order of statement, the apostle tells us that this selfsame One, the Word, the Light, has ever been in the world, even though the world has not known Him.

Then, at last, having made these statements concerning the far-flung splendors of the age-abiding past, and concerning the mystic, mighty processes of all creation, he declares that He, the One from Whom all things came, "came unto His own." The whole tragedy of human sin, if we can but understand it, is packed into the next word, "They that were His own received Him not." The whole glory of infinite grace sings its anthem into the word immediately following, "As many as received Him, to them gave He the right to become children of God."

Now let us try to fix our attention on the last fact. Leaving behind us all the mystery and glory of the eternal fact that He was with God and was God, leaving behind us from this moment all the mystery and glory of the process of creation, and that through all time He was in the world though the world knew Him not, we come to that central fact of human history, that He came, and that He came to His own.

In order to have a clear understanding of the teaching, we need to distinguish carefully between the two phrases which in our versions and in our translations appear to be identical, "His own." The phrase is twice repeated, "He came unto *His own*, and they that were *His own* received Him not." As a matter of fact, there is a very clear distinction between these two phrases, as all those familiar with the Greek New Testament, or the Vulgate, where the difference has been most carefully maintained, will recognize. "He came unto *His own*"—there the word is neuter—"and they that were *His own*"—there the word is masculine—"received Him not." I draw attention to the distinction in order that we may see how inclusive and comprehensive a declaration that is. "He came unto His own"—there the reference is not to people but to place. There are those who suggest that this should read, He came unto His own *land*. Bishop Westcott suggests that it should read, "He came unto His own *home*." I feel that neither is quite final, or quite satisfactory. Perhaps I have no right to say this, because I cannot supply the word that seems to be necessary. "He came unto His own"; why not leave it there? Or perhaps we take it as having application to the Creation, His own creation.

"And they that were *His own* received Him not"; there the masculine form stands for people, and is most certainly used in reference to that peculiar and separated people in the midst of human history which had been created a people for the purposes of God in reaching the world, and witnessing to Himself; and ultimately for the coming of Messiah, Who should be the Saviour of the world, the One for Whom the salvation of Jacob and the calling back of Israel was too light a thing according to Isaiah, and Who should be set for the proclamation of salvation to the ends of the earth.

He came unto His own land, if you will, home if you will; or, in the larger sense which reveals the economy and purpose of God, to His own creation; and His own people—in the midst of His own creation, those to whom after the flesh He did belong, those who constituted God's elect people for the purpose of revelation and who had so disastrously failed—received Him not. He came, the Messiah, Shiloh, the Branch, infinitely more than any prophet had dreamed or known. He came descended from David, according to Jewish genealogy, to exercise His ministry among His own, these people chosen for the purposes of the Divine economy. He spoke in the Jewish synagogues, He referred to the children's bread being given to the dogs; and He lived in the midst of degeneration, and in circumstances of limitation, but in perfect harmony with God in His own life. With what result? "His own received Him not." They tried to entangle Him in His talk, and His very own, the men of Nazareth, would fain have thrust Him headlong down the hill and destroyed him; and, at last, to make the whole tragedy brief in reverent statement, they delivered Him to Roman rule, and clamored for His blood. The end, on the human side, of that which we celebrate to-day, the coming into human history of the Child Who lay in a manger, was the Cross.

I know the difficulty and imperfection of that survey. No man in this house is more conscious of it than I am. The infinite past—to us past, but to God ever present—the beginning; and the word suggests our limitation, for there is no beginning with Him and no end; but therein the infinite mystery of the Person. Then creation, the stars singing, or if we did but dare to translate the Hebrew literally and accurately, the stars vibrating, and the angels singing, and presiding over all the mystic, majestic processes, this same Person. At last, because of human failure, and human sin, He came in circumstances of such lowliness that you may tell the whole tragedy of His human life in brief, brutal chapters. Chapter one, No room in the inn! Chapter two, The foxes have holes and the birds have nests, but the Son of Man hath not where to lay His head! Chapter three, Crucify Him! Chapter four, A borrowed grave in a rich man's garden! If we could come to these things as we ought, and see them as they are, in the light of all the infinite glory with which John's gospel opens, then we should know what sin is, and how far humanity has sunk, and how profound and appalling is the ruin of human nature. "He came unto His own, and they that were His own received Him not."

Was His coming, then, a failure? Were all those years of toil for nought? Was that unveiling of Light, by its veiling, of no avail? Let us go again reverently to the culmination of it all, and behold the Man, despised, rejected, bruised, dead! "His own received Him not!"

But there were some who received Him. There were some who believed in His name. There were those who turned and followed Him imperfectly, but they followed; falteringly, but they followed; unworthily, but they followed! What of them? "To them gave He the right to become children of God." Some of us this morning meditated the anthem of the angels over the new race,

> Glory to God in the highest,
> And on earth peace among men in whom He is well pleased,

that is, among the children of God who result from the presence in the world of this One, those who have the new life. Again, above the glory of the declaration of His coming, and the tragedy of the story of human refusal, we listen to the gospel. Here it is, singing to us even out of the wonders of John's prologue, "As many as received Him, to them gave He the right to become children of God." Let us endeavor to understand this better by considering the privileges and responsibilities of children.

What are the privileges of children? Is my word the best one here? I hardly think so in relation to the first fact, for something deeper than privilege is the first note. Children are such as partake of their father's nature. That is the infinite, profound mystery of the thing resulting from the coming of our Lord. He gave men the right to become children of God. He made those to whom He gave that right, partakers—and do not be afraid of the word, it is Peter's word in his letter—partakers of the Divine nature. Adoption is a word of the New Testament, a great and gracious word, but it is not exhaustive if we attempt to interpret it by what we know of adoption. In very love you may adopt a child which is not your own, you may give it all the things it would have had, had it been your own child; but you cannot give it your nature. So far as that is true, your adoption fails to describe the new relation resulting when a man receives the rejected Saviour, which is that He gives that one the right, not *to call himself*, but to *become*, a child of God.

Let us think of this. Are you a child of God? Then already you are a partaker of His nature. I state it so because it is an amazing declaration. Sometimes the heart is tempted to be fearful and afraid in the presence of such revelations or statements of Scripture because we are so conscious of being unlike God. Think again, and always think patiently of your own life as a believer, with God's patience. What is the Divine nature? It is essentially love. It is therefore holiness. It is also infinite wisdom. Every child of God partakes of these facts of the Divine nature. Every child of God becomes in measure love-centered, in measure holy, in measure wise with the wisdom of eternity. First the blade, then the ear, then the full corn in the ear. Let that principle be remembered by all such as tremble in the presence of the great revelation.

Think again. A man who becomes a son of God, a woman who becomes a daughter of God; men and women who become children of God, immediately share His nature of love. Here is something that has often been pointed out, and it cannot be too often repeated. The first movement of the communicated life of the nature of God to the soul of a human being is a love movement; the first true consciousness of the Divine nature in the soul of a man is one that negatives self and reaches out in strong desire to help another. Children of God, sharers of the Divine nature, primarily, fundamentally, are men and women first of all in whom love becomes the central fact.

It is equally true that the child of God has as desire, as impulse, as the central inspiration, a passion for holiness; but, oh, how we fail, how we sin, those of us who bear His name! But God understands—and it is true—that we do not want to sin. That is the life of God within us, the holy seed that cannot sin, that within us which is against sin. In all the complexity of our personalities that is the deepest thing. We sin against it, violate it, wander into bypaths; but that passion for holiness, the strong, urgent desire after purity, is the sharing of the Divine nature, and it is the result of having become a child of God, because we have received the rejected Christ.

We share also the wisdom of God. This I need not stay to argue, but I ask you to remember it in this way: the moment a man shares His life, becomes a son of God, in that very moment he knows things which before he did not know, he has an absolute assurance and certainty of things which before he wondered about. That is why, if you are not a Christian man, you cannot understand the quietness and peace of the man who is a Christian. I do not say that the truly Christian man has no intellectual difficulty, no problem of the mind; but I do say that no argument can shake his confidence, or remove his trust. It is sharing the nature that brings new wisdom, new comprehension, new certainty.

The child is a partaker of the father's nature. The love of God becomes the central fact in the life of the child of God; His life creates the passion for holiness, and the wisdom of God is communicated to the soul, so that it enters into absolute assurance of things not seen and which never can be demonstrated by the processes of the logician, or be made certain by the argument of the senses. These are some of the first and fundamental values of this great word of John.

But children—and these are the implications of the text—are the recipients of the father's love and especial care. They are the special treasure of the Father, God's treasures. We have sometimes said that God condescends to take our name, "father," in order to teach us what He is. There is an element of truth in it; but I do not think that is the profoundest way to state the truth. I would rather say that God lent us His name, "Father," in order to teach us what we ought to be to our children. Yet it is perfectly fair to take the argument in the other way. If to-night, buffeted, bruised, storm-tossed, lonely man or woman, you want to know what your Father feels toward you, if you are a father or a mother, remember that your care for your child, your thought for your child, your patience with your child, your undying, unquenchable love for your child, all is but the faint shadow of God's love for you. He never forgets us, never abandons us, never gives us up.

Another implication is that children of God are heirs of their Father. That is stated explicitly in Scripture, heirs of God, and joint-heirs with Jesus Christ. All His treasures are ours and are at our disposal so far as we are able to use them. He has treasures He will not give us yet because we do not know their value or use, and therefore possession would but harm us. He withholds nothing from us which would be for our healing, helping, and happiness. He Who spared not His own Son but freely delivered Him up for us, shall He not with His Son freely give us all things? The world with its store of wonders untold is ours. We enter into the treasure-house of snow and ice, and all the wealth of creation. He Who was and is the Word, the Son of God, God the Son through Whom creation came, has brought us into the same relationship to His Father as He Himself is bearing, and we have entered into all the riches of God.

Again, children have a right to the Father's home. One does not often dwell on this fact, perhaps not enough. The saintly Rutherford said, We dwell too much in the wilderness, and lift our eyes too little to the city to which we go. It is good sometimes to enter the city, walk its streets in imagination, and examine the dwelling places, and become familiar with the habits of the home that lies beyond. His home is ours. Homeless the children of God can never be.

> A tent or a cottage, what need I care?
> They are building a palace for me over there.

He is preparing a place, but it is in one of the Father's many places, and all the home of God is ours.

Such privileges bring corresponding responsibilities. The first responsibility of the child to the father is that of the obedience of perfect love. Put it that way, think of it in that way. Think no longer of Him only as King, though King He is; think of Him no longer merely as Judge, though Judge He surely is; think no more of Him solely as Law-giver, though Law-giver He certainly is; but remember He is *Father*, and that interprets the government of the King, and explains the method of the Judge, and unlocks the secret of the law. Therefore, as His child, let me hasten in the way of His commandments and let the answer of my life be the obedience of my love.

We have another responsibility for a little while, not only that of the obedience of personal relationship, but that of the honor of His name and character in the presence of His enemies. As the son of a famous house will move out to the ends of the earth and never forget the name he bears, so surely we who bear His name, and share this nature, must remember that upon us depends the honor of the name we bear, as we move among the sons of men, as children of God.

Now hear this final word. "He gave *the right* to become children of God." The word suggests man's helplessness. The word reveals the fact that having come to His own and being rejected by His own, and being rejected of the whole world, all those who had rejected Him, by that very rejection had manifested the fact of their distance from God. The word, then, first implies man's utter helplessness. How far away man is from God!

The word next implies Christ's power to communicate. "To them gave He the right to become children of God." How? The next verse is the full and final answer to that inquiry, "which were begotten, not of blood nor of the will of the flesh, nor of the will of man, but of God." There we are face to face with the mystic, central miracle of Christianity, which defies all analysis and explains all Christian phenomena; that is the central thing, begotten of God, that which cannot be seen in its happening, but which is demonstrated by the results it produces. The rejected Son of God is received by that man, believed on by that man, and that man is there and then not by his own act or will, but by the answer of omnipotent power, begotten. That is the central secret. This right to become children of God is not merely sentimental; it is not merely a covenant made between two; it is a vital fact.

Some man listening to this word, meditating the word here in the sanctuary, will come to the hour of decision, will receive the Saviour, and even though there be no lightning flash, no roll of reverberating thunder, that man will be begotten, born again, touched in the inner deep mystery of His life with the life of God, changed in his very nature. This is the mystic miracle of Christianity, Christ's power to communicate life.

Wherein lies His power to communicate life? Not in the fact of His eternal nature. Not in the fact of His creative ability. But in the fact of His Cross! Let Him interpret Himself, and let Him do it through this gospel of John, "I lay down My life, that I may take it again. No one taketh it away from Me, but I lay it down of Myself." What for? To give it to the sheep, for that is the setting of this declaration, to communicate His very life to others.

What word shall I use? Suffer me this, it is very imperfect, but I know no perfect word, to *liberate* it through the mystery and tragedy of His death, that He might give it to men, and that they might share it, and come by the Cross and by the Cross alone into living union with Himself, and thus become children of God by virtue of the fact that they have His life, the life of the only begotten Son of God. He gave *them*, who were begotten, not of blood, nor of the will of man, but of the will of God, the right to become the children of God.

That implies our authority, nay, declares it, to be children of God. It is a right based on power, on life, on identification. Unless I share Christ's life I am not a Christian. Though I sing the songs, though I make a great profession, unless I share Christ's life, I am not a child of God.

What, then, is the final word of this meditation? What are the conditions on which a man, a member of the rebelling, refusing, sinning race may become a child of God? "As many as received Him, to them gave He the right to become children of God." Then, in order that there may be no mistake—I am thankful always for this interpretation—"even to them that believe on His name." Take the two phrases and use the one which helps you most, to receive Him, or to believe on His name. What is it to believe on His name? To receive Him. What is it to receive Him? To believe on His name. Avail yourself of that which helps you most, now at this moment. Receive Him, for He is rejected to-day. We sometimes read, If Christ came to Chicago—If Christ came to London. I do not like the suggestion, for it is false. He is in Chicago; He is in London. Yet let me borrow the idea for a brief moment. If He came what would London do with Him? London would not crucify Him in the way they did of old; but it would get rid of Him! Christ is rejected to-day. The human heart is still in enmity against God. Man is still fast bound in sin and nature's night, in spite of all his progress and intellectual advancement. Christ is rejected. We know it. There are whole circles of what we call cultured and refined society which, alas, and alas for the blasphemy of it, are celebrating Christmas who will have none of Christ. His very name is taboo, not to be mentioned! He is the rejected One.

Will you receive Him? Will you find room in your heart and life for the One for Whom there was no room in the inn of old? Will you crown Him Lord of your life? Will you yield all your being, bruised and battered and broken by your sin, incapable of finding God by your own wit and wisdom? Will you crown Him? Then to you He will give the right to become a child of God! And mark the spaciousness of it, whatever your theory may be, whatever your doctrine about sovereignty, elections, reprobations—all of which are true if you understand them—"*as many* as received Him!" Rich or poor, bond or free, black or white, these are incidental things that matter nothing; but a sharp dividing line is running through this audience tonight in the eyes of God between the man who has received Him and the man who has refused Him. Where are you? "As many as received Him, to them gave He the right to become children of God." If you passed into this place to-night, reverent, interested, but nothing more, will you now receive Him, believe on His name and all the name stands for? Will you give Him your life and let Him come into your life and master it? Then, when you pass from this building and walk the streets, you will be a child of God.

What is the application of all this? The first application is to the children of God. Let us answer by unqualified surrender. What is the application of this to those who are His, but are wandering away, backsliding, if I may use the word that we all know? It is this. He is waiting to receive you again. His word to you is, "I have somewhat against thee, that thou hast left thy first love." But this also, "Repent, and do the first works." Come back as you came at the beginning; and the word of gracious promise is, "I will heal all thy backsliding, and love thee freely."

The last word is to the man, the woman, young or old, in this house, who never yet has received Him. You have heard the Christmas bells again, and the Christmas carols, and you are entering into all the merriment of Christmas which may have in it much of blasphemy; but will you open the door of your heart and let Him in? Then He will keep Christmas with you, and you with Him, in the fellowship of the one life, He the Son of God, and you the child of God.

CHAPTER II

THE KING AT THE DOOR

Behold, I stand at the door and knock: if any man hear My voice and open the door, I will come in to him, and will sup with him, and he with Me.
REVELATION 3:20.

THE FIRST AND TRUE APPLICATION OF THESE WORDS IS AN application to the Christian Church; but, with a fine sense of appropriateness, the Christian consciousness has taken the principle involved, and made personal application of it. For while in the letter to the church at Laodicea these words spoken by the Lord outside the Church had application to that church and those within its doors, we do no violence to the principle involved, but indeed come to understand it more perfectly, when, in all simplicity, we listen to these words of Christ as addressed to the individual. The door at which He stood knocking was the door of the Church; yet it was to one man that He made His appeal. If we make our application to the Church we must remember that the call of Christ was to an individual within that church, and that the way back for the excluded Christ to fellowship with those who bore His name and wore His sign was through an individual life. Therefore, the two applications are not only permissible but important.

My principal purpose this evening is to make the second of these applications the personal one. Yet, standing as we do on the threshold of the new year, I feel that I cannot wholly pass over the first value of my text. I have no desire, neither have I the time at the present moment, to enter into any discussion of the application of the whole of these letters; but, taking them in all simplicity, we accept them as letters sent to seven churches then actually in existence; and, moreover, this church at Laodicea was certainly known to Paul, for his references to it in the letter to the Colossians are very striking. An examination of them in the light of this letter is interesting and valuable. The fact that arrests our attention is that here, so soon after the presence of the Lord in the world in the days of His flesh, was a church bearing His name, gathering together ostensibly for His worship, making its boast in its own sufficiency; while His estimate of it was that it was Christless, He was not in the midst, He was outside the door. I say that a picture such as that must cause pause to all of us who are united in church life. "He that hath an ear, let him hear what the Spirit saith to the churches."

To summarize, for I am going into no detail in this application, what is the picture of this church at Laodicea? It is that of an influential church without influence. We should have taken the church at its own estimate, and our Lord made perfectly clear what that estimate was, "Thou sayest, I am rich, and have gotten riches, and have need of nothing." That was the language of the Church. That was our Master's interpretation of the underlying thought of the Church concerning itself.

His estimate of the church was very different. "Thou art the wretched one, and miserable, and poor, and blind, and naked." That phrase, "the wretched one," really means burdened one. We often hear of churches being burdened with debt, but never of churches being burdened with wealth; but that was our Lord's estimate of this church. Therefore, in His view, it was pitiable, for such is the thought of the word "miserable," not that the church was conscious of its own misery; therein lay the profoundest tragedy of its condition, it was not miserable, but it was pitiable, in the old sense of the word "miserable" with which we are familiar in the liturgy of the Episcopal Church, "Have mercy upon us, *miserable* offenders," *pitiable* offenders as the thought really is. We "have need of nothing," said the church; but the Lord said, "Thou art . . . poor and blind and naked." A church without influence, wealthy but poor, satisfied but pitiable. I have no desire to do any other than thus to glance at the picture. As the minister of this church, in the midst of many of my own people, I make no application of it; I dare not, I do not know; but I confront the possibility that a church may bear the name of the Lord, may be perfectly satisfied with its own success and its own influence, may make its boast in the fact that it has now become wealthy and has need of nothing, while yet the Master is outside, declaring it to be pitiable, and poor, and blind, and naked. That is the background of condition.

Now hear His word to such a church, "Behold, I stand at the door and knock." He has not yet abandoned that church. If He is excluded from His own church He stands still near to that church. How near? At the very door, knocking and asking for what? For one man who will let Him in! And promising that if there be one man within the church who comes to consciousness of poverty, and misery, and blindness, and inefficiency, and if that man will admit the Master, He will pass in and set up the table of perfect fellowship with that man. If that should have happened at Laodicea, perhaps it did, I do not know; but suppose some one man opened the door and the Master crossed again the threshold and sat down with that man, what happened in that moment? That man excommunicated the church. We have often heard of a church excommunicating a man; it is possible for one spiritually minded man absolutely loyal to Jesus Christ to excommunicate a whole church.

I now pass to the personal and individual application of this simple and sublime word of Christ. In doing that I am anxious first of all to look at the One Who is speaking. "Behold, I stand at the door and knock." Who is this? Where shall I go for a description of Him in the New Testament? I will confine myself to the writings of John. We were looking at one of them on Sunday evening last, as we found it in the prologue to the gospel beginning with the stately words, "In the beginning was the Word, and the Word was with God, and the Word was God"—then omitting the parenthesis of the next twelve verses and catching up the statement at verse fourteen—"And the Word became flesh, and dwelt among us (and we beheld His glory, glory as of the only begotten from the Father), full of grace and truth." On that description I am not going back. That is the Person referred to here. In this book of Revelation the same One is described for us in symbolic language. In all the symbolism of that description of the One upon Whom John looked we have suggestions concerning His glory and His grace, which as we meditate upon them fill the heart with a sense of wonder and amazement in the presence of this Lord Christ of ours. The first word is an arresting word. "I turned to see the voice which spake with me. And having turned I saw seven golden candlesticks; and in the midst of the candlesticks one like unto *a son of man.*" Bear in mind—this is mechanical, but if you will ponder it, it may be helpful—that description occurs in the New Testament, in the gospel stories eighty-five times, eighty-three of which are occasions when Jesus used it concerning Himself. It was His favorite description for Himself, "the Son of man." I am not going to tarry with the significance of the word save in this one and simplest respect; it brings us face to face with the fact of the humanity of our Master, brings us face to face with the fact that the One upon Whom John looked in Patmos, was, whatever else He was and is—and other facts and forces of His being are symbolically suggested—He was of our own nature, a man of our humanity, the Son of man. Then we find the symbolism of character: the hair white as wool, suggestive according to Eastern symbolism of purity and age; the feet of brass, which burnt as though burnished in a furnace, suggestive of that procedure in judgment in invincible strength which had been spoken of by all the prophetic writings ere the coming of the Christ Himself; the voice as the sound of many waters, the concord of all the voices that had sounded ere His voice sounded, merging into one final truth all the divers portions that had been spoken to the fathers in times past by the prophets; or, briefly and inclusively, the infinite music of the full and perfect speech of God to men through His Son, the Son of man. This is but to touch upon some of the suggestive thoughts of the symbolism of the vision. It was this Person Who said, "Behold, I stand at the door and knock." As we think of the statements of the prologue to the Gospel, and of this symbolic description at the commencement of the Apocalypse, and merge them into one, and endeavor to realize all they suggest, let us remember, however hard it may be to understand it, that the declaration of the text is that the One Who stands at the door and knocks is the Creator, the King, the Lawgiver, the Judge; but He is the Redeemer also, for He says, "I was dead, and behold I am alive for ever more, and I have the keys of death and of hades."

Ere we listen to the word of the text, let us turn to the particular description with which this letter opens: "These things saith the Amen, the faithful and true witness, the beginning of the creation of God."

There is nothing more wonderful in these letters than the fitness of the description of Jesus at the commencement of each one to the peculiar need of the people to whom the message was sent. Here none of the symbolism of the description is employed. Here every word is mystic and awe-inspiring. "The Amen" is a title which by its very simplicity arrests the attention, and of which, when we inquire as to its meaning, we find the root signification is that of nursing, nurture, strengthening, establishment, so that the Amen reminds us that He is the essential, final Truth. It is exactly equivalent to the word which fell from the lips of our Lord when He said, "I am the Truth." Then He is "the faithful and true witness"; and while the Amen is the positive description, this is relative. He Who is the Amen, the essential truth, eternal truth, is, in His dealings with men, the faithful and true witness, not true alone but faithful also, not faithful merely but true also. The thing He will say will be the thing of truth, and He will say the thing of truth however it may burn.

Then the final title, so simple and yet so startling, which links this letter to Laodicea with the teaching of the letter to the Colossians, "the beginning of the creation of God."

Thus it is seen that Christ stands at the door of the Church, or at the door of the individual life, in all the essential grandeur and dignity of His own being, which is far beyond our comprehension; yet in order that we may understand, and be able to hear the knock at the door, and the accent of the voice, "the Amen, the faithful and true Witness, the beginning of the creation of God," is "the Son of Man." All these things are the commonplaces of our New Testament and of our understanding thereof. Yet I have taken time, of set purpose, to remind my own heart of them ere I turn to the consideration of this word of Jesus.

Now listen to the text, "Behold, I stand at the door and knock; if any man hear My voice and open the door, I will come in to him, and will sup with him, and he with Me." There are two things I shall ask you to notice. First, the attitude of Christ described; and, second, the responsibility resting on us in view of that attitude.

What is His attitude? First, He is the excluded One, excluded from heaven by Love, excluded from earth by hate, for "He came unto His own, and they that were His own received Him not." And if we think of the Church, think of Him excluded from the Church, neither by hate nor by love, but by luke-warmness, the tepid condition which is loathsome to the heart of this Christ of ours.

Now let us take this one thought about the Church and make application of it in the case of the individual. They did not know He was outside. They thought they were Christians. They named His name. They professed to believe His teaching. They had His institutions in their midst. They observed the ordinances of His commandment. They were a fully organized church. They did not know, did not dream that He was outside.

The peculiar individual application of this text, then, is not to the man who is openly and avowedly anti-Christian. I believe that at the door of that man's heart and life also Christ is knocking; but the peculiar application of this word of Christ must be to the man who is a Christian in name.

I pray you therefore to place the measurement of the picture of the Laodicean church on your own life, and find out whether in your case these things be so or not. How shall we do this? How shall we find out whether we individually are poor, pitiable, blind, naked, devoid of the essential Christian character? There is one test, very simple, but very suggestive, and very searching. How shall we detect the difference between the church with Christ in the midst and the church with His name in the midst, and Himself excluded? How shall we detect the difference between the man truly Christian and the man who names the name of Christ but is not Christian? What is the testing word, the discriminating thought? This is it, *lukewarm!* May I use another word, far more common, but perhaps more arresting, *tepid!*

That is a startling affirmation to make, yet I make it on the basis of this flaming revelation in the letter to Laodicea. "I would thou wert cold," and the word may be rightly translated frozen—"or hot," flaming, "so because thou art lukewarm, and neither hot nor cold"—are you not appalled by these words of Jesus?—"*I will spew thee out of My mouth.*" That is the test. Can you sing about the Cross without any tears? Can you talk about the holiness of God without any tremor? Are you lukewarm? Then it is more difficult for the Lord Christ to deal with you than with a frozen man. Is it not true? The most difficult congregation in the world to which to preach the gospel is the congregation that regularly listens to it and refuses to obey it! The one man it is hardest to bring into living relationship with Christ is the man who sits right there in front of the preacher sabbath by sabbath, and hears the message but never answers it; admires it, talks to his friend about it, and agrees as to the accuracy of it, but in the center of his own life does not obey it; that man is lukewarm, tepid! Know well that Christ is not within because thou dost only admire Him! Know this, Christ is outside if thou art only prepared to patronize Him. He is the excluded Christ. This is the first picture that my text suggests. Behold, I stand *outside*, and knock. I do not think there will ever be any hope of Christ finding His way into the central life of some of us, until God in His infinite mercy awakens us to the fact that He is not within, but outside!

But this is also the picture of Christ seeking admission. The first is the human side; it tells the story of your condition, many of you who are listening to me. I am not preaching about men and women who are not here, but to men and women who are here, so help me God! Let us hear what the picture suggests about Christ. If He is excluded He is asking to come in. It is so old a story that men do not believe it because they know it so well, and a man does not know how to preach it so as to arrest the attention of the men who know it. Oh that I could so say it that men would be startled by it and believe it; this Lord Christ wants room in your heart and life, notwithstanding the fact that you have excluded Him by your own will, notwithstanding the fact that you have insulted Him by your patronage and admiration while you have withheld your obedience. "Behold, I stand at the door and knock."

What does He want to do if He comes in? To give you gold instead of poverty, to provide you with the white raiment that the shame of your nakedness do not appear; with gentle fingers to do for you what He did for the blind man long ago, anoint your eyes with salve until the light shall stream on them and you shall see. He has described your condition, burdened, pitiable, poor, blind, naked; and He says "Behold, I stand at the door and knock," with wealth for thy poverty, with sight for thy blindness, with raiment for thy nakedness. Thy condition is not My will for thee, says the Lord Christ to this heart of mine; I fain would make thee wealthy with all My wealth; I fain would open thine eyes until thou canst see the vision that I see; I fain would clothe thee with the white raiment that is My very own.

What does He want to come in for? He wants you to be His host, He is asking your hospitality. He wants to be your Host, He desires to give you hospitality. Was there ever statement more perfect than this? "I will come in to him, and will sup with him, and he with Me"; I will be his guest, he shall spread the table for Me. I will be His Host and he shall sit at

My table. I do not suppose there is another figure in the New Testament quite so wonderful as that of a revelation of the Lord's purpose as He knocks at the door of the human heart. How can a man say a thing which in the very saying may be spoiled? Yet let me try! God is robbed of one of His own homes so long as He is excluded from the heart of a man; and that is not a piece of my imagination. I go back to the Old Testament and I find the truth. Let God speak by the lip of the ancient prophet, "Thus saith the high and lofty One that inhabiteth eternity, Whose name is Holy: I dwell in the high and holy place, with him also that is of a contrite and humble spirit." The dwelling places of God, eternity, and the heart of a man! Jesus says, I want to come in to My own home; I built it, furnished it, all the material is My handiwork; let Me in! Be My host, let Me come in and live there. Let Me be the Guest in My very own home, and then I will be Host as well. I will spread the table for thee!

He always wants hospitality. He is very homeless in London by comparison. Will you not make home for Him in your heart? No room for Him in the inn. Let Him in, that He may sup with thee. He is hungry for thy love. He is homeless until a man shall open his heart and let Him in. He shall be thy Host; yet not wholly at His own charges, for thou shalt be His host. And in that perfect fellowship, My heart —as though Christ should say—will find rest, and thy heart will find rest.

What is our responsibility? To admit Him, that is all!

That is all, did I say? It is a very old story, but it will help us now, the story of Holman Hunt's picture. When Hunt painted his great picture, "The Light of the World," the picture of this thorn-crowned King knocking at the door, a friend of his who saw it before the public exhibition said to him, "Hunt, you have made one mistake here." "What is that?" asked the artist. "There is no handle on the door."

Hunt looked at his friend and said, No, that is not a mistake; that is the door of the human heart, and *it must be opened from the inside.* "I stand at the door and knock." He desires to enter, but He will not force an entrance. I am responsible in this matter. If ultimately I should miss the way, I cannot put back the blame on God. I must open to admit Him. You may have heard His voice to-night in some whisper other than any word spoken by the preacher. You may have been conscious of the nearness to you of this Lord Christ; but He is still outside, until you swing your heart's door open and bid Him enter. Why do not men open the door? I would like to tell you another story. My dear friend, Mr. Collier, of Manchester, told me this story, and it made a very profound appeal to me; it is full of simplicity from the standpoint of the child, almost quaint and humorous, but it is a wonderful story. One night they were having a lantern service, and a working man was present with his boy by his side, looking at the pictures of the life of Jesus. When Holman Hunt's great picture was flashed on the screen, they were singing,

> Knocking, knocking, who is there?
> Waiting, waiting, oh, how fair!

and the boy gripped his father's hand and said, "Father, why don't they open the door?" The man said, "I don't know; s'pose they don't want to!" "No," said the boy, "it isn't that. I think I know why they don't; they all live at the back of the house!" Why don't you open the door? Because you are living at the back of the house? You have receded into the baser, meaner, things of your own life, and, living there, you do not hear the knocking at the front door! You have descended in life voluntarily to mean motives, intellectually to limited outlook, emotionally to unworthy passions. You are living at the back. But for this hour some of you have pressed from that back region in the front, and you have seen the light from the windows out of which you seldom look. God grant that you may have heard the knocking. Will you open?

I quoted two lines a moment ago from a hymn, and I am always sorry that the hymn ever appeared in that form. It is the mutilation of a great poem. Harriet Beecher Stowe wrote something far finer than those two or three verses. Let her poem make my appeal;

> Knocking, knocking, ever knocking!
> Who is there?
> 'Tis a pilgrim strange and kingly,
>   Never such was seen before.
> Ah, sweet soul, for such a wonder
>   Undo the door.
> No, that door is hard to open;
> Hinges rusty, latch is broken.
>   Bid Him go!
> Wherefore, with that knocking dreary,
> Scare the sleep from one so weary,
>   Say Him—No!
> Knocking, knocking, ever knocking?
> What! still there?
> Oh, sweet soul, but once behold Him,
> With the glory-crowned hair;
> And those eyes so strange and tender
>   Waiting there.
> Open, open, once behold Him—
>   Him so fair.
> Ah, that door! Why wilt Thou vex me,
> Coming over to perplex me?
> For the key is stiffly rusty,
> And the bolt is clogged and dusty;
> Many fingered ivy vine
> Seals it fast with twist and twine;
> Weeds of years and years before
> Choke the passage of that door.

THE KING AT THE DOOR

Knocking, knocking! What! still knocking?
What's the hour? The night is waning;
In my heart a drear complaining,
And a chilly, sad unrest!
Ah! His knocking! It disturbs me,
Scares my sleep with dreams unblest!
    Give me rest,
    Rest—ah, rest!

Rest, dear soul, He longs to give thee;
Thou hast only dreamed of pleasure,
Dreamed of gifts and golden treasure,
Dreamed of jewels in thy keeping,
Waked to weariness and weeping.
Open to thy soul's one Lover,
And thy night of dreams is over,
More than all thy faded dreaming!
Did she open? Doth she? Will she?
So, as wondering we behold,
Grows the picture to a sign
Pressed upon your soul and mine;
For in every heart that liveth
Is that strange, mysterious door—
Though forsaken and betangled,
Ivy-gnarled, and weed bejangled,
Dusty, rusty, and forgotten—
There the piercéd hand still knocketh,
And with ever-patient watching,
With the sad eyes true and tender,
With the glory-crowned hair,
Still thy God is waiting there.

CHAPTER III

UNDERSTANDING, OR BIT AND BRIDLE

Be ye not as the horse or as the mule, which have no understanding; whose trappings must be bit and bridle to hold them in, else they will not come near unto thee.
                                                    PSALM 32:9.

Be yet not foolish, but understand what the will of the Lord is.
                                                    EPHESIANS 5:17.

THE SIMILARITY BETWEEN THESE TWO TEXTS IS SELF-EVIdent. The Hebrew Psalmist, and the Christian Apostle say the same thing. The method of the former is illustrative and pictorial; that of the latter is more direct and interpretive. Each of these men, separated from each other by centuries, saw two ways of living. The one was described by the Hebrew Psalmist in the figure of the horse and the mule, which must be held in with bit and bridle. That same way was described by the Apostle in a word that really is vibrant with sarcasm —"foolish!" This word, being literally translated, means: having no mind. That is one way of life. The Psalmist describes the method to be adopted with that state of mindlessness; the Apostle simply refers to it. The other way of life is described by Psalmist and Apostle by words which we have translated by the same word "understanding." The Hebrew word translated "understanding" means to separate mentally; or, as to say, to distinguish. The Greek word translated "understanding" means to bring together or, as we say, to conclude.

The distinction between the two statements is that the first illustrates one method, while the second interprets the other method. So these texts complement each other while moving in the same realm and uttering the same injunction. The first declares what has to be done with the mindless horse or mule, or man. Such must be held in with bit and bridle. The second shows what the understanding mind takes hold of. It apprehends the will of the Lord.

In these injunctions a central idea of life is implicated, two methods of life are revealed, and in each case an appeal is made to choose the higher and the nobler. These, then, are the lines of our consideration.

We shall perhaps see the central idea of life most clearly by considering the illustration of the Hebrew Psalmist. What, then, are the functions of bit and bridle in the case of the horse and the mule? Let me say at once, and that for my own soul's comfort, that many of you may know a good deal more about horses and mules than I do. However, I am not proposing to deal with the characteristics of these animals, but rather to take the simplest things, which are perfectly patent to the ordinary person. In the case of horse and mule, the bit and the bridle mean, first, restraint, and second, realization under restraint. The restraint is preliminary, the realization is final. The restraint of bit and bridle is the indication to the will of the animal of the fact of a superior will. If the Psalmist said, and he did say, and that with inspired accuracy, that these animals have no understanding, he did not mean that they have no intelligence. Understanding is something far more than intelligence. Horses and mules have intelligence; they have emotion; they have will. These are the elements of human personality, but in a lower degree and yet very definitely, we find them in what we call the lower animals. No man knows anything about a horse who says that it has no intelligence. And that a mule has will none will deny who has attempted to manage one! The purpose of bit and bridle is to indicate to whatever there may be of intelligence in the animal that it has to do with a superior will.

Thus it becomes the method of compulsion by the superior will, that which keeps all the forces represented in the life of the animal near to the master and under control. That is what the Psalmist says: "Be ye not as the horse or as the mule, which have no understanding; whose trappings must be bit and bridle to hold them in else, they will not come near unto thee." The Revised Version has greatly helped us there. The text is somewhat obscure, but the Authorized rendering: "In order that they may not come near unto thee," is entirely misleading. We put bit and bridle on horse or mule in order to indicate to whatever intelligence they may have that they have to do with a superior will and in order to compel their will to yield to that superior will.

But there is a reason for such restraint; it is always in order to teach realization. In the horse and the mule there are forces of strength, of energy, of swiftness. The purpose of the bit and the bridle is that these forces may be controlled and exercised, that they may become useful, that they may realize something.

For the sake of illustration let us exercise our imaginations and put ourselves in the place of the mule—some of us have not far to travel. The first sense of bit and bridle is simply that of something curbing, hurting, checking, mastering. As to mules I do not know, but I do know that after a while a horse will come to know the very touch of your hand on the bridle. You have but to make your own peculiar movement of the bridle, and it will turn to the right or left, it will halt, trot, gallop, or canter, as you desire. By restraint you have realized its powers, and you have given to the animal itself the sense of power. By the imposition of your superior will, curbing, checking, reining, mastering, you have made its life useful.

Now, what are the implications of that very beautiful illustration from the old Hebrew who loved a horse and a mule I verily believe, or he never would have written this psalm? The first is that life is power, energy, force, having values beyond its mere being. If life be energy, power, force merely, having no value beyond being, then it does not need bit and bridle, it does not need control, it does not need method or direction. In that case, let us merely live. But when a religious singer of the long ago and an apostle of the Christian era charge us not to be mulish, implicated in the charge is the idea that life is power and energy and force, having values beyond being; in other words, that life is purposeful. No human life has come to its realization when it is simply lived. It comes to realization only when it is being lived for purpose.

Again, the figure implicates the truth that life lacks direction within itself for the realization of this purpose. It can exist, but it cannot achieve. The horse and the mule can live in the wilderness and the prairies, but they will not achieve. Lasso them, corral them, break them in, put the bit and the bridle on them; then they will achieve. The bit and the bridle are the means necessary to achievement. Man can live without any control external to himself. He can answer all the impulses of his own being, he can let them have full sway and run riot. He can live, but he cannot achieve. Unless the forces in his being are under some kind of controlling power that will direct and energize, life is nothing more than a putting forth of effort, which is without value.

And so, finally, this figure of the bit and the bridle

teaches us that life needs restraint in order to be realized, it needs impulse in order to achieve, and that such restraint and impulse come, not out of the forces of the life, but from without.

Now let us look at the two methods of life suggested. Neither of these methods is godless. The man who is entirely godless is not in view. Neither writer was thinking of such a man. The Hebrew Psalmist was singing for the people of God, and the whole point of his charge is its application to the people of God. He was appealing to those who had heard the voice of God saying to them:

I will instruct thee and teach thee in the way which thou shalt go; I will counsel thee with Mine eye upon thee.

It was that sense of the Divine relation to the soul, and the soul's relation to the Divine, which led him immediately to say what he did. Because of that, because God is pledged to your guidance, "Be ye not as the horse or as the mule, which have no understanding." So also when Paul wrote this injunction in the Ephesian letter, "Be not foolish." Therefore I say again that neither of these ways is godless. They rather reveal two methods of God with men; which method He adopts always depends on the man. Whether God shall adopt with me the method of the bit or the bridle, or the higher method, depends on me. But to that we will return in conclusion.

Now, what are these methods? The first is the method of compelling pressure; the second is the method of impelling motive. In the first we see life controlled by pressure from the outside; in the second, we see life impelled by the mystic motive of understanding, which is within. The first is the method of conflict; the second is the method of communion. Be not like the horse and the mule, which have no understanding, and must be kept under control with bit and bridle.

The necessity for getting near, and being under control, is admitted; but because there is no understanding, the bit and the bridle, the compelling pressure, the conflict ending in victory for the superior will, are necessary. Be not like that, said the Psalmist; have understanding. More bluntly, the Christian Apostle said, Be not foolish, but understand what the will of the Lord is. Get the deep profound inner secret of your life so related to God that you will understand by the communion of love rather than by conflict the restraint which is necessary for realization. We are offered the choice between the restraint of compelling pressure and the restraint of impelling motive, the restraint of bit and bridle and the restraint of understanding. Bit and bridle mean the fight between two wills, and ultimately the mastery of the weaker by the stronger. Bit and bridle are the symbols of intermediary methods, made necessary because the soul is not consciously near to God, because it has no understanding. Horse and mule must be held in with bit and bridle, for they have no understanding. They are not near to their master in spirit, in thought, in mind. They cannot help it. They are not to be pitied. But when a man is in that state he is to be pitied, nay, he is to be blamed. In the case of a man, the bit and the bridle mean God's employment of compelling pressure to force the will to higher purpose in harmony with His own will. God's method with most of us has had to be that of the bit and the bridle, of adverse circumstances, personal affliction, chastisement; and all because we have not been near enough to God to understand Him.

The method of understanding, the method of communion, the method of impelling motive, is the method, not of conflict between two wills, but of co-operation between the will of man and that which Paul, in another of his letters, so gloriously and adequately described as the good and acceptable and perfect will of God.

The method of understanding is based on the comprehension of these very facts concerning the Divine will, that it is good and acceptable and perfect. To understand the will of the Lord is to love the Lord. Understanding is infinitely more than knowing. It is the comprehension, not merely of what the Lord commands, but of why the Lord commands. Understanding does not mean that we always know immediately the reason of what the Lord commands, but we know the One Who commands so well as to be perfectly at rest, even when we cannot understand the immediate reason of the command. It is good, it is perfect, it is acceptable. If we would finally apprehend the meaning of the word "understand," we may remind ourselves of another great psalm in which the Singer declared: "Thou understandest my thought afar off." That is infinitely more than knowing it. God understands the thought, He knows the reason of it, the genesis of it, how it came to be. Understanding the will of the Lord is the response of the soul of man to God's understanding of the soul. God's understanding is ultimate and final and perfect, and there is no darkness in it. As the soul of man knows these things about God, that soul understands. What it does not know of God's immediate reason or purpose it does understand to be perfectly right, since it is His will. Is there any finer word in the language to express what friendship is than the word "understanding"? Leave all your acquaintances, and think in the narrow circle of your friends. I am not speaking disparagingly of acquaintances; they are very valuable. But no soul has many friends. Fasten your attention on one. The greatest thing you can say to that friend is, "You understand." That does not mean that your friend can explain to you the mystery of the thing you are thinking, but it does mean that your friend understands this mystic call of the soul. Understanding goes out beyond intelligence, beyond emotion, and beyond will. It is a spiritual apprehension. To understand what the will of the Lord is, is to apprehend His motive. It is not always to know what the motive is, but it is to know that the motive is mastered by His infinite and unfailing love.

Now we see why I read that passage in Isaiah for our lesson, which, in some senses, seems to have very little connection with the line of our meditation. I read it for its remarkable suggestions concerning Jesus. The prophet of the olden time, having climbed a great height, having dived into a great deep of understanding, described God's perfect Servant, and in that passage we see Him first as Man, and then immediately as God. The merging of the human and the divine is wonderfully indicated, and in both cases we have this thought of understanding. "He shall be quick of understanding in the fear of the Lord." That is the final glorious word about the Messiah in His ideal humanity. The Spirit of the Lord shall rest upon Him, the spirit of wisdom and understanding, the spirit of counsel and might, the spirit of knowledge and of the fear of the Lord. The Revisers have rendered it: "His delight shall be in the fear of the Lord." The Authorized Version had, and it was a better rendering: "He shall be quick of understanding." Sir George Adam Smith translated it: "He shall be keen of scent in the fear of the Lord." That is understanding! That is the story of the life of Jesus on the manward side, understanding. To my risen and glorified and exalted Lord I render apology for saying the thing I am going to say. There was no need for bit or bridle in the case of Jesus. No compelling circumstances crowded Him into obedience. He went through circumstances that were to His soul as the burning of fire, but not to compel His obedience. He was quick of understanding in the fear of the Lord.

The very next sentence in Isaiah reveals Him on the other side, as God dealing with man. He shall not judge after the sight of His eyes, neither reprove after the hearing of His ears; but He shall judge righteousness judgment. In other words, when the Messiah exercises the judgment of Deity His judgment is not based on the only things that human judgment can be based on; neither according to the seeing of the eye nor the hearing of the ear. His judgment shall be based on understanding, on perfect knowledge, and perfect sympathy. So the light of the great passage comes to help us. This is the higher way of life, understanding. He who understands, yields, not to the pressure of bit and bridle, but to the sweet constraint of the eternal love. Be ye not as the horse or as the mule, which have no understanding. Be not foolish, but understanding what the will of the Lord is.

Both texts make exactly the same appeal. That appeal is based on human capacity. That is the Biblical distinguishing conception of man. He is ever presented as capable of knowing, and of communing with God. Outside the Biblical revelation men have not yet reached that conclusion. They are approaching it. In the days of my youth the physical scientists were telling us that God was unknowable. Science is now beginning to admit that there may be the possibility of communication with a spirit world. That statement, however ignorant it is in some of its applications, is a step towards the ultimate truth that man is fashioned for having communion with God directly and immediately. That is the Biblical revelation. Think hurriedly of its outstanding figures. What are they? The first is that of a man in a garden. It is the story of Adam, the first man. What is the peculiar fact about him which the Bible insists on? That he could talk with God. What is the story of a man who came out from a great civilization that was entirely pagan and became the father and founder of a race that stands to this age in the world for the great monotheistic idea? It is the story of a man called Abram, who heard God speak, who was capable of communion with God. What is the story of a man who was a great lawgiver, and so great a lawgiver that his national code remains to this day the final court of high national morality? It is the story of a man, Moses, who spoke face to face with God as a man talks with his friend. What is the story of all those prophecies of Isaiah, Ezekiel, Jeremiah, Hosea, Amos, Habakkuk? They are all stories of men who heard God, who spoke to God, and in whose very bones the fire of the divine word burned.

Finally and centrally, there is the story of Jesus, and it is the story of a Man Who walked over dusty highways and over our fields, and in the midst of our temptations, enduring our toil, living by trust as we live by trust, but all the while talking with God. The Bible says to every man that he may know God and understand God. The highest function of the human soul is the function of adoration. That goes far out beyond intercession, is greater than thanksgiving, is far more magnificent even than praise which is uttered. It is the function of speechless consciousness of God. For that man is made.

The Biblical idea of man is that out of that exercise of adoration there shall come human inspiration for the carpenter's shop, the commonplaces of life, the doing of the next duty that comes, the taking of the next turning. That is the deepest meaning of Christianity.

The conception of Jesus concerning man is found in the words which John records for us in His final prayer, words perpetually quoted and never exhausted by quotation: "This is age abiding life, to know Thee, the only true God."

The letters of Paul's imprisonment, those to the Ephesians, the Colossians, and the Philippians, breathe his consuming passion that Christian people should come to the full knowledge of God. Again and again we find him expressing his thankfulness for their faith, their hope, their love; and when we read this we are inclined to say: What more could be needed? These people had faith and hope and love. Yet

Paul said: I am praying always earnestly for you. To what end? That you may come to the knowledge, *epignosis*, the full knowledge of God. And there is the Biblical conception. In man is the light of life. In his new birth that light is rekindled. First, it is daybreak; then it groweth more and more unto the perfect day; and so at last it becomes high noon in the life of the soul. If a man will walk by that light, if he will answer that light, he lives by understanding, and the bit and the bridle are not necessary.

The appeal of the text expresses a divine purpose, and the divine purpose fundamentally is that of restraining and realizing life; and the divine desire is that this shall be done by understanding. The divine love, however, says: If you will not walk in the light by understanding, then you must learn by bit and bridle.

So, finally, the appeal of the text offers a great alternative, revealing to the life two methods of God with the soul, urging the higher, that of understanding, but definitely declaring that if the higher is not answered, then God will employ the other, and that for very love.

Now are we saying we have indeed been foolish, we have been as the horse and as the mule, and so we know the bit and bridle? If so, and I speak not to you now, but with you, let us learn to yield to the bit and the bridle, and if we do, because God has created us as He has, we shall come to understanding. Is not that the more common experience of life? Am I not touching the realm of experience when I say that almost all of us pass into the realm of understanding by the way of the bit and the bridle? With the majority of us it has been bit and bridle.

The young I would urge to choose the understanding way at once. This urging comes from one who has known much of bit and bridle through his own folly, through his own lack of spiritual mindedness. Choose the way of understanding. Cultivate your fellowship with God. Make time for the secret place, for the quiet hour, for getting near to God without pressure, that you may know, that you may understand. For the doing of this the great Lord Christ, our Saviour and our King, is ever at our disposal. Take advantage of His comradeship. Watch the glance of the eye, listen to the sound of the voice, observe the activity of the hand. Such contemplation brings the soul nearer to God, to more accurate understanding, and so makes less necessary the bit and the bridle.

CHAPTER IV

THE DIVINE WORKER

Not by might, nor by power, but by My Spirit, saith the Lord of Hosts.

ZECHARIAH 4:6.

THE EARLIER PART OF THE PROPHETIC MINISTRY OF Zechariah was contemporary and co-operative with that of Hazzai. Its burden was that of inspiring the people in the rebuilding of the temple of God. In the book bearing his name there are five great messages, three of them according to internal dating were delivered during the building of the temple; the last two give no indication of the time of their delivery or writing. Of the first three messages the central one is apocalyptic. It consists of eight symbolic visions setting forth the history of Israel from the time of her trouble to the perfect restoration and realization of Divine purpose. The first of the visions was that of the shadowed places among the myrtle trees. The final vision was that of the chariots of might and of magnificence.

The text I have chosen is found in the fifth of these eight visions, that of the golden candlestick setting forth the ideal mission of the chosen people as light bearer to the world. There can be no doubt whatever that the first application of that vision is the prophecy that Israel must finally realize her mission in the world according to the purposes of Jehovah. As I understand this book, none of these visions has been fulfilled. The ancient people of God are still beneath the myrtle trees; they will not abide there; these visions must all be fulfilled.* With this first application of the vision and of the text I am not, however, concerned now. The great principles underlying the history of the ancient people are, for the time being, embodied in the Christian Church. I do not mean to suggest that Israel is forever and wholly cast off, or that in the Church of God are fulfilled all the prophecies spoken concerning God's ancient people Israel. But, broadly stated, it is true that the principle of the Divine government, the illustration of its meaning, the proclamation of its fact, and the propagation of its power, are all committed to the Church of God. Consequently, we do no wrong to the sacred text if we borrow the symbolism intended pre-eminently to show forth the responsibility and privilege of Israel, and make application of it in certain respects to the immediate responsibility of the Christian Church.

There are three things, then, to which I desire to draw your attention. First, the implied mission of the Church, that of scattering light over all the darkness of the world. Second, the refused methods in the economy of God, "Not by might, nor by power." Third, finally, and principally, the secret of fulfilment, "By My Spirit, saith Jehoval of hosts."

With regard to the implied mission of the Christian Church, let us glance at the suggestive and beautiful symbolism of this vision of Zechariah. Wakened as from slumber by the touch of an angel hand, the prophet was challenged as to what he saw, and replied that He saw a candlestick all of gold. We recognize immediately that this was a reference to something in the past economy of the people to which he

* Israel was proclaimed a Free State May 14, 1948.

belonged. Instinctively the mind is carried back to the sacred ritual of the Hebrew religion, through the temple which was then rebuilding, and the temple which had been destroyed, both of which were imperfect, faulty fulfilments of the Divine ideals of worship, to the tabernacle in the wilderness. A part of the central symbolism of that tabernacle was the golden candlestick, found not in the holy of holies, where were the ark and the mercy seat and the overshadowing cherubim, but in the holy place, where were the table of shewbread and, according to the ancient economy, the golden altar of incense. In that suggestive darkness was the great seven-branched candlestick, symbolic to the people who gathered around that holy place for worship of their own responsibility, perpetually suggesting that as the golden candlestick was the means by which the holy place was illuminated—for the holy of holies was illuminated not by the golden candlestick, but by the shekinah—so their responsibility in the world was that of shedding light abroad.

In the mystic book at the end of the New Testament, the writing of the Seer of Patmos, we find the visions of the seven churches unified by the presence in their midst of the living Lord Himself. Every church had as its symbol a golden candlestick, and the seven were unified by the fact that in the right hand of the Master were seven stars, the angels, the ministers of those churches—by that symbolism of light there was carried over into New Testament imagery the suggestiveness of the golden lamp in the holy place of the Hebrew religion. The scene of the revelation is a night scene. The churches are seen fulfilling their function of casting on the darkness of the days the light which is in them.

I go back to the vision of Zechariah, and I see the two olive trees and the oil; and I listen to the inquiry of the prophet, and to his honest confession that he did not understand the symbolism. The angel's answer was strange and mystic, yet surely clear, "This is the word of the Lord unto Zerubbabel, saying, Not by might, nor by power, but by My Spirit saith the Lord of hosts." Thus there is no need for human imagination or speculation; it is definitely stated that the oil supplying the golden lampstand, touched by fire and becoming light, symbolizes the supplying of the Spirit of God in order that the instrument may fulfil her function of illuminating the darkness and scattering light in the world. We remember again the sacred oil of the tabernacle. We remember again the stars in the right hand of the living Lord Who walked amid the churches; and, in this imagery of Zechariah, the sons of oil who stood one on each side of the lampstand, Zerubbabel and Joshua, the king and the priest; and we know how all that was therein symbolized, typified, prophesied, was fulfilled in Christ. We see in Him our Zerubbabel and Joshua, uniting in His own Person the two great offices of King and Priest, and by fulfilling their meaning, supplying to His people the Holy Spirit, that thereby they might fulfil their function of giving light to the world.

Moving a little away from the symbolism, or perhaps a little nearer to it to find its heart, the great truth suggested by the vision of Zechariah, by the golden lamp in the holy place, by the apocalyptic vision of Jesus Christ in the lampstand, the darkness, the light, is that the function of the Church of God may be inclusively and finally expressed thus: She exists to give light.

Have you ever noticed the first occurrence of the word "light" in the Bible? Have you ever noticed its last occurrence? It occurs first in the first chapter of Genesis; it is the word which ends the first Divine fiat, "Let there be *light*." Call to mind that vision of chaos, darkness, disorder, brooded over by the Spirit of God, then the Divine word, "Let there be light." That was the first word, not of creation, but of the restoration of a lost order, and it produced the dissipation of the darkness. The first thing, without which nothing else was possible, was light. The last occasion on which this word occurs in the Bible is in the Apocalypse, in the fifth verse of the last chapter, "There shall be night no more . . . for the Lord God shall give them light." That is the picture, not of the millennium, but of the great and gracious Kingdom of the Son which lies beyond the millennium. It is a picture of the Kingdom of God re-established on the earth. It is a picture of the hour when all human sorrow, sighing, and sinning will be forever ended. It is not a picture of the heaven that lies beyond, but of this world won back to its allegiance to God. It is the picture of that hour when in perfect light, the light of the presence of the Lord God amid the sons of men, all lamentation and all sorrow shall forever have passed away. Between that first fiat and that final word announcing the shining of the light in the earth and consequently in the whole universe, Israel was the light-bearer, Jesus was the light, the Church of God is the light-bearer. The service rendered to God by Israel, by the Lord Himself, and by His people, is that of supplying light by the shining of which chaos turns to cosmos, darkness into light, sin and shame and sorrow flee away, and the great Kingdom of our God comes.

Standing in the midst of human history nineteen centuries ago, this Lord and Master of the race, having emptied Himself of the essential glories of the perpetual manifestation of Deity, and taken upon Him the form of a servant, and being found in fashion as a man, in the midst of His ministry said, "I am the Light of the world." He also said to a handful of faulty, failing, feeble men, men of like passions with us, "Ye are the light of the world"; and He also said to them, "Tarry ye in the city, until ye be clothed with power from on high." Reverently to change the words of the Master that we may in the present hour of meditation understand His message, He said, You cannot be light save in the power of

THE DIVINE WORKER 53

the Holy Spirit; "Not by might, nor by power, but by My Spirit, saith the Lord of hosts."

That takes us immediately to those two words which reveal the refused methods, "Not by might, nor by power." The difference between might and power is not at first easy to determine. There is a difference, but it is very difficult to define it. There is a twofold suggestiveness. First as to the word "might": the Revised Version has as a marginal reading, "*not by an army*." While that is very valuable and helps us, I do not consider it is final. I presume the Revisers made the suggestion because the Hebrew word here translated "might" is more often translated "army" than in any other way. It means force, of men or of means. Sometimes it means an army, the embodiment of might. Sometimes it means wealth. Sometimes it means virtue in the ethical sense, and sometimes virtue in the sense of strength. Sometimes it means valor. Wherever we find it, it suggests resources: of an army, to fight our battles; of wealth, in order that the army may be maintained. All sorts of resources are suggested by this Hebrew word. For the purpose of carrying over what seems to be the special message here, I adopt that word, Not by resources. It is not translation, but I think it is fair interpretation.

Power means force, just as might means force, but never in the same collective massed sense. Power is persistent and purposeful force, as dynamic, strength, vigor. If I use for the first word, "resources," I would use for this word, "resoluteness"; and again this is not translation, but I think it may be accurate interpretation. "Not by might, nor by power"; Not by resources, not by resoluteness. These may be high, pure, mighty; but in so far as they are human they cannot accomplish the work of God in the world. By might and by power, by resources and resoluteness, we may be able to legislate for England; but we cannot build the Kingdom of God. By splendid resources and magnificent resoluteness we can do much upon a human level; but by these things we cannot shine as lights in the world or bring in the Kingdom of God.

Briefly, comprehensively then, this is the meaning of the passage: Not by anything man can do, can man do anything for God. We are very far from believing that. If I were asked to-day to give what I think to be the reason for the comparative failure of the Church of God in missionary enterprise, I would say that we are terribly in danger of imagining that by our own splendid resources and resoluteness we can accomplish the work, and of forgetting the superhuman factor, without which the work of God can never be accomplished.

That leads us at once to the very heart of this meditation, to the most sacred and solemn and strengthening thing in all the word of the prophet, "Not by might, nor by power, *but by My Spirit.*"

"Spirit," how well we know the word, and yet what vast significance there is within it which we have never grasped.

The first value of the word is its indefiniteness, the fact that it makes a suggestion to the mind that the mind can never finally comprehend. The Hebrew word, that wonderful word so constantly translated Spirit, *ruach,* really means invisible force, a force perfectly patent by the results it produces, but a force invisible, intangible, imponderable, which cannot be discovered by any method of the chemist or any cleverness of scientific investigation. The Greek word *pneuma* simply means wind, and is a figurative, poetic word. When Jesus said to Nicodemus, "The wind bloweth where it listeth," to illustrate the working of the Spirit, He employed the word for Spirit which is the same as wind. The Spirit bloweth where it listeth. Wind, we are perfectly sure of it; but no man knoweth whence it cometh or whither it goeth. Yet even that breaks down, it is only a figure of speech. You can weigh the wind, you can register the weight of it, the pressure to the square inch, and it immediately becomes material; but through the material sign there is suggested the great essential reality which is at the heart of the universe and permeates everything.

There is a special value in the qualifying pronoun, "My Spirit." The first occurrence of the phrase in the Bible is in the declaration, "My Spirit shall not strive with man for ever" that word which foretold the limit of the activity of mercy among the antediluvians. It is to be found occasionally in subsequent relations, until we come to the words of Isaiah, "Behold My servant . . . I have put My Spirit upon Him; He shall bring forth judgment to the Gentiles"; and again we find it in the book of Joel, "I will pour out My Spirit upon all flesh." At last we come to that flaming wonder wherein the Church of God was born, and then the great Apostle declared in the midst of the gift of tongues, "This is that which was spoken by the prophet Joel."

By that Spirit alone can men accomplish the work of God in the world. Not by our splendid resources; not by our resoluteness of purpose touched with the dynamic of persistent endeavor, not by anything that is human; but by that selfsame mystic Spirit of God, intangible, imponderable, invisible, but present and potent, "By My Spirit saith the Lord of hosts."

Said Jesus, "I am the Light of the world. He was born of the Spirit, baptized of the Spirit, led of the Spirit into the wilderness; He went in the power of the Spirit to proclaim the Kingdom of God; He offered Himself through the eternal Spirit unto God. Of Him, the meek and lowly, the Galilean peasant according to human measurement, the great central truth may be spoken: "Not by might, nor by power, but by My Spirit, saith Jehovah."

Said He to His own disciples, and through them to the whole Church to the end of the age, "Ye are the light of the world." They are born of the Spirit, baptized by the Spirit, sealed by the Spirit, anointed by the Spirit, filled with the Spirit. They speak with tongues as the Spirit gives them utterance. They receive gifts which equip them for service in the Spirit. They are a spiritual company, and the power which makes them able to shine as lights in the world is the power of the indwelling Spirit of God. "Not by might, nor by power, but by My Spirit, saith the Lord."

Now let us take this great essential truth so familiar to us all, which I have attempted to restate, and make application of it to the present time. *The Decisive Hour of Christian Missions* is the title which Dr. Mott has given to that wonderful little book which we have been studying together in our Missionary Study Circles. Its suggestiveness is full of solemnity. Dr. Mott, who has a right to speak on this matter, believes—and if I may venture to add my own conviction to his, he is absolutely correct—Dr. Mott believes that this is the decisive hour of Christian Missions. We have attempted here to consider that fact. What makes this the decisive hour of Christian Missions? The world's present unrest, the fact that God is saying to His people as never before, Now is the acceptable time; the activities of the Spirit of God everywhere manifest, the fact that the door is opened before the Christian Church to all peoples and nations as it never has been in the history of the two millenniums of the Christian Church. The Decisive Hour of Christian Missions!

What does the Church of God supremely need to remember at this moment? The truth embodied in my text, "Not by might, nor by power, but by My Spirit saith the Lord." Neither by our resources of intellect, of wealth, of enthusiasm; nor by our resoluteness of effort, of propaganda, of cleverness. All these things are necessary, but none of them, nor the whole of them, can do God's work in the world at this critical moment.

"By My Spirit": let us make this particular and immediate. The Church of God can operate in any country or among any people only when the Spirit of God has prepared the way for her coming. If you look back at the history of Christian missions you will find that to be true. Wherever the Christian missionary has come and his work has been successful, bringing men out of the thraldom of darkness into the liberty of light, that missionary has been conscious that the Spirit of God had been at work ere he came; the Spirit of God was at work in the measure of light which existed in the religion of the people before he came; the Spirit of God was at work in proving to these people by generations of failure the insufficiency of the light they had. The Master said to His disciples, "Look on the fields, that they are white already unto harvest." What did He mean? He spoke of Samaria, away from the Jewish covenant. If you had talked to the disciples they would have told you it was the most impossible, hopeless place wherein to proclaim the Kingdom of God. Did they not practically say so? Did they not ask permission to seek for fire from heaven to destroy the ungodly crowd? But that was not the view of their Master. Christ said the fields are white unto harvest, by which He intended to teach us that the fields which we look upon as most disappointing and barren, are white, we have only to reap; our work is not that of plowing or sowing, it is that of reaping. If we are to be successful in missionary work we are to go to a new country, to fresh territory, to unevangelized people, not imagining that we are going to do God's work, but that God has been ahead of us, and not by our might nor our power in this respect, but by His Spirit the work is to be done, and that we simply go, saying as the early apostles said, "We are witnesses of these things; and so is the Holy Ghost."

The Spirit of God must choose and appoint the workers. I have touched on that in this pulpit before. I am almost overwhelmed by the sense of the solemnity of this great truth, and the awful danger there is of forgetting it. Nothing is further from my heart than to discourage anything which is of God; but I do feel we are in danger of hurrying out young people whom God has not called. I think the peril of the Student Volunteer Movement is in that direction. I have often been asked at student meetings to appeal to young men to go to the foreign field, and I always absolutely decline to do so, lest by my might or my power, youth or maiden should be lured to this work uncalled by the Spirit of God. Do we imagine for a moment that our Lord did not understand the sacredness of this whole matter? Did He say to His disciples; "The harvest is plenteous but the laborers are few, hasten therefore through Galilee and Judæa and try to persuade men to do this work"? No, a thousand times no! He said, "Pray ye therefore the Lord of the harvest, that He send forth laborers into His harvest." Any man or woman who goes sent by a missionary board, persuaded by a Christian evangelist, or prophet, or apostle, uncalled by the Holy Ghost, is not only unable to help, but will hinder the progress of the work of God. "Not by might, nor by power, but by My Spirit saith the Lord."

We must also realize in this enterprise that it is the Spirit of God Who overrules occasions and events. We are to depend on Him; but we are also to act with Him. When the Church of God asks the aid of governments to protect her missionaries she is depending on the arm of flesh and is acting contrary to the genius and spirit of the Christian fact. It must be by the heroic, and yet perfectly safe, adventure, that trusts in the Spirit of God for the manipulation of difficulties and the bringing together of circumstances that the mighty work is done.

Finally, we must remember that in all our work it is the work of the Spirit of God to convict of sin, to turn the heart back again toward God; and when in response to His constraint men turn, it is His work to change the character and conform it to the image of His Son.

These things are not for the foreign field only, they are for us who are at home. What dire mistakes have I made in my own preaching because I have imagined that it was my business by argument and appeal to convict men of sin. "Not by might nor by power, but by My Spirit"; by being content to take what He has commissioned me to say, and to utter it, knowing that the thing He said is true, "My word shall not return unto Me void"; and to understand that the word becomes the seed of harvest only as the Spirit interprets its meaning, fertilizes its letter, until it becomes the germ of life in the soul of a man.

I think this great fact explains the solemn injunction of our Lord to His first disciples, to which I have already referred, "I send forth the promise of My Father upon you; but tarry ye in the city, until ye be clothed with power from on high."

I realize that there are certain senses in which that word has no application to us; but there are senses in which it has immediate application and is of paramount importance. The sense in which it has no application is that when He uttered this word the Holy Spirit was not yet given because Jesus was not yet glorified. These men had to wait until Pentecost for the power of the Spirit. Pentecost for us is not in the future, not in the past; *this is Pentecost*. The Spirit of God is here in all the gracious fulness and freedom and force which result from the accomplishment of the redeeming mission of the Son of God. I need wait no ten days for the equipment of power, or ten moments.

But the sense in which that word applies is that unless we have that power of the Spirit, then in God's name let us keep our hands off God's work and especially that most delicate, difficult, sacred work of the foreign field. Unless we know what it is to live the life of fellowship with the Lord in the Spirit, let us neither go nor give: "Tarry ye until ye be endued with power from on high." Let our going and our giving be in and by that Spirit, or let there be no going and no giving.

To my own soul the word is full of solemnity, reminding us as it does of the danger of depending on false strength and strange fire both collectively and individually. Yet the word is full of strength and hope, for that which Zechariah announced as the word of Jehovah to Zerubbabel, "Not by might, nor by power, but by My Spirit, saith the Lord of hosts," comes to us in this age with new meaning and more intimate values because of the fact to which I have referred, that the Spirit has been given in a new way, and new power is available for the doing of God's work. If we will, we may depend on Him and answer the world's woes with the message of His peace, co-operate with the Spirit in that activity in the midst of human life which is so patent at this hour, go through the doors the King has opened to claim the vast territories in His name.

Yet the last statement is this. The matter of supreme importance is that the superhuman factor, God the Holy Spirit, needs the human. Here is the infinite and appalling wonder: the Spirit by Whom alone the work is to be done cannot say the word of Christ finally to the people in darkness unless He can have my lips.

So let us not think of these missionary matters as though they were small and unimportant, or things we can take up as hobbies. We are in the realm of fire, of force, and of eternal things. May it be ours to recognize that only by His Spirit can the work be done, and that His Spirit can do the work only as we are at His disposal.

CHAPTER V

PARDON BY THE CROSS

Redemption through His blood, the forgiveness of our trespasses.
                                        EPHESIANS 1:7.

EVERYTHING A SINNING MAN NEEDS HE FINDS AT THE CROSS. Apart from the fact of human sin, the Cross is indeed foolishness, a veritable stumbling-block. To the Greek, seeking for the culture of uncultured man, "foolishness," something without meaning, a story that can have no moral effect. To the Hebrew, that is the degraded Hebrew, whose ideals are materialized, a stumbling-block, a *skandalon*, something that interferes with progress rather than helps it. And both are right, unless we see the background of sin that makes the Cross necessary, and the foreground of redemption that comes by the way of the Cross.

Unless there is some profounder meaning in the death of Jesus of Nazareth than the end of His life, then the Cross brings me into the realm of the greatest mystery, the deepest darkness, the most unfathomable wonder I have ever known. I will put this as superlatively as I feel, and as carefully as I may; unless there be some meaning in that Cross for others than the One dying on it, then the Cross makes me an unbeliever in the government of God. I cannot believe in the beneficence and goodness and righteousness of God if the Cross is nothing more than the ending of the life of Jesus. We speak of the problem of evil; it confronts us everywhere, but that Cross is the crux of it. If Incarnate Purity must be mauled to death by vile impurity, and God never interfere; if a life absolutely impulsed by love must be brutally murdered by devilish hatred, and God say nothing; and if that is all, then I decline to believe in the goodness of God. There must be some other explanation of the Cross if I am to be saved from infidelity. If in the life of Jesus the Cross was an accident, then the world is handed over to chaos, there is no throne, there is no government, and we are but puppets, and none knows the issue.

But to see the Cross in its relation to the fact of human sin, intelligently to appreciate what the New Testament teaches us concerning it, to see how the experience of nineteen hundred years verifies the doctrines of the New Testament in the lives of countless multitudes of men and women, is at the Cross to become, not an infidel, but a believer. Then at the Cross I see, not chaos, but the dawn of cosmos, not a darkness and an anarchy that appall me and fill me with despair, but a light and a government that make my heart sing amid the processes of a new creation, for I know by that sign amid the world's darkness that God is on the throne, and that at last He must win.

I want to speak of some of the blessings, the advantages, the values that have come to men, and still are at the disposal of men by the way of the Cross. I propose to begin with the very simplest, to begin in the line of experience, with Pardon. That is only the first thing. It is not the last thing, it is not the deepest thing, it is not that after which some of our hearts are supremely hungry. In my next sermon I shall speak of another value of the Cross. Purity. Then I will speak of Peace by the way of the Cross, and after that of Power by the way of the Cross, and, finally, of Promise

PARDON BY THE CROSS

by the way of the Cross. In all this series of studies I shall do no more than touch the fringe. Every day I need the Cross more, and can talk of it less glibly. Every day I live this Christian life I am more and more conscious that I cannot understand the mystery of all Jesus did; yet more and more conscious that by the way of that Cross, and that Cross alone, my wounded heart is healed, my withered soul is renewed, my deformed spirit is built up, my broken manhood is remade; and every day I live I sing in my heart with new meaning,

> Rock of Ages, cleft for me,
> Let me hide myself in Thee.
> Let the water and the blood
> From Thy riven side which flowed,
> Be of sin the double cure,
> Save from guilt and make me pure.

The first thing that a sinning man needs is pardon. The note of preaching may differ in the West from that of the East, but whether in West or East, North or South, amid high or low, rich or poor, bond or free, the first fact that attracts men to Christianity is the fact that it proclaims pardon for sin; and as a man begins to weigh his life by the infinite balances, and to measure it by the undying standards, the first consciousness that breaks in upon his spiritual conception is that he needs forgiveness.

In speaking of the work of Jesus, Paul declares that we have "our redemption through His blood, the forgiveness of our trespasses." "Our redemption," "our trespasses." The former is the foreground, and the latter, background of the Cross. We will begin with the background, "our trespasses."

The particular word here translated "sins" or "trespasses" is a word that signifies actual wrongdoing, and we are restricted this evening, not by my own choice, but by the very terms of the text, to that idea of sin, actual wrongdoing, wrong knowingly, wilfully, done. Sin as a principle we shall consider in a subsequent sermon.

The apostolic word in the epistle to the Romans, which is the foundation epistle of the gospel of the grace of God, declares that all have sinned. The Apostle does not say all are sinners. That is true. He will say that again, and in other ways; but he says "all have sinned." I need take no time to discuss the question of how it comes that all have sinned. I am not speaking of the fall of man, of the fall of the race. I will not now discuss the sins of such men as have never walked in the light of revelation. I speak of the actual sins of men who have broken law definitely, positively, wilfully. That is the aspect of sin with which my text deals. And before we can understand this subject we must go back to first principles. We do not begin to know what sin is until there is a recognition of the government and claim of God in every human life. Exile God from the moral government of His universe, and we shall no longer make our confession of sin or sins. Exile God from relationship to the moral, and then sin will be continuous abnormality, a perpetual infirmity, but it will never be trespass. We must first recognize the throne of God, and the government of God. If you question that honestly and sincerely, then you will not follow my text. We must first take for granted that every man and woman, each one of us, is an individual creation of God, and that for every human life there is a Divine plan, a Divine purpose, and a Divine place. We must come to understand that the purpose of God in every human life is the purpose of perfect love, not merely for the race as a whole, but for every individual constituting a part of the race. Therefore in the economy of God the race is imperfect in the imperfection of any individual, perfected only as every man, every individual, finds his or her place in the great whole, and contributes his or her share to the commonwealth of which God Himself is King. The race is suffering from break-up, and division, and spoliation. But why? Always because the units have broken law, fallen out of harmony, created the chaos. As a whole, the race has no great and immediate responsibility to God. Individual souls have, and so we come down from the race idea, and think of this fact, that if I would contribute my quota to the well-being of all, if I would fill my niche in the infinite purpose of the infinite Creator, the unifying Originator, and the ever-present Governor, I must find what is His will for me and obey it. That is the prime necessity in every human life. Human life is created by God and for God, and the first question of every human life ought to be, What is God's will for me? It is always a larger question than it seems. Find God's will for you, and you have helped to bring in God's will for the world. Walk in the way God has appointed for you, and keep His commandments, and you have made your contribution by so doing to His ultimate realization of the largest purpose of His infinite heart. I sin not only against myself when I break law, not only against God, but against the race. I postpone the golden age. I hinder the incoming of all for which my heart sighs in its holiest moments whenever I sin, for by the breaking of law on the part of the individual there is the postponement of the realization of the purposes of God for the race. Actual sin on my part therefore is not merely something that wrongs me and insults heaven. It is something that harms and injures and blights the race.

If this, indeed, be a fact, that the whole race is under the government of God, but is dependent for realization of His purpose on the obedience of the individual, then we have made one step toward understanding sin. Every human life, every individual life, is conditioned within law, and that law is simply the Divine revelation of the pathway along which the individual may move to fulfilment of personality, and so contribute to the realization of the largest purpose of God in the race.

Do we know anything of these things? We all do. You may never have phrased the thing as I have phrased it. You may have looked at it from the personal position, and never realized your relation to the whole race. But everyone is conscious of having met God, heard His voice, and disobeyed. And here is where some of you will challenge me. You will say, No, I have never met God. I have heard the voice of the preacher, I have read the statements of the Scriptures of the Christian, I have been made familiar with the ethic of Christianity, but I have never met God. Then let me state the case differently. Would you feel perfectly prepared to stand where I stand, and in face of this congregation of men and women, of like passions with yourself—would you be prepared to say, "I have never deliberately done wrong"? Has there never been a moment when you stood face to face with right and wrong, and chose wrong? There is not a man or woman that is honest but will admit the fact of personal wrongdoing. You say, "I was driven by the force of passion I have inherited." I have nothing to do with that now. You say, "The temptation was so subtle and strong I could not help it." I have nothing to do with that. I am asking you one question: Is there a trespass chargeable against you in the light of the infinite Order? For one single moment I will cease to speak of your relation to God, and ask you to speak of humanity as a whole. Have you sinned against your race? Has there not been one moment in your life when you knew truth, and lied; when you knew purity and descended to impurity; straightness and consented to crookedness? I need not labor the inquiry, for I take it I am speaking to those who are perfectly prepared, alone and in silence before God, to be honest; and if you are, though there is no terror in it to you yet, though you do not realize the tremendous meaning of what you have confessed, there is not one that will not have to say, "I also have sinned; I also have committed a trespass."

One step further. If you have submitted to this inquiry in simplicity, you have had to say more than once, "I have sinned." You have been compelled to say, "My sins as mountains rise." They may not have been the sins that society labels vulgar. The policeman's hand has never rested on you. You have not yet lost your character in the eyes of men. But you have descended to the low when the high flamed before you. You have chosen a pathway because it was easy, though you knew it was dishonorable, when the rough, rugged, heroic pathway was in front of you. We all have sinned.

Now I charge this home upon you—and not on you alone, beloved, but on my own heart, as we stand in the presence of this great fact. The moment I say I have sinned, in that very moment, solemn and awful as it is, in that very moment I have confessed that I have been guilty of something that I cannot undo, that I have put myself into relation with disorder, instead of order, that I have contributed to all over which I mourn as I look out abroad in the world to-day. In brief, I have said that I have done something that I cannot undo, and that I cannot forgive myself for doing, unless, perchance, by some mystery that is beyond me, it can be canceled, undone, made not to be.

Sin is not a small act. Sin is something which, once committed, cannot be undone. The broken law means a marring of the ultimate purpose. That is punishment beginning here, but not ending here, unless, by infinite grace, the sin is ended here. I am sometimes told that hell is here and now, and so it is. I am sometimes told that heaven is here and now, and so it is. Both are here and now; but when I am told that hell is here and now, if the deduction I am asked to make is that it is only here and now, by the same reasoning I must decide that heaven is only here and now. If heaven be a condition into which a man enters now, and more largely in the after-life, hell is a condition into which man enters now, and more largely in the after-life.

Hell, according to Scripture is failure, with all that it means in the consciousness and experience of man. Literal fire? No, a thousand times no, nothing so small; but the actual positive consciousness that I have failed, and have contributed to the failure of others. The fire is never quenched, and the worm never dies. The fire is no more physical than is the worm; but they are infinitely worse; they are spiritual, they are the natural outworking of sin. God's plan for man is the ultimate realization of high purpose in the spiritual places. I would not have it. I chose the wrong. I sinned. In that moment, by the irrevocable decree of my own will, I set my face toward the darkling void where God is alienated, toward the awful spaces in which there is neither fellowship nor light, but in which I, with an ever-burning capacity for the high, am doomed to the low I have chosen. That is the outworking of sin. That is the meaning of hell. And I sit, and glibly, quietly, say, Oh, yes, I sinned, I lied, I committed a theft, I dishonored some other human being. I sinned, but it is all right.

Man, it is all wrong! And, having once done the sin, it is not thy tears of repentance or prayer can atone. You cannot undo it. There it is in the past. Ten years ago, twenty— more for some of you—but you cannot undo it. Disorder in the universe, and you created it. No, no, not twenty years, not ten, but yesterday, *to-day*—with God's golden sunlight bathing all this Babel, prophetic of a great resurrection, you sinned under God's sunlight *to-day*. You cannot undo it. You cannot overtake it. You have started discord, and the infinite spaces are catching it up and multiplying it.

Sin is never little. Never talk of peccadilloes—hellish word for the excuse of the thing that aims at the dethronement of God and the spoilation of all His infinite plan. Oh, man, man! if you could but see your trespass, your little sin, in all its magnified meaning, you would cry out to-night, "What must I do to be saved?" "Our trespasses"—and sometimes one wishes only that one could persuade people to put into their prayer the tragedy that ought to be in it. In great congregations we pray, "Forgive us our trespasses," and there is the rustle of soft music about it. Oh, there is tragedy in it, there is ruin in it, there is hell in it. If you and I prayed that prayer as it ought to be prayed, it would escape us with a sob, and a wail, and a cry.

But, thank God, there is the foreground of my text! What is this thing that Paul writes? "Our redemption through His blood." Now again we must get down to the simple things if we would understand the larger things. "Through His blood." Whose? And it is the old, old story. I have no new Saviour to bring you—"Jesus of Nazareth, a Man approved of God among you by mighty works and wonders and signs, which God did by Him in the midst of you: . . . Him, being delivered up by the determinate counsel and foreknowledge of God, ye by the hand of lawless men did crucify and slay." So said Peter in his first Pentecostal sermon. "Jesus of Nazareth, a Man approved of God," the perfect One, the sinless One, the One Who never deviated from truth, or touched impurity, or committed theft, or chose the low, or consented to the dishonorable—the One Who never trespassed, Jesus, the perfect Man; and, if I am tempted to debate it, or discuss it, or defend it, I will resist the temptation. After all kinds of criticism, the ages have set their seal on the testimony of His own age, the testimony of a man in His own age: "I find no fault in Him"; the testimony of a devil in His own age: "I know Thee Who Thou art, the holy One of God"; the testimony of God in His own age: "Thou art My Son: in Thee I am well pleased." Every rolling century has made deeper the imprint of that great truth, that Jesus was the perfect Man.

But I am not redeemed by His perfection. His perfection may lure me to something higher. As I talked of trespasses —and I talked of mine as well as yours—suddenly there came passing in front of my vision the radiant Person of Jesus, so pure, so tender, so perfect, that neither man, nor devil, nor God could find fault with Him. I look at Him and I say: Oh, if I could be such as He! Oh, if from this hour, in this church, I could take this life of mine and live it like He lived His! I will follow Him; I will try; and back out of the years there come to me my trespasses, and suddenly my heart says, It cannot be. His life was perfect from cradle to Cross—no flaw, no deviation, no deflection; and if even from now I could live all the rest of my life perfectly, what am I to do with the scars and the spoiling of the past?

No, Jesus cannot save me by His perfection. Our redemption through His perfection? No. What, then? "Through His blood."

That phrase is not pleasant. It offends our sensibilities. Redemption through blood, and you shrink, you do not like it. You agree with the man who says that this is a religion of the shambles, and you object to it. God never meant that you should be pleased with that word, "blood." God reckoned blood so sacred as to say, "Whoso sheddeth man's blood, by man shall his blood be shed." It is not refined; it is vulgar, this shedding of blood! It shocks you, startles you, appalls you. God meant it should, and especially when you see Whose blood it is. Redeemed not with the blood of bulls and of goats—oh, soul of mine, how canst thou utter it?—but with the precious blood of the Son of God, the dying of the pure and spotless. What happened in that dying I cannot tell. I do not know the mystery. I cannot go into that darkness. Alone He trod the winepress. Alone He bore the pain. You and I must stand outside. Oh, behold Him, the Perfect dying, the Sinless suffering! God in Christ bent to bruising! And as I see the mystery of the human blood I say: What means it, for there is no place for such dying in such pure life?

And now the answer comes, and I dare not give it you in my own language. I will give it you in the language of Holy Scripture: "Behold the Lamb of God, which taketh away the sin of the world." "Who, His own self, bare our sins in His body upon the tree." "He was bruised for our iniquities: the chastisement of our peace was upon Him, and with His stripes we are healed." Oh, God, give us a vision of it! A small thing? Unutterably great! One lonely soul in the centuries! Are you puzzled and say, How can that be for the race? Behold Him! See Who that is! Put thy measurement, if thou canst, on the infinite value of His purity; plumb the depth of His holiness, climb the steep ascent of all that wondrous life, and know that this is God incarnate, and when the vision of it breaks upon you, and the stupendous wonder of it overwhelms you, then listen: "Our redemption through His blood"; and if you dare to take that blood away, you must forgive me if I am angry with you. You knock from underneath my feet the one rock foundation of my faith, you take from my bruised and broken heart its only solace. I come to the infinite mystery, and there, by that scene, by that token, by that unveiling of the Infinite passion and compassion, I know that the trespass I could not overtake is forgiven.

> The joyful news of sins forgiven,
> Of hell subdued, and peace with heaven.

You say, But you have not explained it. Again I say, I cannot, but I know it. I want to say one little word to you, dear man, honestly groping after some solution of this great mystery. If, somehow, you could persuade me that God could forgive my trespass, which was the breaking up of the order of the universe, simply out of pity, well, my heart could not rest in it. I could not forgive myself that way. I should always realize that the thing was there, that its issue could not be overtaken. How can I utter it, how can I tell it, when I see God in Christ stooping and catching that sin into His own heart, and bearing its pain, and exhausting its powers? Then, while the Cross shall ever fill me with grief on account of my sin, it fills me with joy that Christ has triumphed, and that "where sin abounded, grace did abound more exceedingly." The forgiveness of our trespasses can come to us only through His blood.

But, then, there are unforgiven men and women, and to such my final word shall be spoken. How may we obtain the forgiveness provided by the mystery of the Cross? First, I think there must be a sense of need:

> All the fitness He requireth
> Is to feel your need of Him.

And now there are those who feel their need. You say, Of course, I need it; I need forgiveness, I also am a sinner, I also have sinned. That is the first step toward obtaining. And what next? There must be a recognition on your part of the supremacy and sovereignty of God, and that I think is included in your confession of a sense of need. What next? Now there must be on your part repentance, the renunciation of the wrong, the spirit willing, if only the power be given you, to turn from the sin.

Dr. Pierson once gave me a great illustration on this subject. He told me of how in one of the Southern States a man lay condemned to die for having murdered another man; and a brother of the condemned murderer, who himself was a pure, strong man, and had laid the State under obligation to him, went and pleaded the cause of his condemned brother with the authorities, and though the case was one of clear murder, though there was no question about this, for the sake of the brother who had saved lives they consented to pardon the brother who had taken life. Then he went with the pardon of his condemned brother in his possession. He did not tell him immediately, but presently in talking to him he said to him, "If you had your pardon, supposing you had it now, and you were to go out free, what would you do?" And with a gleam of malice and hatred in his eye the murderer said, "I would find the principal witness and I would kill him, and I would kill the judge." And that brother said nothing of the pardon, but leaving the cell he tore it to pieces and destroyed it, and you know that he did right.

Pardon for a man who is persisting in sin is impossible. It would continue the disorder, and make it infinitely worse. God will pardon you even though you cannot undo your past, pardon you without any merit on your part; but if in your heart you still cling to sin, He cannot, dare not, pardon you. And that is why the condition of receiving remission is repentance toward God. And repentance does not mean that a man quits sinning, it means that he is willing to quit if but the power be given him to do it. And that is the condition. You have committed sin. Are you willing to cease, if only the past may be dealt with, and power given to you by which you shall sin no more? That is repentance.

Yes, willing, more than willing, says some tired heart. Then what next shall I say to you? "Behold the Lamb of God." God will give you perfect and full pardon now if you will trust Him, if you will take it of His grace, if instead of attempting to win it, if instead of attempting to merit it you will just come as a poor, guilty, ruined soul—for such you are—and, kneeling at the foot of that Cross, will take God's pardon through Jesus Christ, that is all.

When may I have it? Now. All your sin may be blotted out now. Your neighbor will not know. God will know. But now, trust Him, sinning heart, not on the basis of pity, but on the basis of infinite righteousness wrought out in love, and rendered dynamic in the mystery of His Cross. "We have our redemption through His blood, even the forgiveness of our sins."

CHAPTER VI

PURITY BY THE CROSS

How much more shall the blood of Christ . . . cleanse your conscience from dead works?
HEBREWS 9:14.

IN OUR PREVIOUS STUDY WE CONSIDERED THE FIRST BLESSING that comes to men by the way of the Cross—first, I mean in the line of human experience—the blessing of pardon. We attempted to listen reverently to this note of the great evangel, the glad declaration that forgiveness for actual trespass is provided for men not merely on the basis of pity, but in righteousness, through the mystery of the Cross of Jesus. We all are conscious how great a blessing this is, yet I think I speak for every person here when I say that we do not feel that it goes to the root of our need.

That is not to undervalue the blessing of pardon, but it is to say that mere pardon leaves us lacking something that we do not earnestly desire, and something which we desire the more earnestly as the result of the pardon bestowed on us. I attempted very carefully to limit our previous study to the word which my text contained, "trespasses": sins rather than sin, definite, personal, actual acts of disobedience. Sins as trespasses are pardoned by the way of the Cross, but all such sins are the outward manifestations of an inward disease—a moral disease, of course—the disease of sin.

I am not proposing to enter into any lengthy discussion even now as to how man, using the word in its generic sense, contracted the disease. I simply propose to recognize the fact that it is here, present in human life, that we are all conscious of it, that we feel that behind the deed is a force which impelled us to the deed, and which, strive as we will, struggle as we may, has proved too much for us.

That is not the experience of lonely individuals. It is the common experience of the race. Every man fails, goes wrong, breaks down; and the fact of his actual transgressions results from this deeper, subtler, profounder fact of a tendency toward actual transgression, of a bias in that direction. You may call that original sin or continous abnormality—phrases matter nothing. The fact of which I am conscious and you are conscious and every man is conscious is that in man there is the double consciousness of a desire to do good and of a force which prevents his doing good.

Unless the evangel of the Cross can deal with that deeper thing in my life it does not meet my profoundest need. Great and gracious is the proclamation that my sins may be forgiven, and my hands are open to receive that gift and my heart sings a song of gladness as I receive it; but, oh, my soul, is that all? Must I still be left with this underlying somewhat that drives me to sin? Can nothing be done for me in the actual warp and woof of my spirit, in my moral fiber, to quench the fires of passion, to correct the poison that throbs? Or, again, to use the simpler language, is my prayer, "Create in me a clean heart, O God," to find no answer?

The evangel of the Cross is incomplete unless it meets that great need. My probation is not the probation of an unfallen man, of a man born without these forces and vices within him. The probation that I live is not exactly identical with that of the perfect One of Nazareth, or even of the first man according to the story of holy writ. The father of the race, according to that story, stood upright, erect, began without these forces throbbing through his consciousness. I did not so begin. I was born in sin and "shapen in iniquity." I was born with the need of a redemption that should deal not merely with the sins I have committed as the result of an inherited iniquity, or deviation from the straight, but with the inherited iniquity itself. And I am prepared to say this, even though for a moment it may sound a startling thing. Believe me, I say it most reverently, and yet I am talking out of the deepest and most passionate conviction of my life: Unless God has provided a redemption that touches sin in me as well as the sins that grow out of it, it is an imperfect redemption. All that, as it states the need according to the common experience of men, prepares the way for the consideration of our text, in which the perfect provision is revealed.

God has provided—to quote from the passage I read—"eternal redemption," and eternal redemption is infinitely more than long-lived redemption. Eternal does not finally or necessarily mean continuance without end. Eternal is as broad as it is long, as high as it is deep. Eternal redemption is redemption that meets every possible and conceivable necessity of the case. He has provided that redemption, and, while pardon for sins is its first benefit, everything else that I need is contained within that selfsame redemption. In this passage it is declared that Jesus Christ, who offered Himself through the Eternal Spirit, without spot to God, made a provision by which my conscience can be cleansed from dead works, that I may be able to do that thing that I have not been able to do—to serve the living and true God.

Now let us consider some of the outstanding terms of this text. I want to draw your special attention to the expressions, "conscience" and "dead works." "Conscience" is a word used at this point in one particular sense. "Dead works" is a figure of speech, and we must go back to the old economy with which the writer was dealing if we would understand what the phrase really means in this connection.

According to popular usage, conscience is a faculty enabling men to distinguish right from wrong. Conscience in the Bible has a far wider meaning.

The word is found only once in the Old Testament save once, and then it is in the margin. A careful examination of all the passages in which the word occurs in the New Testament shows that it is used in the sense of consciousness rather than in our ordinary sense of "conscience." The Apostle speaks of "a good conscience," of "a conscience void of offence," of "an evil conscience," of "a conscience branded as with a hot iron." Now, in neither case was he referring to the faculty that discerns between good and evil, but rather to the facts discerned. When he speaks of a good conscience he does not mean an excellent capacity for the discernment of good and evil. When he speaks of an evil conscience he does not mean a conscience unequal to the discernment of good and evil. Conscience is consciousness. To make this clearer let me requote those isolated passages, inserting the word "consciousness" instead of conscience. "A good consciousness," "a consciousness void of offence," "an evil consciousness." In each case the word indicates the fact of discernment rather than the faculty of discernment. "A conscience void of offence," then, is man's inner consciousness, having nothing in it that causes him to offend. "A good conscience" is man's whole consciousness, the whole sweep of his mind good. "An evil conscience" is man's whole consciousness, the whole content of the mind evil.

And here the writer of the letter to the Hebrews says that by the mystery of the Cross man's consciousness is cleansed. Consciousness lies at the back of conduct, is influenced by conduct subsequently, but is first the inspiration of conduct. There is perpetually a reflex action between a man's consciousness and his conduct. My consciousness of anything creates my conduct toward it, and my conduct toward it reflects on my consciousness, and changes it, in that it either defiles it, or lifts it into higher reaches of purity.

Take the simplest thing you know for purpose of illustration. Let us take such a simple thing as the Master would have taken. Bring me a little child, and put this little child in the midst. My consciousness of a little child will create my conduct toward that little child. Let that be my first proposition. What is a little child? What do you think of a little child? Tell me, and I will tell you what your conduct toward that child will be. Is your consciousness of a little child a low consciousness, a mean consciousness? Your conduct to the little child will be low and mean. Suppose you have the same consciousness of a little child that Jesus had, suppose you say, In heaven its angel always beholds the face of the Father, then what? Then your conduct toward that little child will make you say what He said. If you offend that child it is better that a millstone were hanged about your neck and you were drowned in the depth of the sea. My consciousness of a flower will affect my conduct toward it. Young man, your consciousness of a woman will affect your conduct toward her. Now, as God is my witness, there is nothing I crave more than a clean consciousness of things—a consciousness that takes hold upon a flower, a child, a woman, a city, everything, cleanly, purely, and without defilement; if I have that, then have I solved my riddle, then have I found plenteous redemption. And that is exactly what the Cross provides for every man, no matter how depraved he may be, or how utterly his consciousness has become evil. The writer of the letter to the Hebrews says, "If the blood of goats and bulls and the ashes of a heifer sprinkling them that have been defiled sanctify unto the cleanness of the flesh, how much more shall the blood of Christ, who through the Eternal Spirit offered Himself without blemish unto God, cleanse your consciousness from dead works to serve the living God."

Now let us look at that phrase, "dead works." As we indicated before, it is absolutely important that we should notice that the writer is dealing with the old economy, and we remember how strict and stringent were the laws of that economy concerning ceremonial defilement. Both in Leviticus and in Numbers we find clear revelation of how particular God is about small things. To touch the dead was to be defiled, and cleansing was needed. To enter the house where the dead were, and, though they were wandering through the wilderness, and the tabernacle was not erected, and they could not come to sacrifice, they must be sprinkled in water in which were the ashes of a red heifer. If you will ponder well these old Mosaic requirements they are suggestions and pictures of infinite truth, telling us what God thinks of defilement and how easily a man is defiled. So that when I read here, on the page of a letter written to Hebrews, the term, "dead works," I must not pass it over as a mere poetical description. It is a description of corruption, of an evil thing that contaminates and spoils the life. These are the very forces spoiling me; these are the things from which I want a cleansing. My consciousness—how, I do not know; why, I may not be able to tell—is defiled, is contaminated; it suggests things to me which are not pure. Of course, I am speaking of a man by nature, and apart from the grace of God. I am speaking also of many a man who has been born again, but who has never appropriated God's gift of purity. The consciousness is tainted, defiled, spoiled by dead works. It is from that possibility of being contaminated that man wants cleansing.

Let us take some illustrations of things resulting from a

consciousness defiled by dead things, corrupt things. First, in personal life—in the realm of the physical, a perpetual inclination to self-indulgence, to laziness, even to sensuality; in the realm of the mental, a tendency toward sloth, toward covetousness, toward dishonesty in dealing with truth, and even, alas! sometimes toward actual impurity of thinking; or, in the spiritual, proneness to lethargy, to neglect, to compromise between right and wrong. It was such impure consciousness issuing in carnal conduct which made the Apostle urge the Corinthians to purify themselves and cleanse themselves from all defilement of flesh and spirit. It is the defilement of the spirit which lies at the back of these manifestations in the realm of the flesh that we supremely need to have dealt with.

Then, because of this defiled consciousness, this defiled spirit, sin abiding still in the life manifests itself in lack of love, so that envy, malice, and even hatred are present. These are actively expressed by unwillingness to forgive where wrong has been suffered and unwillingness to apologize where it has been done. Or, again, in violation of truth, so that men are given to exaggeration or to prevarication, which is an evasion of truth; or deceit, which is to give another a wrong view of a matter; or fraud, which is to give another a wrong view in order to gain something for oneself; or slander, which is to issue a false report to the injury of another person. Or, again, in the violation of justice, the spiteful disposition, the incivility, the rudeness, the thoughtlessness, and, alas! sometimes the robbery. Now, all these things are to be found, not all in any one person perchance, but in the common consciousness of men and women who have received the blessing of pardon and sing in their joy over that blessing. My brethren, I am talking with you, not merely to you. We know what this conscience or consciousness is which is not devoid of offense, out of which offense comes, so that we do not look on men or things or affairs as we ought to, and the distorted vision of men and things and affairs produces a wrong attitude toward men and things and affairs. We know this is wrong, and we cry out at last, in the agony of our hearts, and say the good we see we cannot do. The vision of the ideal is in front of us, but power to realize it we lack. Or, in the words of the Apostle, when we would do good, evil is present with us.

Now, what we need supremely—what I need, what you need—is that our very inward nature should be taken hold of and cleansed. We need not merely the forgiveness of sins, but a consciousness that is clean. It is a terrible need. It is as deep as our nature, and the cleansing must penetrate as far as our pollution. It must be a cleansing that deals not merely with the surface of sin, but goes down into the warp and woof, into the fiber of the being. Water will not do; fire is needed. Water is not sufficient; the infinite mystery of blood is demanded.

If I have partially voiced your sense of need, as I have spoken experimentally to you of my sense of need, as I have come to know what God is, and what I am, then I bring you the second note of the evangel. It is in the presence of that need that the writer asks, "How much more shall the blood of Christ, who through the Eternal Spirit offered Himself without blemish unto God, cleanse your consciousness?" Christ offered Himself through the eternal Spirit. And by that offering He is able to cleanse the nature of the soul that trusts Him by the mystery of that blood poured forth. He can cleanse the consciousness and make it pure and good. And again I say I am not going to tell you how it is done, I am not going to try to explain to you by speculation of my finite mind or any philosophy of man how through the mystery of that shed blood a man's consciousness can be cleansed as he trusts in Jesus. The writer does not explain it, he affirms it, and all the burden of the teaching of the New Testament is this, that not merely by the mystery of this shed blood a man's sins are forgiven, but he is cleansed from his sin, changed, remade, a new creation, so that the consciousness defiled becomes a consciousness that is pure.

Now, I am perfectly well aware that a great many people who certainly have received the blessing of the forgiveness of sins have never appropriated this blessing of the cleansed consciousness and purity. I am perfectly well aware that hundreds and thousands of us are sighing after it, but not possessing it; and consequently I am driven to ask this question, if that indeed is declared to be a possibility, on what ground can I have that cleansing of my nature which shall change my view of everything, and give me a new outlook on everything, and so remake my attitude toward everything? How, in brief, can I have, instead of an evil conscience, a good conscience, instead of a conscience seared as with a hot iron, a consciousness which is void of offense? How? And the answer takes us back again to the statement of first principles.

The first thing we have to learn to do is to cease attempting to change our own consciousness. We must quit the conflict which is purely personal. A man says, I will come to look upon a little child as I ought to look upon a little child. You cannot do it in the strength of your own willing. That is the very mystery we have been dealing with. How many a man has said, I hate my outlook, this conception which is false and which issues in sinful conduct. I will alter it, I will change it, I will look upon the old things from a new standard, with cleanness of perception. A clean consciousness of the things round about me shall be mine. He was sincere in the vow, but long before the sun went westering, and the night had come upon him, he had looked again with evil thoughts, and impure desire, and debauched conceptions. The first thing, then, to do, strange as it may sound, is that we cease attempting to change our own consciousness. What then? Then we must be ready and willing to abandon once and forever all permitted acts of sin. We are to put ourselves, so far as it is possible to us, outside the place of sinning. That is very concrete if only you will make it so. It means this. If you are going to quit impure thoughts you must begin by burning your impure pictures. If, after long struggle, you are going to enter into the possibility that lies declared in this text and overcome your tendency toward drunkenness—for let us name things by their right name—you must begin by turning out the last hidden cupboard in your house of the thing that has made you sin. "Having, therefore, these promises, beloved, let us cleanse ourselves from all defilement of flesh and spirit, perfecting holiness in the fear of God." "Having, therefore, these promises," what promises? "I will be their God." "I will dwell in them and walk in them." "I will be to you a Father, and ye shall be to Me sons and daughters." These are the promises. Having them, what am I to do? Cleanse myself! But that is what I cannot do. If I try self-cleansing apart from these promises, and apart from the claim that faith makes upon them, I shall fail; but if I claim the promises and neglect the personal cleansing, I shall fail. There must not only be first a cessation of attempt to master the underlying evil in my strength, there must also be what appears to be a contradiction to that first statement, a resolute parting company with all the circumstances and friends and habits and methods which I know have led me into sin.

What beyond? There must be a handing over of the life just as it is, with its defilement, to Jesus Christ. Oh, but you say you are telling us to do what you tell people to do when they come to Him at first. Exactly! When the Church at Ephesus lost her first love, the great and glorious One, walking amid the seven golden lamp-stands, said, "I have this against thee, that thou didst leave thy first love." What shall she do? This is what she shall do: "Repent, and do the first works." Begin where you began, fall in line with the principles you have neglected and wandered from. Remember, when we come for purity we are to come exactly as we came for pardon. First, "Nothing in my hands I bring," the cessation of my attempts to deal with the underlying impurity; second, "Here I give my all to Thee," the utter and absolute abandonment of the life to Jesus Christ—not as a theory to be sung, but as fact. And then what next? Then, dear heart, trust Him for that very thing after which you have been sighing. Accept it as from Him, trusting in Him. The cleansing of the conscience comes whenever a soul ventures everything on Christ and trusts Him absolutely. If you will come now, just where you are and as you are, with your false consciousness, but in strong determination that you will cut every cord that binds you to the old life, burn every bridge behind you, stand out in separation to Him, and then trust Him, He will break the power of canceled sin. He will set the prisoner free. And so, by the way of this Cross, infinite and ever-increasing mystery of God's love, there comes to men not merely pardon, but purity—that for which the heart, quickened by the Spirit, most profoundly seeks.

CHAPTER VII

PEACE BY THE CROSS

Having made peace through the blood of His Cross.
                                        COLOSSIANS 1:20.

PEACE IN HUMAN EXPERIENCE IS THE ISSUE OF PARDON AND purity. There can be no peace so long as sin is unforgiven; there can be no perfect peace so long as impurity remains in the life, dominant and influential. Peace is a necessary sequence in experience; if indeed my trespasses are forgiven, if indeed my consciousness is purged, then issues peace.

The need of peace is created primarily by the fact that man is out of harmony with God. Here I need hardly stay to argue or discuss; I suppose it will be readily granted that this is true. This the Apostle declared in words both blunt and bold: "The carnal mind is enmity against God"; the "natural man" does "not know the things of God." He cannot know them. The natural man is in intelligence dark toward God, ignorant rather than intelligent; in emotion contrary to God, hating rather than loving; in will perverse against God, disobeying rather than obeying.

If instead of stating these things in these terms of doctrine I state them in the realm of experience, the fact is perhaps more patent. Man does not want to talk about God. In the most refined society—using that word in its very degraded and abused sense, for the only final refinement is the refinement of spiritual culture—the one subject which is "taboo" is God. Man is out of harmony with God, afraid of God, unbelieving toward God, and to-day, worst of all indifferent about God.

The reason for this is sin. Find me a man who is afraid of God, and I will find you a man who is a sinner and living in sin. The sin may be manifested in a hundred different ways, but it lies at the back and is the sole reason for lack of harmony with God. It is sin that cuts man off from God, for it is sin that blinds his vision, so that he cannot see God; deadens his emotion, so that he cannot love God; turns his will into perverse attitudes, so that he cannot obey God. Sin prevents the fulfilment of purpose, and thus puts man out of harmony with God.

Moreover, sin reacts on the sinner, polluting the very sources of life, and this pollution prevents communion, so that a man is not only alienated from God by his sin, but by his alienation from God prevented from ceasing to sin. Sin excludes me from the Divine presence. Being excluded, it may be that I want not to sin, but I have lost my power not to sin, for the only power that enables a man not to sin is that of direct communion with God. That is the awful tragedy of sin: its reflex action in human life. Men are coming to understand to-day that if man is to find perfect peace he must find his way into harmony with God. In his *Varieties of Religious Experience*, Professor James tells us that he has come to the deliberate conclusion along lines of scientific investigation that, somewhere, somehow, man has business with God, and that man fulfils his highest destiny only as he submits himself to the call of God.

But men are not having dealings with Him, do not find Him; cannot find Him though they search through the long and misty avenues of scientific investigation, though they spend long and weary years in philosophical elaboration and research. God is never so found. Yet men out of harmony with God are conscious that they lack peace, and the reason of the lack of harmony and the absence of communion is sin, the direct and wilful and personal doing of wrong, when right and wrong have stood confronting man's reason and his will.

Because man is out of harmony with God he is utterly out of harmony with everything else. A man who has no peace with God lacks peace within his own personality. A man who has no peace with God, and who lacks peace within his own personality, fails of peace with his fellow man. The man who has no peace with God, and lacks peace in his own personality, and therefore fails to have peace with his fellow men, is out of harmony with the whole of Nature.

The man who is out of harmony with God is out of harmony within his own personality. My text occurs in one of the stupendous passages of the New Testament: in order that its light may flash on my subject, I ask you to consider the context. The Apostle is dealing with the great subject of creation and of Christ's relationship thereto. He speaks of Christ as being the Image of God, and also as being the Firstborn of creation. He distinctly says that the God-created things were made by Him and for Him. He distinctly affirms that in Him—that is, in Christ—"all things consist." Then he declares, right at the heart of the great argument, that this Christ, Firstborn of creation, Upholder of creation, shed His blood in the midst of creation; and that through the mystery of that blood-shedding, in the midst of the creation held together by Christ, and created by Christ, He will reconcile all things to Himself, both on the earth and in the heavens. That is the majestic sweep of the passage.

In Christ all things consist. Banish from your mind all the larger outlook on creation. Forget the spaces by which you are surrounded: forget even this one little planet on which you stand, and out of its myriad mysteries consider your own life. You are part of creation; the principle that obtains in the whole creation obtains in you. In Him, the Christ Who is the image of God, things consist. In Him they harmonize, part fitting to part, power answering power, joint uniting with joint. If you banish this Christ from the life by sin, if you put God out of count, then you no longer consist, you no longer hold together. You become, within your own personality disorganized, broken up, disintegrated. Every man who is Godless and Christless is disintegrated in his own personality; he is a mystery to himself. He finds the physical—we all know the physical; he finds the mental—we are all conscious of the mental; every now and then he hears, not from without, as though a voice out of the blue addressed him, but from within, the voice of his spiritual nature. This last he stifles, silences, drives back. The mental he sometimes attempts to cultivate and refine; the physical he ministers to with all his power; but he is a broken man. The spiritual, which is the essential, is dethroned, imprisoned within the personality; the mental has the wrong vision, the wrong outlook, and, consequently, is perpetually degraded; and the physical is made the principal; that man lives, as Paul says, "in flesh" instead of in spirit. There is no harmony; and out of that discord of a human life come the questionings and the agonies, and the conflicts, and the defeats that are perpetual in human history. Out of that discord comes the dual cry of a man when he says, I would do good. Evil is present with me. I would climb, but I fall. The man who is Godless lacks peace within. There is passion within, there is power within, but not peace. Passion runs riot, power is misapplied; ambition, aspiration, desire, endeavor, all these things; but no peace. Moments that seem peaceful are broken in on by some rush of passion; moments that seem quiet are disturbed by some new mystery within the life of the man of the world.

Oh, man, thy personality is as marvelous as is God's universe, and the things in conflict are great things, God-made things. Every part of thy personality is the result of a Divine thinking, and a Divine creation; and if thou art living without the Divine Who thought, and the Divine Who created, the great forces in thy life are conflicting and clashing, and there is discord, but no peace.

The result is that man is not at peace with his fellow man. Each man being disorganized within his own personality, social disorganization must necessarily ensue. Are you prepared to say there is peace in the world? Of course, by comparison there are countries that are at peace, but I am not at all sure that the peace of to-day which is perpetually attempting to be ready for war is not more disastrous than war itself.

Is there social peace? Nation is divided against nation, class against class, there is commercial strife, and social strife is rife, and why? Because the units are at strife within themselves. When strife meets strife, strife is perpetuated, and you will never have the peace of a great socialism until you have the peace of a great individualism.

Finally, man is not only out of harmony within himself and with his fellow man, he is out of harmony with Nature. I take up my Bible, and I turn over to that great psalm about man:

What is man, that Thou are mindful of him?
And the son of man, that Thou visitest him?

And now hear the answer:

For Thou hast made him but little lower than God,
And crownest him with glory and honour.
Thou madest him to have dominion over the works of Thy hands;
Thou hast put all things under his feet:
All sheep and oxen,

Yea, and the beasts of the field;
The fowl of the air and the fish of the sea,
Whatsoever passeth through the paths of the sea.

That is a picture of God's intention for man, dominion over Nature, harmony with Nature, mastery of Nature; a beneficent mastery of Nature that leads Nature out to its highest and its best—that is God's thought for man.

At the beginning God put man into a garden; what for? So that he might admire the flowers and pluck the fruits? No! *"To dress it and to keep it."* He put him into the garden in order that man might put his God-made hand on God's unfinished work and finish it. The Garden of Eden was a garden of potentialities, waiting for the touch of man to make it perfect. God placed man in it, and said, Now touch it with labor, and it will laugh at you with flowers. We can see something of this even to-day. One's mind goes to the simplest of all illustrations among the flowers. Who of us has not seen the wonderful development of what in my boyhood's days was a simple country flower, the chrysanthemum? I remember it in my father's garden. It was so old-fashioned that there were gardens that would not have it, but there is not a garden that has not room for it to-day. It has grown since those days, and the petals have run out into wavy gracefulness and tender tints. What has happened? Man has touched it. The potentialities of the chrysanthemum of to-day lay in the old-fashioned garden chrysanthemum, but it waited for man to complete the work of God. At this hour Nature as a great whole is an unconquered territory because man is Godless. You tell me that the most scientific men are Godless men. You tell me that the countries that are most scientific are the most Godless. I do not believe it. Let us study the map of the world; imagine you see it before you. Now put your hand on the places where most discoveries have been made. And while your hands are resting on those countries in which men have done most in the work of mastering Nature and discovering her secrets and giving them to men, they are resting on the countries where the Gospel of Jesus Christ has prevailed most. That is the larger outlook. You bring me to some man whom you call scientific, and he is Godless, and you say that scientific investigation makes a man Godless. I tell you it is a narrow outlook. It is just as narrow an outlook as the outlook of Robert Ingersoll when he said that something happened as naturally as water runs down hill. If you think that is true, read Father Lambert's reply, and see how Father Lambert demonstrated that water does not run down hill, that the vast mass of the waters of the world are piled at the equator.

In the light of Godliness men have mastered Nature; electric light has come directly as the result of Godliness, for if you find lands that are Godless you find them in darkness in every sense of the word. Man remains out of harmony with Nature until he finds his way to God. One man tells me he will climb to Nature and find God. Never. You must find God and then climb into Nature. Neither as to its beauty nor as to its potentiality can you ever be at peace with Nature until you are at peace with God.

And how we long for peace. Oh, the restlessness of the present age! Oh, the friction! Sometimes one pauses to listen and it seems as though surging through the cities, coming up from the quieter country, beating on the listening ear, from all the continents and the isles of the sea, there is the noise of strife and battle, man within himself hot and restless, feverish, lacking peace; man battling with his brother man for territory, for commerce, for advance; man out of harmony with Nature, losing his love of the beautiful, failing to interpret its message of God, but slowly discovering its deep underlying secrets. Peace seems absent, and yet how man longs for it, sighs after it, sings about it, courts it, and fails to find it.

But there are men and women who have peace; there are men and women living at the very center of it. There are men and women who know peace with God, within themselves, with their fellow men, and with all the universe of God. And how has this peace come? I go back again to the first chapter of Colossians, and again ask you to let the great and stately argument of the Apostle pass before you. Christ, First-born of creation, all things held together in Him; Christ bowed to death, to the awful and lonely tragedy of an earthly dying, in the midst of the lack of peace, and making peace through the blood of His Cross.

This is the third time we have come to this central mystery, and for the third time I say to you, I do not know how it was done. I cannot fathom it, but I see the infinite order in the economy of God of which Christ is Originator and Upholder. I see the awful discord and lack of peace that sweep upon men and everything to the utmost limit of the universe. I see at the center the worst disorder of all, the dying Christ, and I see proceeding from that Cross reconciliation, the restoration of peace, men finding God, men finding themselves, because they have found God; men finding their brother men and getting back to them because they have found God; men finding the secrets and beauties of Nature because they have found God. Already I hear across the nations and the continents, war-mad, strife-occupied, the song of an infinite peace. How came it? It began in the mystery of His dying, and the awful darkness of His blood-shedding. I cannot fathom it; I cannot measure it. I cannot tell you all the deep mystery of that outpoured life and flood, but this I know, that through it peace is born.

First of all, peace between man and God. Let us take three phrases of the New Testament. "Justified by faith, we have peace with God." "Peace from God our Father." "And the peace of God shall garrison your heart." "Peace with God," "peace from God," "the peace of God." This is the experience of the soul that comes back to God from sin and pollution by the way of the Cross of Jesus. No man can speak perfectly of this peace. It defies analysis, it transcends explanation, it may sing itself into snatches of song, but the great infinite experience can never be told; it must be known. Peace with God, that is, if you will have it so—judicial peace. I have sinned against Him, and I am afraid of Him. But I come to Him as He calls me by the way of the Cross, and my sin is put away, I am no longer afraid. The fear is gone, that which made me afraid to speak of Him, to think of Him, has all been put away, and small as I am in His great universe, and utterly unable as I know myself to be to comprehend the full meaning of His existence, this at least is true—fear has been banished, I am at peace with Him, at peace with Him Who holds the universe in the hollow of His hand, at peace with the infinite Force and Intelligence. As God is my witness, standing by that Cross, claiming and receiving its pardon, its purity, I have also its peace, and I am not afraid. So the soul that comes to this Cross is first at peace with God.

This peace is also from God, the quietness that comes into the life when man knows that God is pleased. There is no language that can tell the deepest truth here, but as I am accepted in the Beloved, as I am complete in the Christ, the very blessedness of God rests on me, because it rests on Him, the Christ Himself. I have been joined to Him, and "he that is joined to the Lord is one spirit." And as the good pleasure of God was declared with the Christ, it is declared also with all such as put their trust in Him: pardon for the past, purity for the present, and the peace of knowing

> My God is reconciled,
>   His pardoning voice I hear;
> He owns me for His child,
>   I can no longer fear.
> With confidence I now draw nigh,
> And "Father, Abba Father," cry.

And yet once more and most wonderful of all in this connection, not merely peace with God, and peace from God, but "the peace of God." What is God's peace? It is the peace of His omniscience, the peace of His omnipotence, the peace of His omnipresence. Do you not see how all these things must necessarily create peace in the very Being of God? What robs me of peace in the small affairs of life? My limitations. I cannot see the end, and I am afraid. I cannot be where I would be, and my heart is hot and restless. I cannot do what ought to be done, and panic seizes me. God sees the end from the beginning, God is always where He is needed. God is always equal to the demand that is made on Him, even though it be the redemption of a lost race; and, consequently, in the presence of the fall of man, in the presence of the sin of the race, in the presence of the wrong of the centuries of pain, God's peace in its deepest was never disturbed, because He knew how out of it He would bring life and light and glory, until at last heaven would be reached over the mystery of evil, and its mastery come by the way of the Cross.

The perfect peace of God is the peace of the child of God. Not that I now can see the end from the beginning, but I know He can, and so I sing. Not that I now can be everywhere at the same moment, but He is, and so while I stand here, separated by miles from my friend in danger, I speak to Him, and in the act I am with my friend, for God is with my friend. Distance is annihilated in this life of fellowship, power is perpetual, and the things I cannot do, I can do in Him and through Him. The man who is at peace with God enters into the peace of God, for he has found his way, small atom though he be, infinitesimal part of the universe, into harmony with the order of the universe.

This necessarily means that the peace that comes to us is exactly what we need in other respects, not only in relationship to God, but in relationship to self. The whole being is balanced and quiet.

Look at these two men. What is that man? He is a spirit indwelling a body, having a mind. What is this man? He is a spirit indwelling a body, having a mind. What is the difference between them? This man is perturbed, he lacks peace, he is always full of fear, he is hot, restless, feverish. That man is quiet, calm, strong. What is the difference? This man is out of harmony within himself. The essential spirit is starved, dwarfed, driven out, consequently flesh is glorified, and worshiped and served. He lacks balance, harmony, there is no consistence in this man, because he has not found God. That man has found God, his own spirit is taken out of the prison house and put on the throne. The flesh is not bruised, the flesh is not scourged, it is governed, kept under, made servant, instead of master. He has found the true proportion of things. He is consistent within himself, and his life is full of peace. Why? Because he found God, and finding peace with God and from God and of God, he gained peace within his own personality, and his life became strong, free from friction, quiet, calm, powerful.

Watch that man still; that man knows what peace is with his fellow man. I know that Jesus said, "I have not come to send peace but a sword." That is perfectly true. That is the effect produced among Godless men by the presence of godly men; so long as there are godless men they will hate the godly, and so will attempt to destroy their peace. The measure in which professing Christians fail to make peace is the measure in which they are not Christians. I think the day has come when we ought to be more ready to "unchristianize" the man who libels Christianity than to "unchristianize" Christianity on account of such a man. You tell me of a Christian man who is always making disturbances; I do not believe it. Oh, but he is a minister; that does not matter. He is a deacon; that has no signification in this connection. He has been a church member for forty years; I cannot help it. If the influence of his life is not that of peace, he is not a Christian. When once the peace of God possesses a human life, when once the peace of God dominates a human life, the influence of that life is peace. "Blessed are the peacemakers, for they shall be called the sons of God."

And yet that is after all but a negative way of arguing the case. Take the positive statement of truth. There are still those who dare say that war is devilish. There are some of us who still believe that you cannot justify war, and we say so because we believe in Jesus Christ. Thank God for the lonely singers! There is a good deal to be heard beside their song. There are a great many other voices attempting to express in harmony the glory of war; but I hear the singers on the other side of the sea and in this country; and even on that poor war-mad continent there are some foolish souls who believe in peace, and who will try to bring it in.

Where did they learn their song? It was never born or learned anywhere save in living relationship to God. The song of peace, prophetic, expectant, determined, is always the song of godliness, never the song of godlessness; and we know that all the peace that comes in social and national relationships is the outcome of relationship to God, restored in human lives by the mystery of the Cross.

Man finds his way back into the place of peace with nature by this selfsame work of Jesus Christ. As a side light on our subject read again the eighth chapter of Romans, and read it this time not so much in order to learn its marvelous teaching concerning personal relationship to God; listen for the larger thing in it. You will find groaning mentioned three times over. The Apostle says: "The whole creation groaneth and travaileth together in pain until now." "We also groan within ourselves waiting for the redemption." "The Spirit makes intercession for us with groanings which cannot be uttered." The groaning of Nature is everywhere. The Spirit of God interprets the agony of Nature to the godly man, and the godly man groans in the midst of it, inspired by the Spirit into sympathy with it. "Preach the Gospel," said Jesus, "to the whole creation," and the Gospel of Jesus Christ has its application to all the sorrow and the evil there is in nature. Before the Cross has won its last triumph man will be restored to Nature, and Nature will be restored to man. When God's Second Man and Last Adam went down into the wilderness, He met and mastered evil, and at the close we read: "He was with the wild beasts," and we have read it as though it were a message of terror. It means He was with them in company and comradeship, and they were unafraid of Him. Because of His own absolute perfection ferocity ceased; there was no wild beast in the presence of God's Perfect Man. Neither will there be in the presence of a perfectly redeemed humanity. The earth is not old, it is young. This earth effete? By no means. We have hardly begun to realize its resources. The race is struggling still in its kindergarten days, believe me. When by-and-by His reign shall be established, when by-and-by man shall have found peace with God in a larger sense than the merely individual, then he will begin to find Nature and its secrets, then such flowers as men have never looked upon, then such wonders as we would now call miracles, then the resurrection of Christ shall no longer be a mystery to scientific thinking. Do not imagine, my brothers, you know all about Nature. So far, you have just scratched on the surface of things. That is all the race has done. When the Lord of creation, Who is First-born of creation, shall have won His perfect victory and reconciled all things to God, then man will have found peace with Nature. Have you entered into peace with God? If not, you have never seen a flower yet:

> Heaven above is softer blue,
>   Earth around is sweeter green;
> Something lives in every hue
>   Christless eyes have never seen;
> Birds with gladder songs o'erflow,
>   Flowers with deeper beauties shine,
> Since I know, as now I know,
>   I am His and He is mine!

Peace! It can come to you, my brother, personal, social with Nature, only as it first comes with God. I beseech you, "acquaint now thyself with Him, and be at peace." And the only way is at the

> Trysting-place, where heaven's love
> And heaven's justice meet.

The only place is at the Cross, where He made peace through the shedding of blood.

CHAPTER VIII

POWER BY THE CROSS

For the Word of the Cross . . . unto us which are being saved . . . is the power of God.
                              I CORINTHIANS 1:18.

THE ASPECT OF THE CROSS OF CHRIST WHICH IS NOW TO occupy our attention is one that has application only to a certain number of people, whom the Apostle refers to in the words, "to us which are being saved." We have spoken in this series of meditations first of pardon, and then of purity, and lastly of peace by way of the Cross.

We are now to speak of a third blessing—power by way of the Cross. We are often reminded of the fact that in the great experience of salvation there are tenses. I was saved; I am being saved; now is my salvation nearer than when I believed—that is, I shall be saved. The particular aspect of the Cross which is before our minds deals with the present and progressive tense of salvation. Pardon full, sufficient, perfect, is granted in the very moment in which we believe on the Lord Jesus Christ. Purity is in that selfsame moment placed at our disposal; whether we appropriate it or not may be another matter. Power is also at our disposal from that moment and ever onward, but we necessarily come to understand it and make use of it as we live the Christian life. The Word of the Cross is the power of God to those of us who are being saved. The soul pardoned and purified immediately confronts the future, and nowhere is weakness more keenly felt than at that moment. Often men are kept from that great act of surrender to Jesus Christ, which brings them into the position of pardon or purity, or of both, by fear of the future. And though men yield to the call of the Lord, and rejoice in the forgiveness of sins; even though they submit themselves wholly to Him, and claim the great purging of conscience which comes by such surrender; even though the great peace of God is in their hearts, yet when they face the future the sense of weakness comes, perhaps as never before. To that sense of weakness the Cross brings an evangel, and as by the way of the Cross I have pardon and purity and peace, so also by the way of the Cross—blessed be God!—there is power for me.

Let us think for a moment of the need of the soul pardoned, purified, at peace. The new relationship to Jesus Christ does not remove us out of all the old relationships. We are still left on the probationary plane. We shall live in the same store, the same workshop, even though our sins are for-Christ. We shall go back to business in the same office, the same store, the same workshop, even though our sins are forgiven. All the peculiar forces that have played on our personality prior to our relationship with Jesus Christ will still operate to-morrow, though He has forgiven us, purified us, and brought us into the place of peace. All the ordinary conditions and contingencies will recur to the soul that has come into new relationship with the Lord. The old temptations will come again, and will be felt far more keenly than they have ever been felt before. The old temptations will come through the old avenues; there are but three—the physical, the spiritual, and the vocational. Bread—that is the first; tampering with confidence in God—that is the second; attempting to possess the kingdoms in some other way than by treading the Divinely appointed pathway—that is the third. The devil has no other. These avenues are still open when I give myself to Jesus Christ. I still live within the physical tabernacle; I still am dependent on God for everything, and must live the life of trust; I still am called to Divine purpose in the world. And along every one of these avenues temptation will come to me, even though I am forgiven, purified, and at peace. My consciousness of temptation will be far keener than it ever has been; temptation will be more subtle; the tempter will be more busy. The devil is far more eager to spoil that new life dedicated to Jesus Christ than he is to pay any attention whatsoever to the souls that lie asleep in him.

Not temptation only, but suffering will still be my portion. Bereavements will come to me, as they come to others; defeat will sometimes overtake my endeavor, as it overtakes the endeavors of all men; treachery may lurk in the pathway to harm me; I am still in the place of tears, the place of suffering, the place of sorrow. Again, I am still in the place of joy. I now belong to Jesus Christ, but that will not rob me of the rapture of success; I have been pardoned and purified, and am at peace with God, but that will not interfere with the delight I have in the comradeship and friendship for others of my kind. I have indeed seen Him Whom to see is to find light and life and love and liberty; but there is still within me that which asks for gold on the morning sky. Hope will still take hold of every promise and build on it some great expectation. I am still in the midst of the old circumstances. I must still live the old life.

Once again, the dedication of my life to Jesus Christ, and all the answering blessings that come by the way of the Cross: these things do not remove me out of the place of mystery. I am still limited in my outlook. Phantoms will flit across the seas of life, threatening me and affrighting me; questions will still arise in the inner life as they did before.

Yielded to Jesus Christ, I am not at the end of the questioning mind, I have not solved the last riddle or probed the deepest problem.

The man pardoned, purified, and at peace, abides in the place of peril. He must live where he lived, and as he lived, must strive for bread, and prosecute his business, and touch the world. At least, that is the Divine intention for him. And if any man shall attempt to live the Christian life by escaping from these conditions and hiding within stone walls, he will find that he has cut the very nerve of saintship, and has made it impossible to be all that Christ meant him to be. "As is the lily among thorns, so is my love among the daughters." Christianity is not an exotic which flourishes in hothouse atmosphere, separated from all difficulties. Christianity is a hardy perennial that blossoms among the thorns; and if a man moves from such surroundings he will move from the conditions that make him strong.

Yet it is not merely in order that we may meet these things that we need power. When we yielded ourselves to Christ, and received blessing at His hand, we were brought into a new realm of activity. New demands were made on us. When I come to the Cross and receive these benefits, I, by that reception, commit myself to its responsibilities. When I come to the Cross, and there, a lost and ruined soul, see that I am found and redeemed, in the act by which I receive the Christ I take the oath of allegiance to the One Who saves me. In that moment I commit myself to all the enterprises of God. He demands that what there is of my life shall be surrendered to Him, and that from that moment I shall be a worker together with Him, in fellowship, partnership with Him. From that moment I am to stand, wheresoever my lot may be cast, for righteousness, and not for policy merely—I am to put my whole life into the great business of bringing about a reconciliation of men to God. From that moment in which the blessings of the Cross become my own, my life is committed to the publication of the evangel of the Cross to all men; from that moment in which the compassion of God becomes my salvation, I am called on to live in the power of that compassion for the salvation of others. Standing on the brink of the new life of service, with its demands so great and wonderful, the soul says, "Who is sufficient for these things?" Pardoned, purified, at peace, I have to live and serve. How can I live and serve?

What I need is that there shall come into my life a new force that is equal to all the demands. Power to resist temptation, power to endure suffering equally, power to endure joy that I be not spoiled thereby, power to wait amid the mysteries until His light shall shine on the pathway.

For service I need power. If I am called to this new service I need the passive power that will enable me to stand four square to every wind that blows; I need the active power that will enable me to accomplish the work God puts in my hands as a saved man; I need persuasive power to constrain men to this selfsame Cross where I have found my blessings.

Now, I take up this letter to the Corinthians because in face of difficulties and divisions and misunderstanding the Apostle insists on this one thing, that "the Word of the Cross is the power of God."

Now, the question arises, simply and naturally in the heart of each one of us, In what sense can it be true that the Word of the Cross is the power of God to them that are being saved? Not merely the power which enables a man to find salvation, but the power that he needs to live this life, which is in itself a procession and probation of salvation. In what sense can the Word of the Cross be said to be power? If you approach from the standard of merely human intellectual strength you will come to one of two conclusions. You will come to the conclusion of the Jew or of the Greek. You will come to the conclusion that the Cross of Jesus is either a stumbling-block or utter foolishness. These are perfectly natural conclusions. The Jew said the Cross is a stumbling-block, a *skandalon*, something in the way, over which men fall. Put the Cross into its relation to the life of Jesus as the Jew saw it. Take the disciples, not the great crowd that neglected Him: they learned of Jesus, and learned to love Him, and desired to follow Him. What was the Cross prior to Pentecost? It was a stumbling-block; the moment Jesus mentioned it they drew back from Him, and why? Because they thought the Cross would hinder, not help. There was no power in the Cross to the mind of Peter when he said, "That be far from Thee, Lord." It was the thing that ended power, that robbed Jesus of power to the thinking Jew unilluminated by the Spirit of God, who had never seen into the mystery. After the Cross and resurrection, when Jesus walked to Emmaus, two men talked to Him about the Cross. They said, "We hoped that it was He which should redeem Israel." In imagination I will join the group, and ask these men a question. Do you not still hope? No, we have lost our hope. What killed it? The Cross killed it. So long as He was careful, or seemed to be careful of Himself, so long as when men were angry He went away into the country and waited awhile, and went on with His teaching, we hoped; but when He became reckless and set His face to go to Jerusalem, and we could not dissuade Him, that Cross was the stumbling-block; there He fell, there our hopes were ruined. There is no other conclusion; they were perfectly right, judging by natural law.

Or if not, then what? Then, still within the realm of the natural, you say with the Greek, the Cross was foolishness. It means the same thing underneath. It is absolutely foolish to talk about a Roman gibbet lifting a man except that it may kill him. Foolishness to the Greek. When Paul began his ministry in the Greek cities he came to Athens, the center of the culture of the time. They said, "What would this babbler say?" I think that word "babbler" simply means, as they used it, this teller of tales. There were men who traveled through these Greek cities doing nothing but telling tales of travel, adventure, things seen in distant places; and the men of the time who listened had itching ears—and they have successors to-day—men always seeking for some new thing. When Paul came to tell them the story of how Jesus lived and was crucified and rose, they said: This is a tale, and it is just foolishness, we will amuse ourselves and listen to it. The Cross is still that to-day to some. There is nothing that vitalizes the intellect until you are born again; there is nothing in the Cross that helps on the redemption of the race until you are born again. It is a cold, dead, lifeless stumbling-block, and some men are doing their very best to get rid of it. I am therefore limited in all I say now. "To us which are being saved."

What is it to us who are being saved? "The power of God." What is the "power of God"? The "Word of the Cross." Not the preaching of the Cross—one of the most important changes in translation here—not the preaching, but the *Logos*, the Word, exactly the same phrase which you have in John's Gospel, "In the beginning was the Word, and the Word was with God, and the Word was God. . . . And the Word became flesh and dwelt among us." "The Word of the Cross." It is not the preaching of the Cross that is the power. Thank God there is a sense in which the preaching of the Cross is the power of God; it is by the preaching, the heralding, the proclamation of the Cross that men find the Word of the Cross. But it is not the act of preaching that is powerful, it is the thing preached. Some years ago a theological professor said what seemed to be a smart thing to his class. He said, "Gentlemen, remember God has chosen the foolishness of preaching, not the preaching of foolishness." If he had looked a little more closely he would have found he was wrong. God has chosen the preaching of foolishness, foolishness to the Greek. What is this foolishness? "The Word of the Cross." Let us take the phrase and look at it for a moment, very reverently. "The Word," "The Word of the Cross."

Have you ever made anything like careful and patient study of what the Bible says about the "Word of God"? Have you ever taken that phrase and traced it through? The Bible says wonderful things about the Word of God. I go back into the Old Testament, and there is a wonderful amount of New in the Old. I turn to one of the Psalms and I read this:

> By the word of the Lord were the heavens made;
> And all the host of them by the breath of His mouth.
> He gathereth the waters of the sea together as an heap:
> He layeth up the deeps in storehouses.
> Let all the earth fear the Lord.
> Let all the inhabitants of the world stand in awe of Him.
> For He spake, and it was done;
> He commanded, and it stood fast.

Listen to a statement of the New Testament, "Who being the effulgence of His glory, and the very image of His substance, and upholding all things by the word of His power, when He had made purification of sins, sat down on the right hand of the Majesty on high." "He spake, and it was done; He commanded, and it stood fast." "Upholding all things by the word of His power." Hear once again. An angel visitor is talking to the Virgin, and in the midst of her sweet and holy questioning he says, "No word of God shall be void of power." The word of man is a wish! The Word of God is a work! It is always so. I speak, and then I must do it; He speaks, and it is done. I utter a thought that is in my mind; it is a dream, a prophecy, a desire, a disappointment perchance. When God expresses Himself, the thing He expresses, is. The Word of God is the expression of God, the Speech, the Revelation, the uttering forth, the going out, and with the Word is the Work.

In the fulness of time "the Word was made flesh." And what did men do with that Word made flesh? They crucified Him. I know perfectly well that at this moment—God help us to be reverent—we are standing in the presence of the burning bush. It is well that we take our shoes from off our feet, and say to our hearts that we are looking on the ineffable glory, and cannot explain it. We stand and peer into the mystery, and never understand it; yet, I pray you, think a moment in the realm of analysis.

Reverently let me take that great Word of the Cross and see how power is in it, in the mystery of defeat, in the hour of dying, by listening to the words of the Word of the Cross. If you will take the words spoken by the Word in the supreme agony of the Cross, you will find every one of them tells of defeat and of victory, of weakness and of power.

"Father, forgive them, for they know not what they do." It is the word of an unutterable pain, but the pain is the plea that prevails.

"To-day shalt thou be with Me in Paradise." It is the confession of defeat; not often have we said so, but you must take the word and put it into Jewish thinking. Paradise, what is that? The place of departed spirits, and men do not want to pass into the place of departed spirits. He says in effect: I am passing, I am a dying Man, I am going to Paradise. But you will not leave it like that; you know full well it is the passing of a King, that it is the voice of the Master of all defeat, that it is the voice of One Who in supreme defeat utters the word of an eternal victory, "To-day shalt thou be with Me in Paradise."

"Woman, behold thy son," "Behold thy mother." His heart is bereaved, and He knows His mother's heart is pierced through with a sword, and yet He knows that there, through that bereavement and that agony and loss and suffering, the suffering of sympathy for His own mother, there He creates the new kinship, the new relationship, gives His mother a son in the bond of His love, such as she never could have had in any other way, gives Himself back to His mother through John in the new discipleship of John, and begins that gracious work that He has carried on ever since, of healing broken hearts with the new kinship, the new relationship, the new family of God. It is a great triumph through a great sorrow.

"My God, My God, why hast Thou forsaken Me?" That forsaking that so appalls you as it appalls me, what is it but the way of approach? The forsaking is the pathway to fellowship.

"I thirst." Out of that thirst there springs the living water of which thirsty men shall drink, and never thirst.

"It is finished," and we sing of it to-night, not as the declaration of a Man who is beaten and defeated. We know the ending was the beginning. That is the dawning of the new order and the new life.

"Father, into Thy hands I commend My Spirit." The actual passing is the coming back to the Father. Take any of the words, and I will defy you to explain them. Crucified in weakness, and yet throbbing through the weakness rivers of power, which, by the way of the resurrection, have passed out into all human life. "The Word of the Cross" is "the power of God." He spake at creation; it was done. He spoke in Jesus, and it was done. Pardon and purity and peace, and all the power that man needs to live a life and render a service come by the way of the Cross.

Now, brethren, finally, how am I to realize this power as an actual positive fact in my own life? The abiding condition of the manifestation of Divine power is that of weakness. This, carried to its logical and proper conclusion, teaches us that the supreme condition for the working of the power of the Word of the Cross in our lives is that we know what it is to be crucified with Him, to enter into the place of death with Him. It is when I come to the point of the cessation of my activity in the power of the flesh, in the power of my own intellect, that the power of the Cross becomes operative in me, and through me. Here is where we stand away, and do not know His power, even those who are His. Someone writes me. I open the letter, and I read it. It is such an old story. It says: "I am a Christian, and have been one for long years, but I cannot overcome this temptation, this besetment. I want power to overcome." Or the letter says: "I have been trying to work for God for long years in the Sunday school, in the church, it may be in the pulpit, but there is no power. What am I to do?" And my answer in every case must be the same. "The Word of the Cross. . . . is the power of God."

But how am I to make contact with that power, that I may overcome? How am I to appropriate that power in order that I may serve in power? There is only one way, and it is that I get to the end of my own attempts to do without God, that God is able through the mystery of this power of the Cross to come into my life, and work in victory over temptation and sin, and in all the service that His will appoints. "I have been crucified with Christ," said the Apostle, and sometimes one is almost afraid to quote the passage, it has been quoted so often, it has been preached on so constantly. Yet never until I come there shall I know what power is in my own life. That great power of the Cross operates in and through only men and women who are content to die with Him, to be at the end of self, that He may be the one supreme enthroned and crowned Lord of the life. Oh, it is this dying that hinders us. These ambitions must be laid aside, these prejudices must be crucified, this pride must be humbled; that goal toward which I have been running, which is, in the last analysis, pure selfishness, must be swept away, and I must be willing to say, "I live, yet not I." It is that canceling of the "I" in the life of the Christian that creates contact with the power of the Cross. It is only as we are prepared to go down into the death of the Cross that we shall begin to find its dynamic and its thrill, and shall know its mastery in us, over all that is against us, and through us, over all that is against God. Thank God, it is the "Word of the Cross," and it is "the power of God." No human philosophy can explain it, and no human investigation along the lines of scientific method can account for it. Here the fact remains, and the simple illustrations are to be found everywhere. Here is a frail man, battered and bruised by his own sin, who comes at last to Jesus for pardon, claims His purity, finds the peace of God, and then goes out to begin his life anew. Beginning it anew, there is no dependence on himself. He says, "I have tried and failed; I yield myself to Him, willing to be nothing, sinking to the place where I count not my life to be anything. I cast ambition as dust beneath my feet, or, in the words of old, 'I lay my treasure in the dust,' and all I counted as dear is to be counted as dross and dung. I am nothing." Easily said, but not so easily consented to. It is when a man gets there—and now I am out of the realm of explanation, but I am in the realm of faith—that this great Word of the Cross, the Cross that is the death of sin, the Cross that cancels sin, the Cross that brings the power, begins to thrill and throb through that man's life. He is able to sin no more.

God is sufficient for all the life and service of His people. No exigencies can surprise Him, no combinations can defeat Him. But the element of human trouble and weakness has ever been the self-life. Where that ends, God, through the mystery of His Cross, the Cross of His Son, resumes His government, resumes His activity; then the life touches the place of omnipotence. I thank God for the pardon of the Cross. I thank God for purity that is mine by the way of the Cross. I thank God for peace; but, oh! sometimes—and I suppose it is because it is the last thing one thinks of in God's great gifts is always the best—this power that has come into the life and made it equal to the things to which it was unequal, this present power of God, how great and gracious a thing it is! If you and I, who tremble and are afraid as we face our surroundings and our service, will but consent to all that is meant by crucifixion with Him, we shall find that that Cross, which was a stumbling-block to Jew and foolishness to Greek, is to such as are being saved the power of God.

CHAPTER IX

PROMISE AT THE CROSS

He that spared not His own Son, but delivered Him up for us all, how shall He not also with Him freely give us all things?

ROMANS 8:32.

WE NOW COME TO THE LAST OF THESE STUDIES AROUND THE Cross of our Lord and Saviour Jesus Christ, a series in which we have attempted to deal with some of the rich and gracious provisions of the Cross; here we shall consider some phases of that all-inclusive and plenteous redemption which God has provided for us through the Son of His love by the way of the Cross.

We have seen the Cross of Christ standing amidst human ruin and helplessness at the very center of redemption, and as the channel of power.

We have endeavored to watch the progress of its work in the experience of the soul who surrenders to Christ.

We have first seen how pardon is ours, that we "have redemption through His blood . . . the forgiveness of . . . trespasses"; we have seen how purity comes to us by the way of the Cross, seeing that our consciousness may be "purged from dead works to serve the living and true God" by that same most precious blood; we have seen how peace comes to us by the way of the Cross, for He "has made peace" by the blood of His Cross; and, last, we have considered how power comes to us, for "the Word of the Cross," the Logos of the Cross, "is the power of God to such as are being saved."

Let us once more take our stand by this selfsame Cross, and observe how it flings its light out on all the future, and on all possible needs and contingencies that may arise.

This is an aspect full of value to us. We are all growingly conscious of our limitation, of the fact that there are more things in heaven and earth than have been dreamed of in our philosophies. This growing consciousness very often affects our thought of, and relation to, spiritual things, the things of the soul, the things of redemption. There are moments when the trusting soul trembles through its own limitation of knowledge and vision.

Have there not been moments in your own Christian life when the very consciousness of the unending ages has been almost too great a burden to bear, when the consciousness of the illimitable spaces that lie unmeasured and immeasurable around you has almost crushed your spirit? We have all had such moments, in which we have asked questions about those ages, those spaces, those infinite things round about us, and there have been moments when we have asked questions about our own relationship to God in the light of these things.

Let us go back to the eighth chapter of Romans, and if there has seemed to be something of the nature of speculation in my introductory words, I want you to listen to Paul. These are some of the questions he asked: "Who is against us?" "Who shall lay anything to the charge of God's elect?" "Who is he that shall condemn?" "Who shall separate us from the love of Christ?"

It is impossible for any who know the Lord Jesus, and have come into the blessings that have lately occupied our attention to read those questions without the tone of challenge creeping into the very reading of them. I am perfectly sure that this was in the mind of Paul when he wrote them. "Who is against us?" "Who shall lay anything to the charge of God's elect?" "Who is he that shall condemn?" "Who shall separate us?"

Remember where the great questions occur in the scheme of this epistle; they do not come in the early part in which the Apostle is dealing with the need for salvation, nor in the central part in which he is laying down the plan of salvation, but in chapter eight, the chapter of the final triumph, in which life in Christ is so wonderfully described, life by the Spirit, which is life in Christ; the chapter which, as so often has been said, begins, "no condemnation," and ends, "no separation." Beyond the first part of the chapter, beyond the present experience of the power of the Cross, these questions occur. To pardoned, purified souls, at peace and having power, all these questions come sooner or later. Happy and blessed indeed are the men and women who can face them as Paul faced them, so that in the asking of them there is a tone of challenge, the great ring of a sure triumph.

"Who is against us?" What attack may be directed against our souls? "Who shall lay anything" to our charge? Can any other accusation be brought against us? "Who is he that shall condemn?" "Who shall separate us?" They are all questions born of the soul's consciousness of limitation. We are coming day by day to have a widening conception of life; we are living in an age in which the universe is a great deal larger than it seemed to our fathers. The discoveries of science—I say nothing of their speculations, I am always willing to wait while they speculate—have put the horizon back much further than it seemed to be. Theories which sounded like speculations to them are now ascertained facts;

indeed, so great has the universe become that some men deny the relationship of the individual to God. All this is born of the ever enlarging sense of the universe.

These widening conceptions of life, this deepening sense of personal frailty, lead us to ask such questions. Can anyone be against us? I know some of the foes, but are there others of whom I know nothing? I read in my New Testament of "principalities and powers, the rulers of the darkness of this world," and all this phraseology has grown in meaning with the passing of the years. I do not say it means more essentially, but it means more to us than it did.

As one in this little planet, one in this ever widening universe, ever widening to human conception, how do I know what lies beyond in the dim distances? Who can be against us? Is there some spiritual antagonism I have never yet faced, ready to attack me? Is there some accuser who will rise up and set my life in relation with other laws? Shall I find myself a sinner in some deeper sense? Is there any accuser? And the final throbbing, agonizing question, until we come to the Cross for an answer, is, "Who shall separate?" Can anyone?

Every question is in itself a demand, a reverent demand, the demand of the soul; and when I ask, "Who is against us?" I am asking for defense against all possibility of attack. When I ask, "Who shall lay anything to the charge of God's elect?" I am asking that my justification shall be a justification in the presence of any and every possible accusation. When I ask, "Who is he that shall condemn?" I am asking that my acquittal at the bar of Infinite Holiness shall be from any possible condemnation that may arise. When I ask, "Who shall separate us?" I am asking that my communion with God shall be so arranged that all need arising from the new nature and the new conditions and the new demands shall be met.

I tremble on the verge of the eternal, I am, in my own

poor personality, afraid in the presence of the immeasurable and the infinite that stretches out beyond. I stand, a man, a speck amid immensity, and I do not know what cohorts are hidden behind the distant hills ready to come against me. I do not know what traducers may yet bring charges against me. Can anything separate me from the love of God?

These are great questions. They do not always take this form, but they come to us all, sometimes very simply, and perhaps, therefore, the more subtly, with more far-reaching and deep-searching agony of soul.

In view of such questionings the greatness of my text is revealed. It is an answer to one of the questions, but I take it because out of it come the values that answer all the questions. "He that spared not His own Son, but delivered Him up for us all, how shall He not also with Him freely give us all things."

I suppose every man who preaches the Word sometimes feels as though there is nothing more to say when he has read his text. That is certainly how I feel about this. Note its historic basis, "He spared not His own Son." Notice its logical conclusion, "Shall He not freely give us all things?"

When God gave His Son, He gave His best; and now human language must be imperfect. He emptied heaven of its richest; He had nothing more worth the giving. He gave in that moment not something better than the rest by comparison, but something that included all. The Apostle here says, in effect, when God gave His Son, with Him "He freely gave us all things." It is not merely that if He spared not His Son He will give other things. It is really that when He gave His Son He gave all. Take another statement of this same Apostle, from his Colossian letter, which deals with the glorious Christ, and remember his words about Jesus, "Christ, Who is the Image of the invisible God, the first-born of all creation; for in Him were all things created . . . and He is before all things, and in Him all things consist." There is no far distant part of the universe of God that is not held together in orderly array by Christ. No mystic secret of the Divine procedure is unknown to Christ. No foe of humanity lurking in any of the infinite spaces that baffle and affright me is hidden from Christ. God gave His Son, and when He gave His Son, He gave the One in Whom all things consist, from Whom all things came, to Whom all things proceed. In originating wisdom and creating force and upholding power, He gave the sum total of everything when He gave Christ, so that when I ask a question about the infinite spaces I am asking a question about the things that are as familiar to Jesus as are the few grains of sand that I can hold in my hand and look at, and far more familiar, for I cannot tell you the deepest mystery of the grains of sand, and He knows the last mystery of all the universe. When I ask my question about the days that are coming, I am asking a question about things that He will make, for He it is Who fashions not only the worlds of matter, but the worlds of time, the rolling ages as they come. God has given this Son of His love—Framer of the Universe in infinite wisdom, Upholder of it on its onward course to the final goal—given Him freely for us all.

Now, the Apostle says, "Who is against us?" "Who shall lay anything to the charge of God's elect?" "Who is he that shall condemn?" "Who shall separate us?" Notice the questions again, and notice them as they are set against the great declaration.

First, "If God is for us, who is against us?" How do I know God is for me? He gave His Son. There is no other demonstration. If you doubt the Cross you have no proof that God is for us. If you lose the sight of the Cross, and do not hear its message of the Divine good will and favor, there is nothing in Nature to show you God is for you. Nature is red in tooth and claw. We are told sometimes that it is kind, and so it is if we are kind to it; but offend it, break its laws, and it will crush you with merciless severity.

And this also is a merciful provision, for the crushing of anything effete is good for the things that remain. God by salvation has not come to save effete things as effete things. He has come to save things from effeteness and make them new. Nature will laugh in sunshine on the face of your dead child; there is no message in Nature that tells you that the God behind it cares for you.

But this man, weak and frail, suffering the loss of all things, the pity of all worldly-minded souls, says God is for him. How does he know? "He spared not His own Son." That is the infinite proof. The Cross is the revelation of the Divine interest. If I have that Cross, there God has given, in the mystery of that dying, His own Son, and I am prepared to challenge all the universe. "Who can be against me?"

As I learn the lesson and repeat the challenge there will come into it, not merely a tone of challenge, but the tone of contempt for everything that is against me. Circumstances are against me; let them be! God is against the circumstances! Another man says, My parentage is against me. God becoming your Father cancels the evil inheritance with which you entered into life.

But these are things of to-day. What lies beyond? I do not know. What infinite forces will be born in the new ages, the ages that will come fresh as the morning from the wisdom of God? What forces may be born with new principalities and new powers? Perchance some of them will be against me. It does not matter, they will be born of God, and God is for me, and the man who stands by the Cross of Jesus and knows that that is God's gift for his redemption knows that nothing can emerge out of the endless ages, or gather from infinite spaces, that can harm, because by that Cross he knows God is for him. Who can be against us?

As to accusation, "Who shall lay anything to the charge of God's elect? It is God that justifieth." We must interpret this word of the Apostle by his previous use of the word in the same argument. How does God justify? "Being, therefore, justified by faith . . . we have peace with God through our Lord Jesus Christ, through Whom also we have had our access by faith into this grace wherein we stand; and . . . rejoice in hope of the glory of God." Who shall lay anything to my charge? It is God that justifies me. How? By that Cross of Jesus. You may lay to my charge what you will. You may see in me the imperfection that contradicts your sense of law. I am talking in imagination to the principalities and powers which may be created fifty millenniums hence. God has justified me by the Cross, which does not mean for one single moment that He has covered and excused my sin, but by the infinite mystery of the pain borne in that Cross, He has made my sin not to be, canceled it, put it away, and in this justification God acts, not out of pity, but on the basis of eternal justice and righteousness.

I challenge all the accusers. Who are you? Lay your accusation. Yes, it is true, perchance even in the holy service of to-day, perchance even in the service of the ages to come, there will be the falling short somewhere. I do not mean wilful sin. Do you not know that God charges the angels with folly? When I measure my service, even in the infinite hereafter, by the compulsion and propulsion and constraint of the Infinite love, I think that we shall always have to cast our crowns at His feet and say, "Not unto us, O Lord, not unto us, but unto Thy name give glory." If someone shall lay a charge against me that the thing is not as high as it ought to have been, then in the infinite ages the Cross of the Christ abides, God's eternal provision, so that none can lay anything to the charge of such as He shall justify.

Or again, "Who is he that shall condemn?" "It is Christ

Jesus that died, yea rather"—hear the music of it, if death were all, the condemnation would abide—"yea, rather, that was raised from the dead," and in the mystery, and miracle, and marvel of that resurrection there is the demonstration of the truth that the dying was efficacious, that in the dying He accomplished the purpose of His heart, in the dying He put guilt away and bore sin so that I need bear it no more. "Who shall condemn?" The soul, afraid of possible condemnation, hides again in the cleft of the rock, and points to the Cross and the empty grave, and says for evermore, By virtue of that Cross and that empty tomb, there can be no condemnation to the trusting soul.

Once again, "Who shall separate us?" Paul always seems to me, at this stage, as though he had climbed to some great height and was looking out on all the dimensions. "Death," he puts that first, because that is what men are so often afraid of as a separating force. "Life," which is far more likely to separate us than death, even though men do not fear it. "Angels, principalities," the whole world and universe of created intelligences. "Things present—things to come," in simple sentences he sweeps through all the ages. "Powers, height, depth."

Notice carefully this final phrase—"nor any other creation, shall be able to separate us from the love of God, which is in Christ Jesus our Lord." Did you notice the Apostle's outlook on all these things? "Death?" That is a creation. "Life?" That is a creation. "Angels" and "principalities?" Creations. "Things present?" Creations. "Things to come?" Creations. "Powers?" Creations. "Height?" Creation. "Depth?" Creation. All had issued from God. How can created things separate me, says the Apostle, from the Origin of the created things, seeing I am bound to Him through the work of Jesus, His own Son? I cannot be separated by things created by the Creator, for the Creator has bound me to Him by giving His Son, and brings me back with His Son into eternal union with Himself. "Who shall separate me?"

> Jesus, Thy blood and righteousness
>   My beauty are, my glorious dress;
> 'Midst flaming worlds, in these arrayed,
>   With joy shall I lift up my head.
>
> Bold shall I stand in Thy great day;
>   For who aught to my charge shall lay?
> Fully absolved through these I am
>   From sin and fear, from guilt and shame.
>
> When from the dust of earth I rise,
>   To claim my mansion in the skies,
> Ev'n then, this shall be all my plea,
>   Jesus hath lived, hath died for me.
>
> Jesus, be endless praise to Thee
>   Whose boundless mercy hath for me—
> For me, a full atonement made,
>   An everlasting ransome paid.
>
> O let the dead now hear Thy voice;
>   Now bid Thy banished ones rejoice;
> Their beauty this, their glorious dress,
>   Jesus, Thy blood and righteousness.

The Cross of Jesus, the rough Roman gibbet, brutal Cross so far as man had anything to do with it; the Cross of nineteen hundred years ago, which was the manifestation of the great mystery and passion by which God redeems men, that Cross flames with a glory far greater than is needed to illumine the little while, and the here and the now. Its light fills all the universe; its glory rests on all the coming ages. At its birth every new-born age will be baptized in the infinite light that streams from the Cross of Christ. I do not know what they will have in them. One of the joys of the contemplation of the hereafter is that God is infinite in wisdom and power, and my own consciousness of eternal existence becomes bearable as I remember that there can be no monotony with God, always new ages, always new creations, always new manifestations of the one Eternal, incomprehensible Being Whom I call God.

And I do not know what, or how, how long, how brief, how great, how simple. But this I know, that by the Cross I have been brought into the love of God even though I was a sinner; and this I know that nothing He creates can ever separate me from Him Who does create. I know it by the Cross. "No man hath seen God at any time. The only begotten Son, which is in the bosom of the Father, He hath declared Him." When? By the way of the Cross. Men may know the exceeding power and wisdom of God if they study Nature, but they never find His heart.

There is only one way in which men find that—by the way of the Cross. But when a man comes that way, he comes at last to the point where he can write such a chapter as the eighth of Romans, and looking out from the midst of conscious weakness, out into the infinite spaces, as the questions throb through the mind, "Who? . . . who? . . . who?" He can answer them all with a quiet, calm assurance.

A man at the Cross challenges all attack, all accusation, all condemnation, all separation, and ends in the glorious declaration that none can be against, none can dare accuse, that none can condemn, that none can separate.

In conclusion, let me ask, what is the law of appropriation? There is no specific law of appropriation here; this aspect of promise leans back on God and the work accomplished in Jesus. Yet there is a law of appropriation; it is that of the realization of all that we have spoken of before. If I have never been to the Cross for its pardon, if I know nothing of the purity of consciousness that comes by it, if I am not now at peace with God, and within myself, therefore, if I know nothing of the power of the Cross in this life of probation, then the Cross brings me no promise, but condemnation.

The Cross of Jesus brings me all light, or banishes me to all darkness. Our fathers used to preach about the sin of rejecting Jesus. We do not hear very much about that to-day. And yet, believe me, it is the sin of all sins, it is the sin against the Holy Ghost. There is no sin so deep, so heinous, so awful as that. If I will not have its pardon, or its purity, or its peace, or its power, I cannot have its promise. Then if I ask this question, Who is against me? a myriad forces of evil charge on me to destroy me. If I ask, Who is he that lays anything to my charge? the great accuser stands before me and before God. If I ask, Who is he that shall condemn? the very God of love that would redeem, condemns. If I ask, Who shall separate me? I am separated by my own choice; and the question now becomes, Who can unite me? There is none can unite me if I reject the Cross of His dear Son.

Then let us rather come to the Cross, and in submission yield to its claim, and so receive its blessings.

> Beneath the Cross of Jesus
>   I fain would take my stand—
> The shadow of a mighty Rock,
>   Within a weary land;
> A home within the wilderness,
>   A rest upon the way,
> From the burning of the noontide heat,
>   And the burden of the day.
>
> O safe and happy shelter,
>   O refuge tried and sweet,
> O trysting place where heaven's love
>   And heaven's justice meet!
> As to the holy patriarch

> That wondrous dream was given,
> So seems my Saviour's Cross to me,
> A ladder up to heaven.
>
> There lies beneath its shadow,
>   But on the farther side,
> The darkness of an awful grave
>   That gapes both deep and wide;
> And there between us stands the Cross,
>   Two arms outstretched to save,
> Like a watchman set to guard the way
>   From that eternal grave.
>
> Upon that Cross of Jesus
>   Mine eye at times can see
> The very dying form of One
>   Who suffered there for me;
> And from my smitten heart, with tears,
>   Two wonders I confess,—
> The wonder of His glorious love,
>   And my unworthiness.
>
> I take, O Cross, thy shadow
>   For my abiding place;
> I ask no other sunshine than
>   The sunshine of His face:
> Content to let the world go by,
>   To know nor gain nor loss—
> My sinful self my only shame,
>   My glory all the Cross.

The Cross is God's giving, and the proof of His giving. His giving, "He spared not His Son." The proof of His giving, "Shall He not freely give us all things?"

The Cross is the place of my receiving. I look back, and the Cross brings me pardon. I look within, and the Cross brings me purity. I look up, and the Cross brings me peace. I look around, and the Cross is the Word of power. I look on and out at the infinite and unknown possibilities of eternity, and the Cross is the message of promise. Here and now, as I know my own life, as I know my own heart, I have no hope for to-day or to-morrow, for life or death, for time or eternity, but in the Cross of my Saviour. I have that hope, for

> In the Cross of Christ I glory,
>   Towering o'er the wrecks of time,
> All the light of sacred story
>   Gathers round its head sublime.
>
> When the woes of life o'ertake me,
>   Hopes deceive and fears annoy,
> Never shall the Cross forsake me:
>   Lo! It glows with peace and joy.
>
> When the sun of bliss is beaming
>   . Light and love upon my way:
> From the Cross the radiance streaming
>   Adds more luster to the day.
>
> Bane and blessing, pain and pleasure,
>   By the Cross are sanctified;
> Peace is there that knows no measure,
>   Joys that through all time abide.

CHAPTER X

THE HOLY SPIRIT THROUGH CHRIST, IN THE CHURCH, FOR THE WORLD

Being therefore by the right hand of God exalted, and having received of the Father the promise of the Holy Ghost, He hath poured forth this, which ye see and hear.
ACTS 2:33.

CHRISTIANITY'S SUPREME CREDENTIAL IS CHRISTIANITY. Of all miracles it is the greatest. There are two historic facts which are indisputable: first, the death of Jesus, and, second, the Church of Jesus. Or to put that in another way, history attests the fact that somehow or other out of death came life, that after the death of Jesus there began in human history a new order of men and women, a new order of society, new ideals, new impulses, new forces. That is the supreme wonder. We look back again to the Cross of our Lord, and we may say of Him reverently in the language of the writer of the letter to the Hebrews concerning Abraham, but with more definiteness, Here is One, not only as good as dead, but dead; nevertheless, His thoughts, His teaching, He Himself, guide and govern those movements of the race which tend toward its perfection and its permanence. This is the supreme wonder, the wonder of all wonders.

When we turn to this last historic pamphlet of the New Testament and read the story of the new beginning of the

Christian movement after the resurrection and ascension of our Lord we find the secret of the victories that have resulted. In this second chapter of the Acts of the Apostles we have the account of the first blaze of light, and the first thrill of power following the resurrection and ascension. The story is always full of fascination. We can never read this chapter without feeling the thrill of it, and the power of it. The ideals suggested and revealed constitute the reason of this perpetual appeal rather than the realization of these things by the men of apostolic times, for the book of the Acts is as surely a revelation of failure as it is of victory. I do not know how far it is wise to take comfort from that fact, but I do find my own heart perpetually comforted by it. In these days of lamentation and wailing over the failure of the Christian Church I go back to the beginning and find the same story still. Through all the centuries victories seem to have been in spite of unfaithfulness rather than as the result of faithfulness.

That which began at Pentecost is abiding. There is no need to pray for a new Pentecost. There can be no new Pentecost. Pentecost was the occasion when the Spirit of God came to create and abide with the Church of God, and He has never been withdrawn. This place of our assembly is as full of the presence and power of that Holy Spirit of God as was the upper room at Jerusalem. We may not hear the sound of a rushing mighty wind, but the Spirit is proceeding from the Father through the Son into the lives of believing men and women, and still is that selfsame Spirit poured upon all flesh.

Then it may be said, Where is the secret of present failure? How is it that we are not conscious of the same experience? In answer to that, two things must be said. First, that there were experiences of the day of Pentecost that were not intended to abide. Things that were necessary at the moment have passed, but the spiritual facts have not passed. We do not ask for the sound of the rushing mighty wind, we do not seek—if we have spiritual apprehension of the true meaning of this Pentecostal effusion—for manifest tongues of fire upon the heads of the assembled saints. But, second, we do ask for the power itself, and we do most earnestly desire to know something of the experience that came to these men, that filled them with ecstasy, with joy; that irradiated their faces and put songs on lips which had perhaps never sung before. We do desire to know the secrets of that power which made prophecy prevailing in those olden days and constrained men to obedience to the Lord Christ. To know the power of this Pentecostal effusion surely we must discover its laws, and any measure of present failure is the result of failure in that particular.

The first symbol of the Christian Church was the tongue of fire. The first experience of the outpoured Spirit was fulness of life and fulness of joy. This fulness of life and joy was expressed in that strange, I had almost said weird, manifestation in which men in various tongues praised God. The tongue was not a gift enabling men to preach or prophesy, it was a gift for praise. The first function of the Christian Church is that of praise. The first function of the Christian priesthood is eucharistic in the true sense of that great word, that of the offering of thanksgiving and praise. When the Spirit of life fell on these men their eyes were opened, and they saw as they never had seen, and understood as they never had understood, things concerning Christ and concerning God; and the multitudes listening heard them in their own tongues showing forth the mighty works of God. They had become a company of priests offering praise. In fulness of life there was fulness of joy, and out of that came the words which magnified the name of God, and sounded His praise abroad.

The first impression this Church produced on the city

was that of mental arrest, they were compelled to consider; it was that of mental defeat, they were unable to explain; it was that of mental activity, they attempted to explain. The city was arrested, not by a preacher, but by a Spirit-filled church. That church, manifesting the fulness of its life in great joy, in great ecstasy, and in praise, created the opportunity for the Christian preacher to proclaim the evangel of Jesus.

The first activity in the power of the Spirit on behalf of men outside the company of the saints was that of this discourse of Peter. Observe the scheme of it. The people of the city said, "What meaneth *this?*" Peter replied, "Be *this* known unto you, and give ear unto my words," and then proceeded to detailed explanation, of which the central declaration was, "*This* is that which hath been spoken by the prophet Joel." The address culminated in the word of the text, "He hath poured forth *this,* which ye see and hear." The city said, "What meaneth *this?*" Peter replied, "Be *this* known unto you; .... *This* is that; .... He hath poured forth *this.*"

Now let us confine our attention to the last word of the answer of Peter to the inquiry of the city. We shall dwell on the "He" and on the "this," speaking first of the relation of the Pentecostal baptism to Christ, and, second, of the meaning of the Pentecostal baptism for the world.

The relation of the Pentecostal baptism to Christ is most clearly declared. Having quoted from the prophecy of Joel and having declared that the signs which they saw and the circumstances in the midst of which they found themselves were in fulfilment of that prophecy, Peter arrested the attention of his hearers anew as he said, "Ye men of Israel, hear these words." Then in an orderly sequence he told the story of Jesus. First, he named the Lord, Jesus of Nazareth. This was His most familiar name, the one by which He had been known, the one which had been used by the disciples in love, and by other men in contempt. Second, he declared the witness of the miracles to the perfection of His nature as he spoke of Him as "a man approved of God among you," not a man that God approved, but a man that God demonstrated "by mighty works and wonders and signs," not which He wrought, but "which God did by Him in the midst of you, even as ye yourselves know." The miracles and wonders were works of God wrought through the absolute perfection of Christ's humanity. Then, immediately, he came to the last fact of which these men had been conscious: "Him"—and after a parenthesis, "being delivered up by the determinate counsel and foreknowledge of God," which the men who heard him certainly could not understand—"ye by the hand of lawless men did crucify and slay."

In these words so far the Apostle had massed all that these men knew of Jesus, the manifest things—Jesus of Nazareth, a Man demonstrated among you by God in miracles and wonders and signs, a Man crucified. Beyond this these men who listened were unable to go of their own knowledge.

But the Apostle had much more to say. He followed the mission of Jesus into spiritual heights which these men could not understand; he told them, if I may use the terms of time in relation to eternity, of the events which had followed the Cross, which for them had ended the career of Jesus, "whom God raised up"; and "being therefore by the right hand of God exalted, and having received of the Father the promise of the Holy Ghost, He hath poured forth this." He has given to these men this fulness of life which expresses itself in the praises which have arrested the city, amazed, and made it critical.

As we read the story there is evident throughout conflict between grace and sin; the Divine activity beneficent in its intention toward men, and human activity in its intention hostile to God. As we watch the course of our Lord's ministry revealed in this wonderful paragraph we see Him as the center of perpetual conflict between sin on the one hand and the grace of God on the other.

Mark the movement of sin. Sin first expressed itself in blindness in the presence of the revelation of the life of Jesus; His words and His works witnessing to truth Himself demonstrated by God by the wonders He wrought; men were blind, not seeing, not understanding. Blinding their own eyes, hardening their own hearts, they moved ever more persistently into the mental mood of definite hostility. Sin expressed itself finally in the Cross, as there it refused the Kingship of the Christ. That Cross was man's answer to everything Christ had said, to His spiritual conceptions, to His severe and awful moral requirements, to His offer of pardon and of grace. The Cross of Jesus Christ is the very center and ultimate of human sin.

At that point in the history sin had done its worst, it had crucified the Lord of glory, and laid His body to rest in the tomb. Sinning man could do no more, he had become impotent, he had wreaked his vengeance on Jesus. One can hardly feel anything other than contempt for the rude superstition that watched the body of a dead man.

But now through all the movement observe the activity of grace. In the life of Jesus grace revealed God and the will of God concerning man. Through that life of Jesus God was calling man back to Himself. What of the Cross? Has sin there won a victory? Is that the ultimate word, is grace defeated, is the intention of God defeated? In the course of the declaration we find that which was a parenthesis so far as the men who listened were concerned, "being delivered up by the determinate counsel and foreknowledge of God." None knew the Cross like that until after Pentecost. None saw the Cross so until he looked back at it in the light of the resurrection. But looking back through the resurrection and in the light of the Spirit, Peter and the rest saw God acting in the Cross in determined love, mastering sin in a mystery that baffles us, in darkness that we never can enter, darkness which has at its center light unapproachable. In that hour and mystery of the Cross God is seen dealing with the sin that had expressed itself ultimately therein, and so dealing with it as to be victorious over it.

We now take the next step as suggested in the address of the Apostle. The victory was won, the Lord was raised from the dead and exalted. Then followed the ascension. As in all reverence we follow the Man of Nazareth into the light and glory of the heavenly place, the Spirit through Peter interprets the activity of that sacred hour in words which entirely transcend our explanation. The declaration that the Lord "received of the Father the promise of the Holy Ghost" can be understood only as we follow our Lord into the light of the heavenly place and realize that He passed in as the representative One. In that moment man returned to God, and God returned to man in Christ. By the mystery of the wounds He bore He asked, as He said He would, for the Spirit that He might bestow it upon all trusting souls. Not by right of His sinless humanity did He claim the Spirit, but by the right of His passion. Not for Himself did He claim the Holy Spirit, for was not the whole history of His earthly career the history of fellowship with the Spirit? Born of the Spirit, baptized of the Spirit, in the power of the Spirit, He entered on His ministry. In the great mystery of the passion was it not also true that through the eternal Spirit He offered Himself to God? Now risen Man and ascended Lord, in the presence of God He received the Spirit as the representative of those whom He had left behind, representing them by the very wounds He bore, representing them by the passion through which He had passed. When the Father gave Him the Spirit, to use still this mystic figurative language, He gave the Spirit to Him as representing those for whom He had been wounded and bruised, whose place He had taken in the mystery of the Cross by which He had overcome sin. He represented humanity as humanity's Saviour. Then we reach the final word, descriptive of the final movement, "He hath poured forth this."

Thus the Spirit on the day of Pentecost came to these men in answer to the prayer of Jesus, not in answer to their praying, not even in answer to their obedience, but entirely and absolutely in answer to the request in heavenly places of Christ Himself, the One Whose wounds told the story of His conflict, and Whose presence there proclaimed the fact of His victory. The Spirit thus given through the Son united those on whom He fell to the Son in a life of absolute identity, ultimately making those to whom He came like the Son.

If we have received the Spirit we have received it from the Father and through His Son. If we who name His name are receiving His Spirit, we are receiving the Spirit through the Son, not in answer to our praying, not as a reward for some sacrifice we are making. All these may be conditions which we fulfil, but this great Pentecostal gift of the Spirit, making men and women one with the Lord, indwelling them so that the very life of the Lord is dominant within them, expressing the power of the Lord through them, is in answer to the prayer of the Lord and the result of what He did.

What, then, was the meaning and what the value of this Pentecostal baptism for the world? It was the creation of the Christian Church of God. That is a phrase I used carefully, *the Christian Church of God.* The Church of God, if you will; but there had been a Church of God in some senses before this. In the seventh chapter of this book of the Acts we have mentioned the Church in the wilderness, that is the assembly, the congregation, the *ecclesia* in the wilderness. This, however, was the *Christian* Church of God. It is an interesting fact that the phrase, the Church of Christ, is used only once in the New Testament, and then by an apostle speaking of local churches. This Church of God, the Christian Church of God, is a new entity, a new nation, a new people. The differences between this Church of God born at Pentecost and the Church of God existing before are vital differences, but we need not now stay to look at them. In that moment, when those who had been individual disciples were brought into living union with the Lord Himself and so into living union with each other, the Christian Church was born.

What, then, is the Church in the world, considering it as a whole? It is God's institute of praise, God's institute of prayer, and God's institute of prophecy. The whole Church is, first of all, an institute created to praise God. "Ye are an elect race, a royal priesthood, a holy nation, a people for God's own possession, that ye may shew forth the excellencies of Him Who called you out of darkness into His marvellous light." The first purpose of the Church is that she shall praise God. I think we need to remember that in its first application and its simplest the first function of the Christian life is that of praising. Yet let us take the larger outlook. The Christian Church exists so to reveal God as to utter forth His praise, so to make God known to men who know Him not that in the presence of the revelation they may be filled with awe, and wonder, and amazement; so to make God known that God shall be attractive to humanity. Whether we are prepared to accept the declaration or not, the experience abides. Men of the world can know God only as God is revealed to them through His people. The Word of God can be powerful only as it is incarnate. Is not that the meaning of the central mystery of our holy religion? God came no nearer to humanity when Jesus was born in Bethlehem, but He came into visibility, into manifestation. In proportion as in this Church of Jesus Christ His life is reproduced, God is being revealed anew. Our first business is that of praising Him, praising Him with lip and with life, in the actual songs we sing, in the hallelujahs we lift; praising Him by all the habits of our life, by the perpetual testimony of our ways as they announce the fact of His being, the fact of His love. That was the first effect the Church produced. Filled with life, light flashed from the eyes of the disciples, songs were on their lips, they magnified the mighty works of God, and the city was compelled to listen. In that hour of Pentecost God created for Himself by the coming of the Spirit through Christ a people for His own praise and glory, a kingdom of priests that they might offer to Him sacrifices of praise and thanksgiving. Unless Pentecost produces in our life fulness of joy and makes us a people filled with praise we are failing sadly. The first function of the Christian Church is that she should be to the praise of God.

In that hour, moreover, God created in the world a great institute of prayer, for the function of the priesthood is not only eucharistic, it is intercessory. By the coming of the Spirit He created a people able to pray. Surely this is what the Apostle meant in his Roman letter when he spoke of creation groaning and travailing in its pain, and then spoke of the Church in the midst of the groaning creation, the Church groaning and travailing together with creation in pain; and at last declared that "the Spirit maketh intercession for us with groanings that cannot be uttered." The Spirit of God understanding the pain of creation is grieved thereby, sorrow is caused in the very heart of God by the agony of humanity; that Spirit indwelling a company of people interprets to them the agony of creation, so that they enter into a new compassionate sympathy with all the suffering of the world, and thus in the midst of the groaning creation they constitute an institute of prayer. No man can pray for the world unless the Spirit interpret to him the world's agony, and the Spirit cannot interpret the world's agony to any man unless that man live in the midst of the world's agony. Not by retirement from the world, not by hiding away within a monastic institution, not by seeking to develop my own spiritual life by removing myself from the agony of the world, can I ever pray for the world; but because I live every day in the midst of its busy life, am close to it and know it, and because the Spirit of God in me leads me into the secret of the deepest meaning of the world's agony and pain so that I no longer treat it as a superficial disease that can be dealt with by the nostrums of humanity, but as a great heart trouble that needs blood and sacrifice to deal with it, am I able to pray. Out of that revelation of the meaning of the world's agony created by the Spirit in the hearts of believing men they are able to pray. The Church of God in the economy of God was created an institute of prayer.

But more, not for praise alone was the Church created, not alone for prayer, but also for prophecy, in the highest use of the great word, for proclamation. As with lip and life the saints praise, so by lip and life the saints should preach. The Spirit came uniting these men to the Lord, disannulling orphanage and canceling distance to make the risen and ascended Christ a living bright reality. By so doing He enabled these men to speak to the Lord familiarly as those who have constant comradeship with Him, and by so doing enabled them to reveal the Lord of Whom they spoke in tone and temper and habit and speech, and in all activity. Reverently and superlatively, He came to multiply and unite in the perfect Humanity of Nazareth all the scattered members of the one great Christ o'er all the earth that in the case of all of them, and not only in the case of the overseers, bishops, deacons, both by their preaching and their living they might show forth the glory of God and proclaim the power of His great evangel.

In conclusion, let us recognize that our possession of this power of Pentecost depends on our relation to Christ. Glancing at the description which Peter gave of the progress of our Lord toward the heights, we described it as a conflict between sin and grace. The question for our hearts is this, In such conflict, on which side are we? Are we in true fellowship with God in the determination of His grace to deal with sin in its opposition to the way and will of God, refusing to come in obedience to the revelation of life, refusing to yield ourselves to the claims of the Christ? Such questions must be left unanswered in great assemblies. They are for answer only in the privacy of the individual life.

Perchance the question may be stated in another way. Let it thus be asked in individual lives. What is the influence we exert? The answer to that is the answer to the question whether or not we have this Spirit of Christ. "If any man have not the Spirit of Christ, he is none of His." If any man be living still the life of blindness to all the will of God, the life of rebellion against the will of God, the life which in its practical activity refuses to crown Christ, that is demonstration of the fact that such a man lacks the Spirit of God. On the other hand, are we conscious that we have seen the glory, that in some measure at any rate already we have put the crown on the brow of Christ, and that the deepest passion of heart and life is to crown Him and make Him known to others? Then we may take heart and know by that sign that this Spirit of God has been given to us. As to whether we may be living in all the fulness and privilege of the Spirit is another question. The question that demands our earnest attention is, Are we ministers who praise His name in lip and life, do we know the secret of prayer that prevails in the midst of the world's agony, are we proclaiming the evangel in our words and in our works? If not, then let us search our hearts now and discover whether we have been self-deceived and lack the Spirit of God. As the Spirit comes we receive all that we need in order to praise and pray and prophesy. He comes in response to our belief in the living Lord at the commencement; He perpetually comes and proceeds, flowing in, filling and overflowing, in response to the attitude of belief maintained. The celebration of a festival is of no profit save as we yield ourselves to all the facts which we celebrate. May it be ours, then, to know that union with the Lord in life and service which can come only by the presence and power of the Spirit.

CHAPTER XI

JUBILATION IN DESOLATION

> *For though the fig tree shall not blossom,*
> *Neither shall fruit be in the vines;*
> *The labour of the olive shall fail,*
> *And the fields shall yield no meat;*
> *The flock shall be cut off from the fold,*
> *And there shall be no herd in the stalls;*
> *Yet I will rejoice in the Lord,*
> *I will joy in the God of my salvation.*
>
> HABAKKUK 3:17, 18.

THIS IS AN ARRESTING TEXT. THERE IS RHYTHM IN ITS movement and a vividness in its description which compel our attention, yet that which is most impressive is the contrast between the conditions described and the experience claimed. The conditions are these:

> For though the fig tree shall not blossom,
> Neither shall fruit be in the vines;
> The labour of the olive shall fail,
> And the fields shall yield no meat;
> The flock shall be cut off from the fold,
> And there shall be no herd in the stalls.

And the experience is this:

> Yet will I rejoice in the Lord,
> I will joy in the God of my salvation.

The earlier part of the text constitutes one of the dreariest pictures man ever drew. To summarize in a word, it is the picture of a scene of desolation. Yet that is preliminary, it is the introduction to something that is to follow. As we read the statement through, we find that the figure in the foreground is radiant and exultant, and all the dreariness in the background serves but to fling up into clear relief this figure in the foreground. As we proceed, we discover that the dirge is but the prelude to a plan, and if we summarize the conditions by the one word "desolation," we may express the experience by the one word "jubilation." This is the mystery, the arresting wonder of the text, that these two things are brought together, jubilation in the midst of desolation. If we were reading this for the first time, or if we found it in any other literature than this, we should be driven to inquire, Was this man a fanatic? Was he deluded? Or did he speak a wisdom of which this world knows nothing when he crowned the song which describes desolation with the song which expresses jubilation? We believe that this is a song of the higher wisdom, and that the singer was a philosopher in possession of the true secret of life.

Let us observe at once that he did not begin on this level. I turn back to the opening of this prophecy, and I find the same man speaking in other terms and in other tones:

> O Lord, how long shall I cry, and Thou wilt not hear? I cry out unto Thee of violence, and Thou wilt not save. Why dost Thou shew me iniquity, and look upon perverseness? for spoiling and violence are before me: and there is strife, and contention riseth up. Therefore the law is slacked, and judgment doth never go forth: for the wicked doth compass about the righteous; therefore judgment goeth forth perverted.

That is the tone with which the prophecy begins; yet it ends with the song of jubilation in the midst of circumstances of desolation. To that matter we shall return again presently.

Having affirmed our belief in the wisdom of this man, let us consider the ground of his confidence as it is suggested in his psalm; and let us consider the joy of his experience as it is expressed therein, and then turn again to a consideration of that process of faith by which he rose to this height from the depth which is revealed in the opening of the prophecy.

First, then, as to the ground of his confidence. At the head of the third chapter of the prophecy of Habakkuk we find these words: "A prayer of Habakkuk the prophet, set to Shigionoth."

We are at once arrested by this strange, mystic, suggestive word "Shigionoth" at the opening of the psalm. There have been many opinions concerning the meaning of this word. It has been suggested that it was a description of poetry that was almost incoherent, a series of expressions having little connection with each other. In that suggestion there may be an element of truth, but it is by no means finally satisfactory. The word is found in only one other place in our Bible, and that is over Psalm 7, where it appears in the singular form, whereas in this case it is in the plural. In a comparison of these two psalms we cannot now indulge, but such a comparison reveals two qualities which seem to be quite opposed and yet to be an underlying unity. Dr. Thirtle, in a recent volume on the Psalms, has suggested that the title means loud cries merely and that the thought must be interpreted by the nature of the psalm. In Psalm 7 we have the loud cries of a man who had passed through a period of pain and anguish and trial, and was celebrating his deliverance therefrom. If we take the whole of this psalm of Habakkuk we shall find that it is a series of extollations of God.

Its first great note is the uttering of the name of Jehovah:

O Jehovah, I have heard the report of Thee and am afraid;
O Jehovah, revive Thy work in the midst of the years.

The prayer is, "Keep alive Thy work" rather than "Revive Thy work." This opening cry was the prophet's reply to the revelation which had preceded it. Let us go back briefly over the whole prophecy. Habakkuk was confronted by the problem of prevalent anarchy; he declared that there was no justice, no equity, no right dealing; and out of the midst of his overwhelming sense of the iniquity of his own times he cried to God, and, in effect, he said, Why art Thou doing nothing? God answered him in the secret of his own soul, as He declared to him, I am at work, but if I told you what I was doing you would hardly believe Me. I am employing the Chaldeans, people outside the covenant, as My instruments to punish My own people. When the prophet heard this, with new astonishment he argued with God, How canst Thou employ a man more wicked than these Thy people in order to punish them? Then he said, I will away to my watch tower and wait and see! And while he waited God declared to him the true principle of all life: the puffed up soul is destroyed, but the righteous live by faith.

This is the history of Habukkuk's triumph over the appearances of the hour. The man had cried to God, and God had answered him. Now he said:

I have heard the report of Thee, and am afraid:
O Lord, revive Thy work in the midst of the years.

The method of that work I cannot understand. I thought Thou hadst forsaken us. I made my protest. Thou hast told me how Thou art working, and I am still puzzled! But, O Lord, keep alive Thy work, even though I do not understand its method and cannot observe its secret. "In the midst of the years make it known, only in wrath remember mercy."

Then, immediately following this opening prayer, there is a great psalm of worship of God:

> God came from Teman,
> And the Holy One from mount Paran,

and so in mystic sentences, many of them defying all our attempts at exposition, he rose to the heights of Divine contemplation and extollation; until at last from the heights, turning his eyes again to the desolation, he said:

> For though the fig tree shall not blossom,
> Neither shall fruit be in the vines;
> The labour of the olive shall fail,
> And the fields shall yield no meat;
> The flock shall be cut off from the fold,
> And there be no herd in the stalls:
> Yet I will rejoice in the Lord,
> I will joy in the God of my salvation.

Thus out of the midst of adverse, perplexing circumstances the prophet had been brought face to face with God, and in communion with God he had reconsidered the present in the light of past history and of the presence of God. If you will examine the psalm at your leisure you will find that while there are things in it which defy exposition, this man was clearly looking back, reviewing the way along which God had led His people, even to that hour of darkness and difficulty. As he looked back and remembered the way along which God had led them, he said, in spite of all the desolation, my heart shall be filled with rejoicing, and I will extol God.

Can we not see some of the things that were presented to his mind? Attempting to put ourselves back into his place, to stand side by side with him in the midst of the desolation already apparent, and presently to be even more so, I think we can discover some of the sources of his confidence.

JUBILATION IN DESOLATION

This song is in the future tense; the prophet was describing the terrible desolation that would come with the coming of the Chaldeans. How dare he rejoice? It seems to me that these are some of the arguments which produced his joy.

First, he knew that if everything were destroyed, God is able to create anew all that shall be needed for the sustenance and fulfilment of life. To grant the first miracle of creation is to see that everything is possible, that even the desert may blossom as the rose, that even the high mountains of difficulty may be brought low, that even the deepest valleys of life may be lifted to the height of the everlasting hills. That is the simplest proposition that the man of faith will make when his eyes are turned from the oppressive circumstances of the hour to God Himself.

As this man reviewed the history of the past he was warranted in believing that God was able to send supplies from sources other than he knew. Although the fig tree shall not blossom, nor fruit be in the vine; although there be no promise of spring, although all that we have done shall wither and produce no fruit, God is able to supply our need from resources of which we know absolutely nothing. Habakkuk would remember the way God had guided His people; he would remember how in the wilderness, which the great Leader Himself had described as a great and terrible wilderness, God had hidden resources; that quails were supplied, and water provided from the flinty rock. This prophet would remember also the experience of another prophet, who in the reaction after a tremendous victory sat beneath the juniper tree and said, Let me die, and not live. And he would remember that in that hour of strange desolation angel ministers brought him bread and water. Consequently he said in his heart, God can supply all that is needful from resources of which we know nothing, and this song was the result.

Did he not also know as he sang this song that God was

able to multiply the little and make it last through the distress? That was the wilderness experience, in which the shoes of the pilgrims did not wax old. That had been the experience of the widow who found that the little meal in the barrel and the oil in the cruse had never grown less until the distress had passed. Or may he not also have argued that, if there should be no supply of his need, no meeting of the physical need of the people who put their trust in God; if He created nothing new, sent no supplies from sources other than he knew, if He did not even make the little last till the distress were overpast, then, if necessary, God could sustain without food?

Unbelief springs in the heart of this congregation when the preacher suggests that; but it is unbelief! Sight will never believe such a thing possible when faith affirms it. Faith does not affirm that to be the ordinary method of God; faith does not declare that it is likely God will sustain men without food; but faith does declare that it is possible for God to do so. This man would remember how Moses on the mount for forty days had been sustained, how Elijah on Horeb had been sustained, and he would say, Although all physical means of support and sustenance are denied, I will rejoice, for if it be necessary for the fulfilment of the Divine purpose and the carrying out of the Divine intention, God—and the emphasis must always be there—is able to sustain life even without food.

Yet I do not think that this method of argument created the full inspiration of the song. It was the song of a man who, having seen all these things, yet rose to higher heights. It was the song of a man who had come to the conviction that although all these things should fail, God Himself could not fail. It was the song of a man who but a little while before had imagined that God was inactive, indifferent, but who had discovered in the process of honest communion with God that He was active in spite of the appearances of the hour.

JUBILATION IN DESOLATION

He had discovered God anew in communion, and now he rose to the height of this great song, and declared that although material support of life should be withdrawn entirely, yet in God is still found fulness of life, a complete joy, permanently satisfying, and absolute and undisturbed peace. Rising above the surrounding desolation, he extolled God, and though in different language, expressed exactly the same philosophy as did Job when, in a moment of rare illumination, he exclaimed, "Though He slay me, yet will I trust in Him."

In the second place, let us consider the joy of this man's experience;

> I will rejoice in the Lord,
> I will joy in the God of my salvation.

His knowledge of God produced his confidence in God, and that confidence in God immediately and inevitably produced joy. The words he made use of are remarkable words; "I will rejoice in the Lord." I hope I shall produce no shock when I translate them literally. Take the first Hebrew word and express it quite literally, and this is it: I will *jump for joy* in the Lord. Take the second of the words and translate it with equal literalness, and this is it: I will *spin round* in the God of my salvation. Does that seem as though I were spoiling a great passage? I think some of these passages need spoiling in this way in these pre-eminently respectable days when congregations are shocked if a man say Amen! Exuberant joy, a bounding joy was this man's experience, and in these words we have such joy expressed. This was no cool, calculating word. I will jump for joy in Jehovah, I will spin round with delight in the God of my salvation. Do we know anything of that emotion in the midst of desolation, not when the ordinary activities of everyday life are prospering, but when it seems that there is the most calamitous failure everywhere, no blossom on the fig tree, no fruit on the vine, the labor of the olive failing, the flock gone from the field and the herd from the stall? It is all Eastern; I should hardly know how to express that in the language of London, but you business men know. Perhaps we might employ a modern word, *bankruptcy*. Everything gone, yet will I jump for joy in the Lord, I will spin round with gladness in my God. I believe that one thing the Church most sadly lacks to-day is exuberant, buoyant joy in the Lord God. I do not forget that a woman laughed at a king who danced before the Lord; but I thank God that the king danced before the Lord. This word of Habakkuk was compelled by the joy that sprang within him. This was not imitation joy. It was that of a man filled with delight even in the midst of circumstances of desolation.

If I have thus laid my emphasis on the nature of the joy, let us carefully mark the sphere of the joy. "I will rejoice *in the Lord.*" "I will joy *in the God* of my salvation," not in circumstances but over them, not in the part that is seen, but in the whole that faith alone can comprehend. Not in circumstances can I rejoice oftentimes, but if I have this clear vision of God it is given to me to rejoice over them; if I simply look at them my heart will be depressed, filled with a sense of sorrow; but if I see the whole, the ultimate, the unveiling of the purpose of God; if I really believe that the bud may have a bitter taste but sweet will be the fruit; if I have seen God and know that His purpose is a purpose of great love, then surely I may triumph over circumstances, not in self, but in God.

That takes us to our last consideration, that to which I referred at the beginning, and on which I have touched incidentally. How did this man climb to this height from the level on which he began? The whole value of this prophecy on the side of human experience is its revelation of a process. As a revelation of the method of God it is a most surprising prophecy and one which we need to study. So far as man's experience is concerned, the prophecy is of value because it shows the process. How did Habakkuk arrive here? First, through doubt in which he was absolutely honest; second, through trial in which he waited; finally, through communion and the revelation of a secret which he obeyed.

First, through doubt in which he was honest. The picture presented at the commencement of the story is that of prevalent anarchy, the silent God and a man doubting. Let no man be angry with Habakkuk for doubting. I would utter a paradox: it is only the man of faith who really doubts. There is no room for doubt unless you believe in God. Blot out God and everything is certain, mechanical, fixed; twice two are four—and you may as well be buried. If the eye has ever been lifted, and the soul has ever been conscious of more than the dust, then there must be the hour of questioning—if you are afraid of the word "doubt." What is God doing? Why is He so silent? That is where this man started. Forgive me if I modernize my story. He did not then start a society of men who had found relief in doubt. He did not talk to other men about his doubts. He talked to God about them. That was his first step toward the heights. If a man is oppressed by the difficulties by which he is surrounded, if he talk to the dwellers in darkness he and they will abide in darkness. If, on the other hand, he will tell the doubt to God there will always come an answer. That is the way of triumph, that is the first upward step, that when a man doubts God he tells God so. That is fine agnosticism. Habakkuk was in the midst of doubt, and he said, O Lord, how long shall I cry of vioence and Thou dost not answer?

The answer was very surprising, so surprising that we cannot understand the surprise until we get right back into the Hebrew atmosphere and realize the exclusivism of these people. God said, Behold, the Chaldeans; I am bringing them to do My work, I am employing forces outside the covenant. That was the first answer. If some of us will begin in the midst of a dark outlook to talk to God like this, telling Him we cannot understand what He is doing, it is very probable He will give us the same answer: Do not try to measure all My going by the statistics of the Christian Church; find Me at work beyond the borders in which you have thought confine Me. We still say that God must do everything through His Church. He wills to do so; but if the Church fail, God cannot; and He will then gird some Cyrus outside the Church, and employ the very wrath of men outside the covenant to praise Him, and make the remainder to be restrained. So this man beginning in the depths dared to speak the thing he thought, that God was not at work, and this was the answer.

Second, he found his way higher through trials during which he waited. There was the approaching foe, the Chaldeans actually coming; presently they must sweep over the country, and everything must lie in desolation. He looked on the coming desolation, and saw that God was acting, but he could not understood God's method. What then did he do? The most difficult thing of all:

> I will stand upon my watch, and set me up upon the tower, and will look forth to see what He will speak to me, and what I shall answer concerning my complaint.

I have complained that He is using the Chaldeans, I know He is doing it; I will wait the interpretation of events in explanation of the mystery that I cannot fathom. I will wait. I think some of the apparently simple injunctions of the Bible are the most difficult to obey. Take this one: "Be still, and know that I am God." It sounds so simple, until I begin to do it, and then I find that it is the hardest thing in the world to be still. The most perfect exercise of faith is to wait, to wait patiently for Him. That is what this man did. I will look forth to see what He does. I will wait.

In that waiting God came again, and said to him:

Write the vision, and make it plain upon tables, that he may run that readeth it. For the vision is yet for the appointed time, and it hasteth toward the end, and shall not lie: though it tarry, wait for it; because it will surely come, it will not delay.

God thus said to the waiting man, I will give you a secret that will enable you to wait; I will strengthen you in the process of your waiting. This is the secret: "Behold, his soul is puffed up, it is not upright in him; but the just shall live by his faith." That was the secret of all secrets. The final step to the heights is that of communion with God, and a secret given, which must be obeyed. The righteous shall live by faith. Apply the principle, Habakkuk, to all that puzzles you. Yonder are the Chaldeans coming, the scourge of God; they are coming in pride, their soul is puffed up; know this, they cannot abide, they also must pass and perish. I will make their wrath to praise Me, and the remainder restrain. Let the principle of your life be faith, and you shall *live* . . . a great word without any qualification, because qualification almost invariably lessens the grandeur. My righteous shall *live* by faith.

Immediately the word was spoken the man answered it. He believed and rested on God, with no explanation of the circumstances in the midst of which he found himself other than the declaration of the overruling of God, the abiding government of God. He experienced no amelioration of the conditions, desolation was imminent, but the song reveals him acting on the secret whispered to his soul; and there rose loud cries of rejoicing, extollings of God, and all this out of the rapture of a soul that by faith had taken hold on God, and knew—if I may use New Testament language to interpret Old Testament experience—that "to them that love God all things work together for good."

This is a study of Old Testament times. Let me, therefore, quote to you from the words of a New Testament apostle:

> We have the word of prophecy made more sure; whereunto ye do well that ye take heed, as unto a lamp shining in a dark place, until the day dawn, and the daystar arise in your hearts; knowing this first, that no prophecy of Scripture is of private interpretation.

Peter was here thinking of the vision of the holy mount, and referring to all the ancient prophecies, he declared that in Christ they were made more sure. The great principles revealed in this Old Testament story abide, only to us they have been made more sure in Christ. In Christ we have the ratification of everything we find suggested in this psalm of ancient Hebrew time.

Let us be personal and particular in the case of our own need. This is not a message primarily for those who are in circumstances of prosperity, and who see light everywhere. Let them rejoice in the Lord for prosperity, and walk in the light by His fear. Some are in circumstances of adversity, confronting apparent desolation. I speak with such, and in all tenderness and all reserve, not out of an experience which is in perfect harmony with that of Habakkuk. I do not think I have ever risen to his height, but I see the glory of it. Can we rejoice in the midst of desolation? All the arguments in favor of his rejoicing are made more sure for us by Christ. Suppose all be swept away on which we depend. Our Master is able to create for our sustenance. He has resources of which we know nothing out of which He can meet our need. He can lay His multiplying hand on five loaves and two fishes so that they will meet the need of thousands. He can, if it be necessary, sustain without bread. If all these things are to fail, and by reason of this failing, this transient physical life of ours shall droop and wither and die, yet there will be infinite music in our Master's word to us: "I am with you alway." If Habakkuk of old could rejoice in God revealed to him, as by comparison in the twilight only, how much more may we rejoice in Him as He has been revealed to us in the grace and truth and glory of the only begotten! "Rejoice in the Lord, and again I say, Rejoice."

How shall we rise to this height of triumph over all circumstances? First, by recognition of the fact that amid the prevailing conditions which appall us Christ is at work. Is not our Master making this appeal to us to-day, that we trust Him even though He seem to be using strange instruments? Let us see the goings and victories of Christ, and dare to affirm them as such, even though we may not have been the instruments in His hands for the winning of these victories.

To summarize our meditation in a final word, What is the value of it? I would state it thus. Our joy is in proportion to our trust. Our trust is in proportion to our knowledge of God. To know Him is to trust Him. To trust Him is to triumph and excel. May we be led into fuller knowledge and so find fuller faith and so enter the fuller joy.

Then shall we be able truthfully to sing:

> Though vine nor fig-tree neither
>   Their wonted fruit shall bear;
> Though all the fields should wither,
>   Nor flocks nor herds be there;
> Yet God the same abiding,
>   His praise shall tune my voice;
> For while in Him confiding,
>   I cannot but rejoice.

CHAPTER XII

THE FIRST MESSAGE OF JESUS

From that time began Jesus to preach, and to say, Repent ye, for the Kingdom of Heaven is at hand.
MATTHEW 4:17.

That is the way in which Jesus always begins. His first message to men is always, Repent! He does not end there. He has much more to say to men than this; and even after He had said much more to His disciples, He finally confronted them, and said, "I have yet many things to say unto you, but ye cannot bear them now. Howbeit, when He, the Spirit of truth is come, He shall guide you into all the truth." But there is nothing Jesus can ever say until this first thing is said, and until this first thing is done. He began to preach, and said, "Repent ye, for the Kingdom of Heaven is at hand."

It is not only true that this is always the first message of Jesus to men. It is equally true that it is perpetually the first note of the Divine message to men. Through all the messages of history, utterances of prophets, visions of seers, and songs of psalmists, the almost monotonous burden of the Divine call is, Repent, repent. The herald, the forerunner of Jesus, came preaching, and saying, "*Repent* ye; for the Kingdom of Heaven is at hand." Jesus Himself began to preach, and to say, "*Repent* ye; for the Kingdom of Heaven is at hand."

Presently He gathered round Him twelve men, and sent them out on their mission, and they went and preached that men should *repent*. Presently the new era dawned, the new order came, and Pentecost flooded the world with new light and new life, and in the first message delivered in the power of the indwelling Spirit, Peter said, "*Repent* ye, and be baptized every one of you in the name of Jesus Christ unto the remission of your sins." When Paul stood in the heart of Gentile culture in Athens, he said, "The times of ignorance, therefore, God overlooked; but now He commandeth men that they should all everywhere *repent*." It is the perpetual keynote of the Divine message to men.

If I seek illustrations outside the Book of Revelation, and come down through the ages, I find that every subsequent visitation of power has had the necessity for repentance as its keynote. The Reformation under Martin Luther was a reformation based on the great and glorious doctrine of justification by faith. But the Reformation, based on the doctrine of justification by faith, was a revolt against the pernicious teaching that by indulgence men might continue in sin. The great revival under Wesley and Whitefield had this as the very keynote. The whole missionary movement of the last hundred years to the far-distant places of the earth has had this as its message to all men, Repent. That also was the keynote of the visitation that came to this country a generation ago under the preaching of Dwight Lyman Moody. Whereas the tone of his preaching was that of a great winsomeness, a definite call to repent sounded in every message. Wherever God has come to men in restoration, renewal, and regeneration, the first word has always been Repent. That is the keynote of all true ministry. It is the message that we are called on to deliver to all those who are outside the covenant of promise, outside the Church, and apart from Jesus Christ. There the chief emphasis must be laid, because on the repentant and regenerated individual we may build society, cleanse municipal affairs, and create the national outlook. "Repent, for the Kingdom of Heaven is at hand," is the message to the individual. It is the message to society both in the proper use of that great word and its popular and improper use. It is the message to the nation in its home and foreign policy. It is always the first message of Christ, the one in which He arrests men on the threshold, coming to the individual, the society, the nation, always with the same monotonous burden, Repent, Repent, Repent.

It is well, then, to consider this initial note in the form in which it is stated here at the commencement of our Lord's own public ministry; and, therefore, I shall ask you to think with me, first, of the great need declared, "Repent ye"; second, of the direction indicated, "the Kingdom of Heaven"; and, finally, of the possibility affirmed, "the Kingdom of Heaven is at hand."

The need is declared in the words, "Repent ye." Our very familiarity with this message, because it is the message of Christ, is in danger of making us mistake its point and misunderstand its meaning. We have been affected in our thinking on this word by the teaching of differing schools of theology, in each of which I believe there is some note of truth. Let us attempt to dismiss from our mind all the messages uttered concerning repentance by inspired writers before Jesus; let us turn from every attempt to explain the message of Christ in the terms of accepted theologies, and let us endeavor to listen to what Jesus said, praying that God will help us to understand this initial message. Not that they of the past were false, or that the messages were unimportant, but because this word of Christ is absolutely all-inclusive; moreover, because His message is not the property of one age, but is for all time, and this message is complete.

Let us, therefore, first of all attempt to look at the

Speaker, and consider the occasion on which He uttered these words.

Those familiar with the Gospel of Matthew will remember that it falls naturally into three great parts, and this is one of the great dividing points. In the first part you have the story of the preparation of Jesus for His work; and here it says, "From that time," when the preparation was complete, "He began to preach." Now it was here, at the parting of the ways, between His private and His public life, that our Lord uttered this first note. Jesus of Nazareth, the One who most perfectly fulfilled the human ideal, after a life of thirty years of observation, began to preach, and He said: "Repent." He had observed individual life in a small township, where individual life is always best seen and best known. We cannot study individual life carefully if we live in London. Men are hidden there by each other, and we never get to know the real force of individual life in a great city. But there in little Nazareth up on the hillside, far enough removed from the great centers and the great movements to be isolated from them, and yet near enough to know them, this pure Man lived and listened and watched, and came to know men by careful observation; and in preaching to the men and women He knew individually He said to them, "Repent." That is the connection. It was the first note of His preaching, born of His consciousness of the need of the people, first as the outcome of this personal and individual observation of them. Yet living there in Nazareth, remember, He had lived close to the place where the great forces of worldly ideals and methods passed and repassed. Professor Ramsay in his little book on the boyhood of Jesus, a fascinating and interesting book, reveals how the great world powers passed along the road at the foot of the hill—the Hebrew priest, the Roman soldier, the Greek merchant and traveler. Jesus had watched, and perceived, and measured. And now He came to preach to Hebrew, the religionist; to Roman, the man of power and government; to Greek, the man of culture and merchandise; and He had one word for each of them, the word "Repent."

But this is to say very little. It was not merely the message of the Man of Nazareth, due to His observation of individual life in Nazareth, and of the great currents of the world thought and action. This was the Son of God, and this was the message of the infinite and mysterious One, who was familiar with all human history and all human life; this was the message of One who presently would say, "Before Abraham was, I am." This was the message of One who did not need to ask what was in man, "for He Himself knew what was in man." This was the message not merely of the Man of Nazareth, who had lived and observed, but it was the message of the ordained Messenger, who was none other than the Son of God, clothed in human garb, that He might utter in the words of human speech the fundamental truths of Deity. Standing at the parting of the ways, and beginning to utter the great message for which men had been waiting, the infinite music, for which the world had been sighing, the great prophetic message toward which every prophetic message had moved, He said, "Repent ye, for the Kingdom of Heaven is at hand."

Having thus noticed the occasion and the Speaker, let us consider the need. I want to speak about the simplest meaning of the word "repent," for as we know what this word really means, we shall understand the message of our Lord.

In the New Testament there are two Greek words translated "repent." They have quite different meanings. One of these words means to sorrow for or regret a deed. The other word means very simply and very literally to change the mind.

Around these two words a great conflict was waged between the Reformers and the Roman Catholic theologians.

The Reformers maintained that the second word, which means a change of mind, was used of the change which is necessary to salvation; while the former word, which indicates sorrow after an event, was in some cases indicative of a change of mind, and in other cases it was not so. Such was the contention, in brief, of the Reformers. On the other hand, the Roman theologians maintained that the words were used interchangeably, that the elements of each were present in both, and they taught that the prevailing value was that of sorrow. The whole battle was waged around two Latin words, *pœnitentia*, which means the sense of sorrow, and *recipiscentia*, which means the recovery of the senses. The Reformers maintained that the essential repentance demanded by Christ and His Apostles, as well as by prophets, was a change of the senses, or a change of mind. The Roman theologians, on the other hand, maintained that the prime element indicated by the word "repent" was sorrow, and from that Roman theology we have gained our word "repent" and the associated idea that sorrow is the prime element in repentance.

I have the profoundest conviction that the Reformers were right, and that the Roman theologians were wrong. A careful examination of the New Testament use of these two words will show that the essential quality that Christ called for was not sorrow, but a change of mind. Now do not understand me to say that the change of mind will not be followed by sorrow. My experience is that the sorrow grows with the Christian life, and is not part of its initiation. I do not say there is no sorrow; I am sure there is. What I do say is that a man may be sorry, and at last be damned. We may be sorry for sin with the meanness of motive, which means that we are afraid of punishment, and no fear of punishment ever had in it the evangelical value of repentance. The repentance that Christ preached, and His Apostles preached, the repentance which is demanded of every man is always indicated by the use of the word that means a change of mind.

When Christ used that word, and when, as I have no doubt in the hearing of the men who listened to Him, it had exactly that meaning of change of mind, He had passed beyond the outer circumference of things into the inner center of a man's life. He began by declaring to men that their thought was wrong, that their conception of life was wrong. Now we say to a man, alas, too often, Change your conduct. Jesus never begins by telling a man to change his conduct. That is to begin in the externalities of human life. He comes to a man, and says, Change your mind, and by that word He means that men hold wrong views at the very center of their being. The word "repent" passes into the fundamental realm, the thought of a man's life. We are not accustomed to think about this deepest fact, and even in preaching we are too often more occupied with conduct than with creed. I use the word "creed" very carefully; I am not referring to the creed prepared for us to recite, I am referring to the creed of our life, to the deepest conception of it, to the underlying and overmastering thing that we absolutely believe.

We all believe something, and it is the something which a man believes that makes his conduct and finally makes his character. "As a man thinketh in his heart, so is he," and when Jesus came and began His preaching, instead of starting a society to correct the conduct of men, He faced men, and He said: Change your mind, repent, get right at the center of things.

But the word that demands a change in the thought or mind, or conception, does not tarry there. For the moment a man has really changed his mind or his belief his conduct will be changed. Let me take a concrete, very simple, and familiar illustration. A man declares, "I believe in God the Father

Almighty." I do not know whether he believes that; I may have heard him say it, but I do not know whether it is true. How shall I find out? I shall be able to find out on Monday, Tuesday, Wednesday, Thursday, Friday, and Saturday. A man's creed is not to be measured by the occasion when he recites it, but by the life that follows its recitation. When Jesus takes hold of a man, and says, Change your mind, He changes the conduct of the man, and then the character. That is the order of procedure. If a man's conception of life is wrong his conduct will be wrong, and, finally, his character. Jesus does not begin by changing conduct, for He cannot do it from the outside of things; but passing behind the character, and beneath the conduct, He says, Change your mind, get right in the deepest and profoundest fact of your life.

This call of Christ is revolutionary. It calls for upheaval, change, and the alteration of all things. It is radical, passing through the external to the internal. But it is also regenerative, declaring the only way in which it is possible for man to live a new life. This is always the call of Jesus: Repent. For human life, social life, national life, Jesus Christ is the most revolutionary teacher the world has ever had. Looking into the face of the priest, He said Repent; you have a conception of life which is false, change it. He looked into the faces of the pleasure-seekers, and said: Repent, change your mind. Jesus Christ confronts you. You are interested in Him, and speculative about Him; perchance you are even daring to patronize Him. There is no blasphemy greater than the patronage of Jesus Christ. He says: Repent; your conduct and character are wrong. They are wrong because your thought is wrong; your conception is wrong, change it. That is revolutionary. It is radical.

Let us pass to the second point. Jesus in this great word did not merely say, Repent. To leave the word at that point would be to reveal all I have attempted to say as to its revolutionary and radical nature, and to leave unsaid the thing of chief importance. He indicated a direction. "Repent . . . *the Kingdom of Heaven* is at hand." Repentance there may be, and yet the life be hopelessly wrong, for repentance means a change of mind; and a man may change his mind, and his new conception be as false as was the old conception. There was a time when that brilliant and gifted woman, Annie Besant, changed her mind and announced that she was no longer a secularist and a materialist. She repented, she changed her mind, and she became a theosophist, believing in Mahatmas among Himalayan heights. She repented, but the direction of her repentance was wrong, the nature of the change was wrong, a false conception gave place to another false conception. Jesus does not come to men and say, You are wrong, get a new idea of life. Said He: "Repent, for *the Kingdom of Heaven* is at hand." Herein is direction. Herein is the indication of what the change is to be.

The phrase is suggestive. There occur in the Scriptures of truth certain terms, which we need to consider; the Kingdom of God, the Kingdom of Heaven, the Kingdom, the Church. Now these terms of Scripture are quite distinct in their application. I absolutely differ from the teacher who tells me they are synonymous terms. They mean different things in different relationships and different applications. But they are related by a common principle, and it is by that common principle that the direction of repentance is indicated.

The Kingdom of God means the universal sovereignty of the Almighty. Everything is in it, and never gets outside it. Hell, as well as Heaven, is in that Kingdom. In Scripture the phrase, the Kingdom of Heaven, is always used in relation to the establishment on the earth of a heavenly order; and it is used wholly in connection with the redemptive work of God through His Son Jesus. The Hebrew theocracy culminated in Christ, the King; and in the coming of Christ the Kingdom came, and that is what He meant when He said, "The Kingdom of Heaven is at hand." But men said, "We will not have this Man to reign over us," and they flung the King out, and they have never admitted Him since, save to individual hearts and lives. But there were a few souls who said: "We will have Him for King"; and He said, "You shall be Mine"; and there began the Church in which the principles of the Kingdom are revealed, even though the King is absent from His world as to manifestation. That is the period in which we live. But the King cast out is coming back, or else this is all untrue! That Kingdom is being prepared for and is to be set up here, under the direct reign of Jesus of Nazareth.

Now, without following these lines, what is the common principle in all these? The rule of God, the authority of the Most High over the affairs of men. The permanent principle in all these phrases is the direct right of God to govern individual life in its entirety, social life in all its relationships, and national life in its purposes and its policies. Do Christian people realize and believe this? The permanent principle, that for which Jesus came, and for which He stood, is that of the absolute right of God to govern every man's life in every part and detail of it. That is the Kingdom of Heaven. The absolute right of God to govern social life in all its interrelationships, husband and wife, father and children, master and servant, capital and labor. The absolute right of God to govern in national life, in its purposes and in its policies. We must believe this. Dr. Frank W. Gunsaulus has said in one of his books, "True statesmanship consists in finding out which way God is going, and getting things out of the way for Him." That is the whole truth. That is the principle. Now, Jesus did not say merely, Change your mind, but Change your mind toward that, and in the phrase that indicates the direction there flashes the light that reveals the failure. We can put the whole call into very simple phrases and words. Change your mind about God, and Change your mind toward God. God is exiled, enthrone Him! That is all, and that is everything. It is a call from godlessness to Godliness. I leave the national outlook, I leave the social application, and I listen while Jesus says to us, and God help us to hear Him: "Repent ye, for the Kingdom of Heaven is at hand." We have lived under other lords. We have obeyed the impulses of sin, of self, of passion, of pride; we are wrong. We have wakened in the morning, and we have said: "What will please us to-day?" We are wrong. Change your mind, learn to understand that you never can live, till with the break of day we say: "Teach me to do Thy will, O my God." "Repent ye, for the Kingdom of Heaven is at hand." It had its local application, but I take out the eternal principle, the right of God to govern human lives, to direct, immediate, positive, drastic, interference with every man. This is the keynote of the preaching of Jesus.

Some have dared to suggest what they would do if they were God. Oh, the blasphemy of it, whether it comes from brilliant novelist or neurotic essay writer! Jesus Christ has no dealing with a man who takes up this attitude. He says to him, "Repent." The first thing is that we enthrone God, and kiss the scepter, and bow the knee, and learn that we have no right at all except the right of being where God would have us be and doing what God would have us do. Jesus comes to enthrone God in human life, in human society, in national affairs, and in the world; and the line of repentance is indicated when He says: "Repent, for *the Kingdom of Heaven* is at hand." When men repent in that direction what will happen? Their conceptions will be Godly, their conduct will be Godly, and their character will be Godly.

And, finally, let us consider the possibility affirmed, "Repent, for the Kingdom of Heaven *is at hand*." The prophets had all testified to the abiding fact of the Divine Sovereignty, and yet had looked forward to a centralized manifestation of that sovereignty in a person. Read them all; what is this they sing of, what is this they thunder about, what is this that makes the wail of their agony, and creates the passion of their hopefulness? The Sovereignty of God. But, Isaiah, what is your hope? Has the King come? No, harlotry and evil, abounding wickedness, are about us. What, then, is your hope? The coming Deliverer, and wistful eyes from mountain tops strained eagerly for the break of day and the coming of the Person in Whom and through Whom this Kingdom should be set up.

At last, the final prophet came, rough John the Baptist, and he said: "I indeed baptize you with water, but He that cometh after me shall baptize you with the Holy Ghost and fire." The great cry of the Baptist rang over the plains about Jordan, and then another voice was heard, meek and low, gentle and sweet, and yet uttering the same drastic word, but now whispered with wooing winsomeness, "Repent." Who is this? He does not speak of another, He utters no prophecy of someone yet to come. He says "The Kingdom of Heaven *is at hand.*" The Kingdom came when He came. "At hand" as to manifestation, the Kingdom was realized by this Teacher, this Man. "At hand" as to administration, the Kingdom was executed by Him in the affairs of men in proportion as they yielded to Him. "At hand" as to discrimination, He opens and closes the doors of the Kingdom, and by Him alone men enter it, and by refusing so to enter, He will exclude them from personal realization of blessing. Said He one day, "the Kingdom of God is"—not *within* you, a mistranslation absolutely, and yet a whole system of teaching has been based on it—"the Kingdom of God is *among* you." He meant literally, I am here, and where the King is, there is the Kingdom. Obey Me, and you have entered the Kingdom; trust

Me, and I will unlock the doors of the Kingdom to you. It is by the way of the King that men come into the Kingdom. And, oh, let me discuss it no longer as a theory, but let me announce it as the evangel. Dear man, dear woman, dear heart, "Repent"—the word is stern and fiery—"for the Kingdom of Heaven"—and the word indicates the need of your repentance. But, ah, me, it merges and melts into an infinite music—"the Kingdom is at hand." Just where you are. The King is there. Turn to Him, and that shall be repentance. Believe on Him, and that shall be thy passing into the Kingdom. Trust Him, and that shall be the dawn of the veritable day of God in thy soul.

We have attempted to consider this great initial word of the Lord. Wide-reaching circles have stretched out around us. God grant that their infinite significance may have impressed us. And yet now here is the difficulty of it, here is the point at which the preacher becomes utterly helpless, save as the Spirit of God will use the human word to deliver the Divine message. Oh that I could so constrain you that you should forget the messenger and your neighbor and let these far-reaching circles of the Divine Government contract until you find yourself alone, standing face to face with Jesus Christ in solemn isolation before God His King.

Oh, man, for a moment shut out the nation, for a moment shut out society, shut out this congregation, and now hear this voice as it says to you, "Repent, for the Kingdom of Heaven *is at hand.*" Oh, the good news! The Kingdom is at hand. Repent; change your mind and so your conduct, and so your character, and so your destiny, for the King who calls you bears in hands and feet and side the wounds that tell of how He opened the Kingdom of Heaven to all believers. Trust Him utterly, and enter into His Kingdom even now!

CHAPTER XIII

THE WORK OF FAITH

This is the work of God, that ye believe on Him Whom He hath sent.
JOHN 6:29.

THE MESSAGE OF THIS TEXT IS A SEQUEL TO THE SUBJECT of our previous consideration. I then spoke from the first words our Lord uttered when He began His public ministry. The keynote of the preaching of Jesus called for a change of mind in its initial word, "Repent," and indicated the direction of that change in the phrase, "for the kingdom of heaven," and proclaimed the possibility of that change in the declaration, "is at hand." That was how He began His preaching.

The words of our text were uttered at a crisis in the work of His ministry. These wonderful discourses from which the text is taken were delivered in Capernaum toward the end of the second year of His ministry, and they constitute the close of the Galilean part of that ministry. He was speaking His last words in Galilee, uttering His last message to that particular region and to those particular men, and the very atmosphere in which He breathed was alive with criticism.

Yet there was a species of interest in Him, born of low motive, manifest on this occasion. He had recently fed the people, and then, escaping from them over the sea, had been found by them on the other side. They came to Him with a question that seemed to be very simple and very natural—a question that was purely geographical, "When camest Thou hither?" There seemed to be no boat to bring Thee, how didst Thou reach this point? Immediately in the most startling way Jesus Christ flashed on His questioners a great light. "Ye seek Me, not because ye saw signs, but because ye ate of the loaves, and were filled." Having thus rebuked the low level of their interest, revealed the materialization of their passions, with wooing tenderness and winsome softness He called them to something higher. "Work not for the meat which perisheth," work for the bread that is "unto eternal life." And these people, willing to be religious if He wanted them to be—how many men are so, until He begins to reveal to them what religion is!—willing to discuss religion as a metaphysical question, said, Tell us, what work must we do to work the works of God? He answered, and perhaps men were never much more startled, "This is the work of God, that ye believe on Him Whom He hath sent." The keynote of their question is to be discovered in the phrase, "Work the works." They asked, "What must we do that we may work the works of God?" That was their idea of religion, of spirituality—to work works; and He said to them, "This is the work—believe."

Let us pay special attention to this word of Christ. In common with all His words, it was not spoken for a day but for all time; it is not only a message to the quibblers concerning Him, but also one to us. It came not only as an answer to the peculiar form of their rationalistic thinking; it comes as an answer to every sincere or critical soul who asks, What is the work of religion? What is the secret of relationship between God and man? I bring you this further word from the teaching of Jesus, as in advance of the one considered previously, on the need for repentance, and I pray you hear the Master as He says, "This is the work of God, that ye believe on Him Whom He hath sent."

The first matter of importance in order to have a full appreciation of the value of these words of Jesus is that of their presupposition. Postponing the consideration of its philosophy to the second place, I shall ask you first, then, to notice the presupposition of this declaration, that Jesus was sent by God. We shall never understand the meaning of our Lord's strange declaration that belief is work and that work is belief until we have taken some time to consider this underlying thought, that He who was speaking claimed to be sent by God, "This is the work of God, that ye believe on Him Whom He hath sent."

Looking at this inferential claim in the light of other passages of Scripture, I find that here, breaking into the text, is a principle which recurs throughout all the teaching of Jesus, and around which everything else gathers.

Turning to the Gospel stories, we find that our Lord distinctly declared that He had been sent of God. There are three references in Matthew's Gospel showing that Matthew heard Him make the claim. In Mark's Gospel are recorded two occasions on which our Lord declared Himself to be sent of God. In Luke we have four such references. Thus each of the Synoptics gives occasions when Jesus declared He was thus sent.

But when I turn from the Synoptics to John, which is the Gospel of the One revealed from heaven, Who also was the Revealer, I find an accumulated and remarkable testimony to the truth I am trying to emphasize. We may omit chapters 1, 2, 18, 19, and 21; but in every other chapter Jesus is reported as declaring that He was sent. In chapters 18 and 19 man was sending Him back, and there is no declaration that He was sent from the Father.

But why do I emphasize this fact? Because I want to

utter a definite protest against the idea that Jesus was a man who dreamed His way into Messiahship, that Jesus was a man who lived a pure life, and one day, as a recent writer has, to my mind, almost blasphemously said, woke up to imagine He could be Messiah and so became Messiah. No, He was sent from God, and throughout the whole of His mission there was the tremendous consciousness surging within Him that He was the sent One, the anointed One of the Father.

The matter of supreme importance for us in this connection is that of the bearing of this fact on the text. This is a distinct claim of personal authority based on the direct authorization of God. He was where He was because God had sent Him. That was the meaning of all the things He said in the ears of men. He was perpetually attempting to arrest the attention, and enforce the claim that men ought to hear Him, not because of what He thought Himself, not because of what He thought of Himself, not because of any testimony He bore to Himself, but because He was in the world, the One sent of God with a message to men, that He was the Sent of God.

The value of His presence in the world was twofold; revelation and reconciliation. Revelation of God, revelation of man, revelation of evil. Men never knew God perfectly until He revealed Himself. Fallen man has no conception to this day of what humanity is save as he sees his possibility in Jesus. The world never knew the truth about Satan; no writer had ever been able to say, "We are not ignorant of his devices" until Jesus dragged him out of the darkness and held him in the light of His own pure life.

Jesus was the Light of the world, flashing truth on men concerning God, flashing truth on men concerning their own nature, and in that light of truth concerning God and man setting evil in the light that man might know it, and know it as it really is.

A great revelation, and yet the purpose of His mission was infinitely more. A great reconciliation was the intention of His being sent, and that reconciliation was threefold, consisting, first, of mental conviction; second, of moral cleansing, and, finally, of mutual communion between the soul of man and God.

The reconciliation that Jesus came to bring comes first by this revelation, which results in mental conviction. When mental conviction has been realized by the revelation man is ashamed and conscious of his moral failure. Then he receives moral cleansing by blood, for He makes reconciliation by the blood of His Cross, and on the basis of that moral cleansing He restores man to the One Whom man has seen in Him, and there is mutual communion or fellowship between God and man in Christ.

This is a great claim that Jesus made. He stood amongst men and He said: You want to know the work of God? This is it: "Believe on Him Whom He hath sent," the authorized and appointed One, Whose work is that of revelation and reconciliation. You begin your religion when you believe in Me, said Christ; you work the work of God when you believe in Me.

This leads us to our second point. I ask you to notice the philosophy of our text. Jesus declared that belief is an act, that it is not a frame of mind that comes unconsciously to man without the activity of his own will. Yet you find men who tell us to-day that they cannot help what they believe. I think I may say scores and hundreds of young men have said that to me, and said it honestly. It is partially true. But Tennyson says:

> A lie which is all a lie may be met and fought with outright,
> But a lie which is part a truth is a harder matter to fight;

and that is true of this statement. Many a man is saying that he cannot help what he believes, and because he persists in saying that, he is uttering half a truth, and the half-truth is blinding him and preventing him from coming into the possession of all the fulness of the suggestion of the word "believe." What is it to believe? Let me take that word that lies in my text: "This is the work of God, that ye believe." What is that word "believe"? I do not mean now merely how we commonly use it, for we cannot understand the use of the word until we understand the true meaning of the word. What is the simplest meaning of the Greek word translated "believe" so constantly in our New Testament? In the last analysis, to believe is to be convinced. You may take this word, which has to be translated trust, or faith, and trace it back to the root meaning, and it will be found that the essential value of the word is to be convinced. A man believes when he is convinced, so that, after all, belief is a matter of the reason. Never trust any teacher who affirms that you must believe against your reason. God calls man to the exercise of every faculty He has given him. To believe is an act of reason, and the simple meaning of the word "believe" is to be convinced that a statement is true. Belief is conviction, and a man may believe a lie or he may believe a truth; but he himself believes it to be true. In the simplest analysis of the meaning of the word, belief itself is conviction.

You say, Then is a man a Christian because he believes something? Not at all, and that is exactly the point to which I am coming. The New Testament never tells men that they can be saved by belief. It always indicates the line of belief, always declares the facts that must be believed, and indicates an action of the will as accompanying the conviction of the mind. It is belief *in* or *on* Jesus Christ that saves. Well, but you say, surely we are still in the presence of the same difficulty. If belief is, in the last analysis, to be convinced, and it is belief on Jesus Christ that saves, I cannot help whether I believe on Him or not.

In my text this word "believe" is used with a little Greek preposition, translated here "on"; and forgive me if for a moment I quarrel with the translators and use the word "in." Everyone knows there is a whole realm of value in prepositions, and this preposition, when used with the accusative case, always means motion into something. Every man will see that if he will take Thomas Newberry's *Englishman's Bible* and study that simple, yet wonderful, diagram of prepositions at the beginning of the New Testament. There it is clearly shown that this little preposition means motion into.

What is the work of God? Belief, but belief in Him Whom He hath sent. The work of God is the acceptance of conclusions on testimony concerning Jesus Christ. The faith that saves a man is that act of the will by which he says, Yes; the evidence is conclusive. I will believe. And that is the act that brings a man into living relationship with Jesus Christ.

It is an act of the will. I need not argue that. Anyone who has read Professor James' *The Will to Believe* will not desire me to argue that the will acts in belief.

I suppose there is no single canto of Tennyson's "In Memoriam" more quoted, or in many respects more beautiful, than that which deals with doubt. Shall we have it all, that we may have the truth of the text in its context:

> You say, but with no touch of scorn,
>   Sweethearted you, whose light blue eyes
>   Are tender over drowning flies,
> You tell me doubt is devil-born.
>
> I know not. One, indeed, I knew
>   In many a subtle question versed,
>   Who touched a jarring lyre at first,
> But ever strove to make it true.

> Perplext in faith, but pure in deeds,
>   At last he beat his music out.
>   There lives more faith in honest doubt,
> Believe me, than in half the creeds.
>
> He fought his doubts and gather'd strength,
>   He would not make his judgment blind;
>   He faced the specters of the mind,
> And laid them; thus he came at length
>
> To find a stronger faith his own;
>   And power was with him in the night,
>   Which makes the darkness and the light,
> And dwells not in the light alone.

The arresting and most often quoted line of that poem is: "He would not make his judgment blind."

Now, forgive me, I am almost tired of hearing that line quoted by one class of men. It has been quoted to me north, south, east, west, in my own country; it has been quoted to me from the Atlantic coast to the Pacific, and almost always by the man who is critical, who does not accept certain truths which I accept, and who in vindication of his skepticism says, I will not make my judgment blind. I am not angry with him. I believe there is such a thing as "honest doubt." But "He would not make his judgment blind" is not merely a line that describes honest doubt, it equally describes honest faith. There is such a thing as making judgment blind by receiving credulously a statement that you cannot believe with your judgment; but there is such a thing as dishonesty in refusing to receive testimony. I will not charge you with that. There is such a thing also as neglecting to consider testimony. There is a peril that when men boast they will not make their judgment blind they are so boasting to cover intellectual indolence or moral failure. It is not always so. There are men who are fighting "the specters of the mind," men who cannot be convinced at present. But, oh, I am a little tired of the man who comes to me and says, I do not believe in Jesus. I say to him, How much time have you given to attempt to consider the arguments? And I sometimes find that he once heard some lecturer say something smart about Jesus, or else he heard some preacher cast reflections on the person of Christ, and, without taking one solid day out of his life, to say nothing of weeks and months of toil and thought, to find the truth, he says, I will not make my judgment blind. Why, man, you are making it blind, and you have no business to say you do or do not believe on Jesus Christ until you have taken time to hear the testimony and to weigh the evidence. The one thing Jesus said in the age when men were criticizing Him was, "Believe Me," examine Me, or else "believe Me for the very work's sake." Consider the arguments, take time to look into the whole question: this is the work of God, that you believe in Him Whom God hath sent. The claim is, God has sent Him, and here is the imperial claim Jesus Christ makes. If you will take time to consider Him you will have demonstrated to you the fact that He is sent of God, and there will begin your faith.

Jesus spoke one very terrible parable among many that were beautiful. He spoke of one lost soul crying out to Abraham that somebody should be sent to his brethren. You remember the answer Abraham is represented as giving to the lost soul. I pray you, think of it carefully: "They have Moses and the prophets . . . if they hear not Moses and the prophets, neither will they be persuaded, if one rise from the dead." There "persuaded" is the word translated in other places "believe." So that our Lord said, in effect, that there is such a thing as being willing to be persuaded. The evidences are with them: they have Moses and the prophets, and if they will not hear them it will still be the same—they will not believe, they will not be persuaded. There is the element of will, and that is the element for which we are responsible in the matter of faith. Faith will not come as a sentiment creeping over the life, or if it so come it will be worthless, anemic, faithless. Faith is a great act in response to a great claim. Here is a man who says: I will listen and consider; I will not be persuaded by anything short of conviction, but as the conviction comes I will not make my judgment blind to that; neither will I, because the growing conviction is going to make claims upon me, shut it out. I will believe the thing of which I am convinced by yielding complete obedience to it.

We need to plead for this honesty to-day. I repeat that half the much-talked-of agnosticism of the present hour is due either to intellectual indolence, or to the desire to cover up some moral defect; and, if not, then, in the name of God and humanity, there is no Gospel. I stand here to declare that, if you will consider Christ, consider Him honestly, listen to Him rather than to the exponents of His teaching, bring your life into the light of the revelation He makes, as to its possibility—if you will measure your creed by His revelation of God, I think you cannot possibly do so without finding that there grows on you the conviction that He is right.

What, then, is belief? Belief is the action of the will whereby you accept the conclusion and abandon yourself to Him. The belief that saves a man is the attitude of will of a man who looks into the face of Jesus and says: At last, oh, Nazarene, Thou hast conquered.

> Here I give my all to Thee,
>   Friends and time and earthly store,
> Soul and body Thine to be,
>   Wholly Thine forevermore.

THE WORK OF FAITH

This is belief in Him: the motion into Him of all the life, under the impulse of an honest conviction which will not make its judgment blind.

Finally, and briefly, let us listen to the proclamation of the text: "This is the work of God: believe." It is the initial work making possible a new life. It is an inspirational work that goes forward through all life. It is an inclusive work that takes in the whole sum of things for a man.

It is the initial work of God. Jesus Christ is God's new point of departure, and from the moment when He came and lived and taught, God swept everything else away. The law and the prophets are no longer necessary, as they are no longer sufficient. Men had lived under conscience, men had lived under law, men had lived under the interpretation of the will of God by the messages of the prophets. God swept them all away when Christ came. The law made nothing perfect, and God, with the sending of Jesus, put His hand on every other method of human salvation, and from that moment until now God refuses to meet any man save through that Man. If the resurrection of Jesus Christ—if I may put this superlatively and finally—was demonstration of the fact that God accepted Jesus, it was also a demonstration of the fact that He rejects everybody else save as they come to Him in and through Jesus Christ. If you ask me whether a man can possibly be saved except through Jesus Christ I say absolutely, No. No man can be saved except through Jesus Christ. You say, Can I be saved by some educational, ethical method? I tell you, No. This is the work of God, that you believe on Him. This is not a mere caprice of Deity. It is not merely because God will not receive you on any other basis, but because you cannot come to Him on any other basis. Your highest ethical code appears sullied when held in the light of heaven's unsullied purity. Your educational method is the education of devilry when compared with the purpose of God. What He asks is truth in the inward parts, a pure unsullied spotlessness, and there is no man who can bring it to Him. And so, in His mercy, God, sweeping away all other methods, sent forth this Man to be at once Example and Saviour, Revealer and Reconciler; and the first thing in life and religion is that men believe in Him.

But it is not true that God saves a man on the basis of an intellectual assent. This work is not merely initial, it is inspirational. The work of belief is not one act, it is a maintained attitude. I believe on Him, and by that belief I am received of God. But that belief is not then over. It begins then, and it runs through all life; and real Christian living is living by faith in the Son of God all the time. Faith means not merely an intellectual assent; it means a moral obedience, a whole-hearted surrender, and a perpetual yielding of the whole life to Jesus Christ. If a man really believes in Him Whom the Father hath sent, that belief will affect all his thinking, all his speaking, all his doing. To work that initial work of belief is to bring forth all the works that are meet for repentance and manifest the fruit of the Spirit in all its diversity of beauty and of glory.

This work of belief in Jesus is also inclusive, including all the territory of the being, including all the forces of the life, and, thank God, including the utmost reach of the coming ages. This is the work of God. Not that God is mindful of the thing that you believe intellectually and unmindful of the actual doings of your life; but because God would correct the external conduct by the internal creed, because God would set right the last detail of daily activity by setting right relationship to Him.

I ask, therefore, in conclusion, Have you believed in Him? And if not, why not? If you tell me your difficulty is intellectual, then, I pray you, do not make your judgment blind. By that I mean, do not profess a faith you do not possess. But, in God's name, do receive the testimony and consider it, and do not treat a matter so weighty as this with trivial attention, and then profess that you are a skeptic. Think, man, think! Face this claim of Jesus, face all the evidence, do not make your judgment blind.

But is there not a deeper reason? Is not the reason of your unbelief moral? Be honest to-night and answer that question as between God and your own soul. Do you not know that if you believe in Him it means that you must obey, and that means the going out of your life of the cherished thing that is wrong. I do not ask you to confess to me—may God deliver you from such folly! But, as the messenger of the Cross, the messenger of the living Lord, I charge you, look within. Why have you never yet abandoned your life in honesty to the conclusions that have come to you as convictions long ago? Remember that if in the inner shrine of your heart you are now facing some evil and immoral thing, then I must take you back to the former word: "Repent ye, for the kingdom of heaven is at hand."

But let my last word be spoken to the man who is close to Christ and is conscious that Christ is close to him. Right there where you are, without outward sign or sound as yet, believe in Him, trust Him, venture everything on the conviction that is in your heart of what He is and what He can do.

I have often told the story; I will tell it again; to me it illustrates faith so beautifully. It was an old Scotch woman who had been following the Lord for many years, and her minister said to her—I don't know whether it was wise or not, but yet, for the sake of her answer, I am glad he said it—"Maggie, supposing, after having been a Christian for forty years, the Lord should drop you out of His hand, and you should be lost, in spite of your faith." And Maggie, with a radiant smile, looked back into his face and said, "Nay, then

I would just lose my puir wee bit soul, but He would lose the honor of His eternal Word." That is the faith that saves a man.

Oh, men, at this moment in the presence of God, I will risk heaven and eternity on this One sent from God. Will you do that? Then there will come into your heart the sense of His peace, the sense of His power, and you will find that in that initial work there lie all the forces of the works, and out of the creed of honesty will come the conduct of purity.

CHAPTER XIV

ETERNAL LIFE

He that believeth on the Son hath eternal life.
                                                            JOHN 3:36.

THE FIRST WORD OF JESUS IS, "REPENT." WHEN MEN, hearing that call, indeed change their mind, and ask, "What must we do to work the works of God?" He answers, "This is the work of God, that ye believe on Him Whom He hath sent." The question then arises, What is the issue of such belief? The answer is, "He that believeth on the Son hath eternal life."

No question can be more interesting or more vital than that which inquires the meaning of this phrase, "eternal life." A partial definition narrows the outlook and gives half a conception which may be false because partial. For instance, eternal life has been thought of too often as though it were a quantity. It is a quantity; but if we think of eternal life only as a quantity we miss the profoundest and most wonderful truth about it.

Eternal life is a quality, and therefore a quantity. A man who has eternal life never dies, he cannot die; death for him is abolished, made not to be, is swallowed up in victory. He may fall on sleep with regard to one manifestation of his life, the purely earthly and physical, but he never dies.

John says more about eternal life than any other of the

New Testament writers. Let us take two parentheses, one in the beginning of his gospel, the other in the beginning of his first epistle.

That in the Gospel reads: "And we beheld His glory, glory as of the only begotten from the Father" (John 2:14).

That in the Epistle reads: "And the life was manifested, and we have seen, and bear witness, and declare unto you the life, the eternal life, which was with the Father, and was manifested unto us" (I John 1:2).

John declared in each of these passages that if we would know what eternal life is we must know Jesus Christ. He declared that he saw eternal life in a Person—in Jesus. Very remarkable are the words he used, suggesting a merging of the tangible and the intangible. "The Word of life," seen, touched, handled, all which means that John came to know eternal life by knowing Christ. Eternal life is no more a mystery, but a revelation, no more something concerning which we have to speculate; it has been revealed in a Person. Those words from the great intercessory prayer of Christ contain the same thought: "This is life eternal, that they should know Thee, the only true God, and Him whom Thou didst send, even Jesus Christ."

Then we may reverently examine eternal life as it is revealed in Jesus. First, we will look at the essential quality thereof, and then consider its relative consequences as manifested in Jesus.

The essential quality is marked by the word "eternal." Eternal means not only unending; it means of the ages. Life which is of the ages lacks the quality that makes for ending; and is a life undying, because there is nothing in it of the element of break-up or decay.

The writer of the letter to the Hebrews declared that we have not a High Priest "after the law of a carnal commandment, but after the power of an endless life," that is, a life that partakes of the very spirit and nature out of which the ages come. Ages come and ages go, but this life is the dividing principle of them, and continues while they rise and fall. It is endless life, eternal life, the life of the ages. It is the very life of the eternal God Who fashioned and framed the ages themselves.

The difference between eternal life and temporal life is that when a man is living eternal life his intellect operates in the consciousness of eternity rather than in that of time, his emotion is actuated by infinite values and infinite issues rather than by present or perishing reasons, and his will is dominated by the supreme and undying truth rather than by transient currents of thought. In his epistle, Peter says of certain persons, they are "blind," more correctly, they are near-sighted, "seeing only what is near." Eternal life enables man to see the things that are near in the light of the things that are far. The peculiar wrong and disaster of human life as it is being lived in the world to-day is that all our ideals, apart from the Christian revelation, are ideals that look on things in themselves, and not in relation to the larger issues. I am told sometimes that certain men in this age are far-seeing men, and I am somewhat amused when I hear it. When I ask how far can they see, I am told that they see exactly what is to be the result of a war scare on the market! How far is that? Far enough to buy up all the steamship lines and merge them! That is to say that they see nothing beyond the place where blue sky dips into blue sea. Such men are blind, near-sighted! They are burying their vision in the dust of to-day, they have not begun to see; they are living temporal life. If we take their philosophy, rub away the tinsel of it, and bring it down to the dead level of truth, it may thus be expressed: "Let us eat, let us drink, for to-morrow we die." But here is an old woman, a church member, who has been praying for forty years. She never saw far enough to make provision for old age; but she has "endured as seeing Him Who is invisible." That is far-sightedness, that is eternal life.

Jesus did not measure the movements of His time by the men of His time, He did not lay on the affairs of His own age, the measuring line of His own age. He lived eternal life.

First, His intellect operated in the consciousness of God and eternity. I love to think of this in small things. Flowers, what did He say about them? One passing reference is enough. "God so clothes the grass of the field." Years ago I walked into my father's garden with a young man who had been led to Christ under my father's ministry. Picking up a common nasturtium leaf, and putting it in my hand, he said, "Is it not beautiful? God made it." That man was a far-seeing man. He was looking through the delicate tracery of the nasturtium leaf to God behind it. You tell me this is old-fashioned! Yes, old as the everlasting hills, white with the hoariness of eternity, and unless we have that vision, we are near-sighted. God open our eyes in order that we may see! When Jesus said God clothed the grass, He talked in the language of the eternal, not in the language of the temporal. We might follow Him through all the gamut of interest in life. Birds? "Not a sparrow falls to the ground without your Father." Children? He declared that every little child has an angel who beholds the face of God. Home? When they came to Him with their casuistical questions concerning divorce, He said, "From the beginning God made them male and female," sweeping past the dictum of Moses to the infinite purpose of God. Whether He touched a child or a flower, a problem or a pain, He thought and taught in the infinite consciousness of God. That is eternal life. He lived with feet squarely planted on dear old mother earth, but brow lifted high into the infinite light, while the light of the ages of God played on His temporal pathway.

His emotion also was actuated by infinite values and infinite issues. Behind all failure He recognized possibility. He saw in every man the image of God, marred, bruised, battered by sin. He knew that behind the ruin lay the possibility, and when He looked on a man He saw him not only as he stood there in the degradation of his sin; He saw him a being having come out of the infinite, traveling toward the infinite, and He knew that the little hour which He was spending in Jerusalem or Jericho was but a part of the infinite whole. His life, coming out of eternity, embraced eternity, until of His own it is said, "having loved His own, which were in the world, He loved them unto the end." That is love eternal.

His will was dominated by the Supreme Truth. Every man's will is dominated by his intellect and his emotion. No man's will is finally free. A free will is evidence of fitness for a lunatic asylum. Man's will is never free so long as he is rational. It must be dominated by reason. You cannot cross the road without saying or thinking, "I will cross the road," but you never say, "I will cross the road," without meaning, "I will cross the road, because . . ." Back of the will is a reason, and your will is dominated by something behind. No man ever exercises his will save under the impulse of intellect or emotion. The impulse that controlled the will of Jesus was an intellect homed in eternal principles, an emotion impulsed by infinite love. That is eternal life. Eternal life is not narrow, not of long continuation merely. It is as broad as it is long, as deep as it is high, as magnificent and splendid as it is severe and straight.

Let us briefly notice the relative consequences of this eternal life in the case of Jesus. Seeing God, He used the world. He was no ascetic; He never did violence to Himself, He never took a whip of cords to lacerate His flesh. Whoever imagines he is spiritual because he is bruising himself with cross or cords or hair shirt is sensual, not spiritual. Jesus "was bruised for our iniquities." In the mystery of eternal life, He handed Himself over to bruising by His enemies, but He never bruised Himself. He lived a life so perfectly natural and artless that men said of Him, He was a wine bibber. Instead of retiring from them, He sat down with publicans and sinners, and ate bread with them, until the alarmed Pharisees and Sadducees said, "This man receiveth sinners and eateth with them." He lived His life amongst men, loved flowers, birds, and little children; He was perfectly simple, perfectly artless, perfectly natural. He took His place in the God-filled natural order; seeing God everywhere, recognizing that all things were of God and for God, He took them as God's great sacramental gifts.

Being God-indwelt, He loved infinitely, and so with a searching severity against sin and an infinite tenderness toward the sinner. These are the two notes of real love, of eternal love. It is temporal love that never says a severe thing. Eternal love is severe. Listen to Jesus Christ, and watch Him. How scathingly He dealt with sin! "Woe unto you, scribes and Pharisees, hypocrites! Ye whitewash the tombs of the prophets, ye yourself are whited sepulchres, but within ye are dead men's bones." Never language was so white-hot and scorching as the language of Jesus against sin. "Woe unto you, scribes and Pharisees, hypocrites! For ye devour widows' houses, even while for a pretence ye make long prayers." If you are a hypocrite, He scorches you with His glance. You will not dare to stand in the purity of His presence, for you will find the fire of His glance the very consuming fire of perdition. And all that was born of love. It is only love that can be severe. Why was He severe? Because He saw these men were injuring other men, ruining their own lives, spoiling the Divine order, bringing discord where harmony ought to be. Out of His love came the fire of His wrath. It was out of His consciousness of the eternal that He spoke such withering words of scorn to the men who in the temporal were violating eternal principles.

Yet, again, the eternal dominating the will was proof against all merely temporal impulses. I have looked at my Lord, and I have wondered at His victory over temptations, subtle, insidious, that swept on Him like a hurricane in the moment of His weakness, that came whispering to Him through the voices of His friends, temptations unmasked in all their fierceness in the wilderness, temptations coming disguised again and again, and yet He was always victorious. How was it? Because the voices of temptation were for Him voices that spoke in the language of the temporal, the small voices had asked Him to act as though this moment were all. Temptation never dare take eternity into account. How was it that He overcame? Because He thought, loved, and willed in relation to infinite things.

Let one illustration suffice. High on the mountain the arch enemy of mankind flung before Him in panoramic vision the kingdoms of the world and the glory of them. He said in effect to Christ, "Do something *now*, get something *now*. Fall down before me *now*, and I will give Thee the kingdoms of the world *now*." What was the answer of the Man who lived eternal life? "It is written, Thou shalt worship God, and Him only shalt thou serve." Do you see the measurement He put on the present moment? Jesus knew that to take those kingdoms in the temporal *now*, and have them as temporal kingdoms *now*, was to lose them in the hereafter. In effect, He said, I will take the way of God to the kingdoms, though it be the way of the Cross, of shame and blood, and I will come into the kingdoms by the way of God's appointing along the line of the spiritual and the eternal.

Are you face to face with some temptation in the *now?* If you are haunted by a suggestion that you should do something dishonorable *now;* if you are haunted by a face luring you to do something *now,* for pleasure *now,* I beseech you to remember that the only way to deal with the *now* is to flash on it the light of eternity. Every moment winging its way past you is offspring of the ages, and what you do now, stands related to the eternities. Feel the searching fires of eternity in your life, and you will be able to overcome. It is this bringing to bear of the eternal on the now, of the infinite on the small, that is the secret of victory. Eternal life is life that takes account of eternity, refuses to set the horizon at any moment where sky kisses ocean; but sees out beyond the horizon the infinite, the spacious, the unending. I am only child of dust in material life for a little while; but I am offspring of God in my essential being. What I am, I am by the fact of the inbreathing of God, and my life must be conditioned by infinite things.

Now let us hear the Great Announcement. "He that believeth on the Son hath eternal life." I long for the return of the days when men believed as the Word was preached. Believe on Him *now.* Say I have heard for a long time; I will not make my judgment blind any longer. I know this Man of Nazareth, this Jesus Christ, can save me and give me eternal life. I believe on Him now. I will become His now.

Immediately He will give you eternal life. That is not a mere sentiment; it is a great fact. Eternal life in the present moment, eternal life positively possessed, this is God's declaration. "He that believeth on the Son hath eternal life."

Or, again, in words almost more startling, and striking and beautiful, "If we receive the witness of men, the witness of God is greater: for the witness of God is this, that He hath borne witness concerning His Son." What is this witness of God? "He that believeth on the Son of God hath the witness in Him: he that believeth not God hath made Him a liar: because he hath not believed in the witness that God hath borne concerning His Son. And the witness is this, that God gave unto us eternal life, and this life is in His Son."

So I put the matter thus for myself—perhaps it is the best way to help others. God declares that if I will believe in His Son, if I will believe into His Son, if I will refuse any longer to make my judgment blind, and will abandon myself to Him, He gives me eternal life here and now.

It is this venturing on the Word of God that will bring a man into conscious possession of eternal life. "He that hath the Son hath the life." If you believe on Him He gives Himself to you. He in you will illuminate your intelligence with the light of eternal life; He will dominate your affection with the love of God; He in you will master your will, to do the will of God. That is eternal life. He will interpret to you the will of God, and so illumine your intelligence that you will go out, and to-morrow you will look again at the old scenes, the old facts of your life, but you will see them with new eyes. Christ's estimate will put on everything.

Jesus living within by the power of His Holy Spirit, illuminating the intelligence, inspiring the emotion, and mastering the will; suddenly we shall know the horizon put back, the dark sky illumined, things that once were wild babel become resonant with the evangel of life, everything will be enlarged and corrected by the enlargement. This is the experience of eternal life—not a magnetic thrill, but a great spiritual consciousness that makes a man at last able to say, "I know I am born again—first, because God says it, and I believe it; but, second, because in me life moves to new impulses, new desires, new passions, new enterprises; and the things I loved I hate, and the things that mastered me like vipers have dropped off, and I am free who once was bound." Such is the consciousness of life, but it never comes to man until he believes in the Son of God.

Now, very reverently and solemnly, hear the final

words of my text: "He that obeyeth not the Son shall not see life, but the wrath of God abideth on him." "Believeth not" it is in the Authorized Version; the word is changed in the Revised Version, because a different Greek word is used. Yet I am not at all sure that this word "obeyeth" covers all the ground. I give you this, not as translation, but as interpretation; he that will not be persuaded, he that refuses conviction, he that declines to believe into, in obedience to a conviction, "he that obeyeth not the Son, shall not see life, but the wrath of God abideth on him." Mark the negative condition: "He that obeyeth not the Son," he that believeth not into the Son of his will, he that will not be persuaded. But all that goes back on our previous subject to those solemn words of Jesus, spoken in the parable in answer to the cry of the rich man in hell, "They have Moses and the prophets. If they will not hear them, neither will they be persuaded though one rose from the dead."

There are men and women who refuse to be persuaded, who will not believe, who will not believe into and obey the Son of God. What of such? "They shall not see life." Here, first, is a reference to something they are hoping for—the life beyond; they shall not see it. But here, in a simpler way, as a profounder truth, is the declaration that such people have not begun to live at all, that the very life they now live is a living death.

That is not the last word, nor the most solemn word, and I have no more right to omit the last word than I have to omit the first. If the first word is a great evangel, so also is the last a great evangel. The first is the evangel of salvation made possible. The last is the evangel of solemn warning, and it is always an evangel when truth utters a warning. "The wrath of God," terrific word, terrible phrase, not occurring here only, but often in Scripture. I am here to preach the Word, and not to philosophize concerning it. This word wrath means anger, which includes the purpose to punish. There are other words used for wrath that have not that purpose, but this one has—the wrath of God, anger, which includes the purpose of punishment.

"The wrath of God abideth." It is not merely that men are coming into that wrath by-and-by; they are in it at this moment. If you have heard the evangel and have refused to obey, God is angry with you, angry with you, not on the basis of caprice, but by the very necessities of the case; angry with you as you would be with any man who might dwell on the heights of health, but who chose to dwell in the midst of putrefaction and disease; angry with you, first, because you ruin His fair work in yourself; angry with you because by living where you do, outside the life eternal, you spread the contagion of your moral leprosy and lead other men to ruin. Do not imagine when you refuse Christ that there is nothing round about you but the love and mercy of God. "The wrath of God abideth upon the children of disobedience." I am not entering into any argument concerning the attitude of God toward the men who do not know the Gospel. I am talking to people who know it. The Son is calling you into eternal life, and you know it. If you do not obey, you can neither see life, nor enter into life; but, instead, the wrath of God, the anger of God, that holds within itself the purpose of punishment, abideth on you.

And yet, thank God, He calls! He calls to mercy. He calls to life. "I call Heaven and earth to witness against you this day, that I have set before thee life and death, the blessing and the curse; therefore choose life, that thou mayest live."

CHAPTER XV

THE EXALTED CHRIST

Wherefore God also highly exalted Him, and gave unto Him the name which is above every name; that in the name of Jesus every knee should bow, of things in Heaven and things on earth and things under the earth, and that every tongue should confess that Jesus Christ is Lord, to the glory of God the Father.

PHILIPPIANS 2:9-11.

He raised Him from the dead and made Him to sit at His right hand in the heavenlies, far above all rule, and authority, and power, and dominion, and every name that is named, not only in this age, but also in that which is to come, and He put all things in subjection under His feet, and gave Him to be Head over all things to the Church, which is His body, the fulness of Him that filleth all in all.

EPHESIANS 1:20-23.

THE WORD WITH WHICH THE PASSAGE OF SCRIPTURE from the Philippian letter commences is the word "wherefore." Necessarily our minds are thereby turned back to the preceding statements. The subject we now propose to consider is that of the exaltation of Christ, and His investiture with a name to which every knee is to bow and every tongue confess. But as we approach our subject, the word "wherefore" forces us back. Ere we consider the fact of His exaltation we ask, Why was He so exalted? We ask that because the writer of these words based the fact of exaltation on certain reasons which he had already declared.

The declaration of those reasons is contained in a passage than which there is no more wonderful in all Holy Scripture in its revelation, in language at once simple and sublime, of the pathway by which God moved to the redemption of men. It is an incidental passage—I do not say accidental. The Apostle was urging the Philippian Christians to be of one mind and of one heart, was calling them to certain disposition, to certain tone and temper: "Have this mind in you, which was also in Christ Jesus," he wrote. What, then, was the mind in Christ? In order to reveal it he gave the story of the Christ.

The story begins in a great mystery of light, out of which light there appears One, Who descends until we see Him in the awful and tragic agony of the brutal and bloody Cross. And the end of the story is that same One's return to the highest throne in the universe of God, leaving behind Him a highway along which multitudes will follow Him to share His glory.

"Wherefore" lies at the middle of that descriptive paragraph. Let us look first, then, at the things that precede, in order that we see the relation between this ascent and descent of the Son of God.

The first words are: "Who, being in the form of God, counted it not a prize to be on an equality with God." That is the blinding light of the past. It is

    . . . . light too bright
  For the feebleness of a sinner's sight.

We have looked into it, we have attempted to understand it. We have sometimes, perhaps foolishly, attempted an explanation of it. Let us at once confess that it says something about the Christ who transcends all human explanation. No translator has yet been satisfied with his rendering of the passage. All kinds of attempts have been made, and none of them is perfectly satisfactory or successful. "Being in the form of God," He "counted it not a prize to be on an equality with God." Mark your margin, and see another suggestion, "counted it not a thing to be grasped to be on an equality with God," counted it something to be kept. I am growingly thankful when I find a passage I cannot translate, and no one else can. When my attempts at exposition and exegesis are alike baffled, then I worship.

But emerging from that dazzling light, that strange mystery of illumination, emerging from it I read: "but emptied Himself." I do not understand it. He "emptied Himself, taking the form of a servant, being made in the likeness of men." I understand that. Here is a Man. I can see that, I can handle that, I can listen to that. John will write for me what I feel now: "That which we have heard, that which we have seen with our eyes, that which we have beheld, and our hands handled"—the Word of life, the intangible, imponderable mystery of life. But we saw it, we touched it, we handled it, we felt it. It is a Man. And there is no more gracious word in all the Book of God than this, "The Word was made flesh." I wanted, I needed it. The word eluded me. The mystery of Divine self-existence and revelation was beyond me. It was a whisper, a thunder, a gleam, and a glory. None of them came near me. But it became flesh, a Man. We cannot fathom these distances; we cannot measure them. Out of the mystery of an infinite light, into the simplicity of a human life. Oh, in the name of God Almighty, I charge you, do not think the Christ began to be in that life of Jesus. We must have the mystery behind, this unfathomable wonder, this Being Who thought it not something to be snatched at to be on an equality with God. It is He that is clothed in the warm flesh of humanity. Now I can follow Him, or I think I can. Presently I shall find I cannot. I will begin. "Being found in fashion as a Man," He humbled Himself here, "and became obedient unto death," yea, the death of the Cross. Forgive my halting; I cannot speak of this agony. More and more it crushes me and overwhelms me. This Cross, this rough, and rugged, bloody and brutal Cross, hateful Cross, is as great a mystery as that light behind. "He became obedient unto death, yea, the death of the Cross." You ask me if I will not explain atonement. I cannot do it, dear heart. You ask me to measure the Infinite Light; when I can do that I can plumb the infinite darkness; both elude me. But we have at least seen this Person, immeasurable within our measurement, going to that Cross of pain and sorrow and suffering.

Now I come to "wherefore." On the basis of that mystery of humiliation and pain, and because of the mind that brought the Person out of mysterious light into mysterious darkness to work redemption, "wherefore also God highly exalted Him, and gave unto Him the name which is above every name, that in the name of Jesus every knee should bow."

Again the glory breaks with new light, and in meaning still defying my analysis, still shining with such radiant splendor that all attempts to paint it are of no avail, all attempts to describe it are utterly futile. We had better confine ourselves to a consideration of that which God gave to aid us, the Man Himself. As we were able to look at Him for a little on the pathway of His obedience, humbling Himself, and as we were able even to get some brief glances of Him in His dying in the tragic, awful, and inspiring mystery of His pain, what shall we do now? Has He ceased to be as Man? Has the personality that made it possible for me to apprehend Him passed away? Nay, verily, if so, I have lost all my power of comprehending God. God exalted Him. Who? The Man Who died. If we would know the measurement of the exaltation, we must take also the passage from Ephesians. God "made Him to sit on His right hand, in the heavenlies, far above all rule, and authority, and power, and dominion, and every name that is named, not only in this world, but also in that which is to come."

Let us endeavor to come face to face with that exalted Person. We cannot exhaust Him in the human Person even in the glory. He is more than a Person that can be seen. That Person is the Revelation of the Infinite Mystery; that Person is coming again to gather His people to Himself, and to be the localized King and Judge of humanity, but the infinite and the eternal and the immeasurable quantities will abide there and here. All the localization is for our frailty, and our understanding, the method by which we touch that which could not be touched, and see the unseen, and hear the unutterable. That is the essence of my creed, the foundation of my faith, that the same Jesus whom John saw and handled and heard is at the center of the universe of God, highly exalted, and that same One is to come again. With the story of His coming I am not now dealing, but only with the fact of His exaltation.

Mark the statement: "God highly exalted Him." In writing to the Philippians, Paul said, "God highly exalted Him." In writing to the Ephesians, he said, "He made Him to sit at His right hand." That is a figure of speech, and yet so simple that there can be no misunderstanding of its meaning. He exalted the Man of Nazareth by resurrection and ascension to His own right hand. That is the place of infinite and unfading glory, the right hand of God; the place of rest, where weariness never comes; the place of power, where weakness is never known; the place of glory, where there is no shadow cast by turning, and no darkness—and all these also are figurative expressions. As a matter of fact, we cannot express the true position of the Man in any language at our command to-day. We shall need the heavenly speech, the heavenly language, the heavenly method of expression to explain it. But there, placed at the point in the universe of God, which is the central point of Divine manifestation, is this Man of Nazareth, highly exalted to the right hand of God. He was weary here. He is beyond weariness now, knowing still my weariness, perfectly acquainted with it there, but never wearied by my weariness. In all my affliction He is not afflicted. It is a great passage of Scripture that tells me that in "all their affliction He was afflicted." Many of you have heard, doubtless, that it is a great question whether it was ever so written. It is far more likely that it was written, "He was not afflicted," which does not mean to say He was not acquainted with the sorrow and did not share the affliction, but which does mean that He came into the midst of it, and affliction never mastered Him, never tired Him, never wearied Him beyond the power of renewal and regaining of strength. Whether that be true as to the past I will not argue, but it is true now.

> In every pang that rends the heart,
> The Man of Sorrows hath His part.

But He is strong, He is in the place of rest.

He is, moreover, in the place of unlimited power, and to my weakness, which He knows, from His place of rest there comes the power that is His. He is in the place of glory, exalted to the right hand of God. Think of it, figure it forth in what language you like. This at least is true, that the Man of Nazareth, because of the suffering and victory of the Cross, has been crowned by God King of Kings and Lord of Lords, and is at the center of the whole universe of God, its glorious Master and King.

If God indeed has highly exalted the Man of Nazareth we may argue therefrom one or two matters of importance concerning Him, and of value for ourselves.

First of all, this exaltation of the Man of Nazareth by God implies the absolute perfection of His life, as revealing to me a pattern. I go back to some of the Messianic Psalms (Ps. 22, 23, 24). Listen to some of the words of the last, which speak of His triumph:

> Who shall ascend into the hill of the Lord?
> And who shall stand in His holy place?

And the question is answered:

> He that hath clean hands, and a pure heart;
> Who hath not lifted up his soul into vanity,
> And hath not sworn deceitfully.

Mark the fourfold description. First, "clean hands," right action. Behind that "a pure heart," purity of thought and of motive. "Not lifting up the soul to vanity," reality in all his dealings. "That hath not sworn deceitfully," truth in the inward parts and in the outward expression. They are pregnant phrases which describe the man of absolute integrity, in the moral fiber of whose personality exists no taint of evil. Who fulfils that ideal?

The Man who ascends into the hill of the Lord and stands in His holy place. Who is it that is exalted to the hill of the Lord? Who is it that stands in His holy place? None in the right of his purity, save this Man of Nazareth. He it is whom God highly exalted, placed Him on His right hand, on the holy hill of Zion, in the midst of the light of the infinite and unsullied purity. And from the exaltation of this Man I argue the absolute perfection of His life. That life is the pattern life for humanity. If you want the one ideal that is perfect, you must take the ideal Man that God has lifted out of the centuries, and put at His right hand, because of the perfection of the pattern. He exalted Him, the Man of clean hands, the man of the pure heart, the Man Who never lifted up His soul to vanity, the Man who dwelt in realities, the Man who never swore deceitfully, the Man in whom there was no cunning, no double-dealing. Straightness in speech and action. That is true greatness. That is the character which ascends the throne, and sits at the center of the universe of God, the one perfect pattern of human life.

There is more than this, for notice that the "wherefore" with which my text opens leans back, not merely on the obedient Servant, but on the obedient Servant Who suffered to death, even the death of the Cross. When I lift my eyes by faith, and look toward those distant hills, to that high and holy place, I see the Man Jesus perfect, but I see Him as a "Lamb having been slain." There are wounds. There are the marks of this very dying which the Apostle has described with a great reserve of description. "Yea, the death of the Cross." It is not merely the exaltation of a perfect pattern, it is the exaltation of a perfect pattern which has been wounded, bruised, afflicted, and has passed to death.

And now I ask again, what does this exaltation mean? Why was He wounded? Why was He bruised? Why was He afflicted? "He was wounded for our transgressions, He was bruised for our iniquities: the chastisement of our peace was upon Him." He went to the Cross, intending to bear the sin of the world. Did He succeed? Oh, behold the exalted Man! And as I see that wounded One lifted up out of death by resurrection, lifted back to Heaven by ascension, placed by God at the heart and center of all the universe, I know that He succeeded, that He bore my sin, that He made it not to be in the mystery of His dying. The exalted Christ is not merely the revelation of a perfect pattern. He is the assurance of a perfect salvation.

And yet one other thing. This exaltation does more than argue the perfection of His ideal and demonstrate the success of His work. The fact that God has taken this Man and set him there at His own right hand is to me the word that speaks of my security; for seeing God has set Him there, I know that none can ever dethrone Him. To do that has been the attempt of all the centuries since he lived. The work of evil, the work of His enemies has been to dethrone Him. Devils and demons, fallen principalities and powers, through one organized and persistent effort have attempted to dethrone Him. Blessed be God, they have never succeeded. The perpetual attempt of man in his opposition to Christianity has been to dethrone Christ. Say anything of Him you like, only dethrone Him, says evil through man. Say He is not there, that He has ceased to be. Say, if you will, He was a good Man, hoping to do well, but He died. Admire the fair example of His life if you will, but do not let Him be enthroned.

Let us go back to the Psalms again:

Why do the nations rage,
And the peoples imagine a vain thing?
The kings of the earth set themselves,
And the rulers take counsel together,
Against the Lord, and against His anointed, saying,
Let us break their bands asunder,
And cast away their cords from us.
He that sitteth in the heavens shall laugh,
The Lord shall have them in derision.
Then shall He speak unto them in His wrath,
And vex them in His sore displeasure.
Yet have I set my King
Upon my holy hill of Zion.
I will tell of the decree:
The Lord said unto Me, Thou art My Son;

This day have I begotten Thee.
Ask of Me, and I will give Thee the nations for Thine inheritance,
And the uttermost parts of the earth for Thy possession.

Let us catch the message of it. God has exalted Him. The rulers take counsel together, but the Lord has them in derision. They may attempt to break the bands and cast away the cords, but it is useless. He is the crowned Lord of all, and Jesus seated at the right hand of God—to use the exquisite figurative language of these New Testament writers—is at once the revelation of perfection, the demonstration of salvation, and the assurance of ultimate victory. So God highly exalted Him.

Then the Apostle passes on, and writes a thing full of tenderness and beauty. "And gave unto Him the name which is above every name." What name is this? He had many names here. They were all beautiful. They called Him Messiah. Prophets spoke of Him as Immanuel, the Branch, Shiloh, Dayspring, Daysman, Daystar, King, Prophet, Priest, Shepherd, names and titles all full of beauty. What name is it that He has as He sits there on the throne of God's universe? Is it some new name I must wait for until I reach the land of light? I think not. My own conviction is that the Apostle intends that we shall understand that he explains his own statement in the words that follow. He says, "God . . . gave unto Him the name which is above every name; that in the name of Jesus every knee should bow." I am quite aware that there are great diversities of opinion concerning this passage. So eminent a scholar and so correct an exegete as the Bishop of Durham holds that it does not refer to the name of Jesus, rather that God invested Him with His own great name forevermore. And I bow very largely to Dr. Moule's exegesis and interpretation. But, with all humility, I do not at all agree at this point. I believe that what the Apostle wrote admits of no interpretation except this: that God gave Him when He exalted Him the name which is above every name, that in the name of Jesus every knee should bow. Not that He then gave Him the name, but that he gave Him, in the moment of His exaltation, the right that every knee should bow in that name. So He did give Him then the name of Jesus in a sense in which He had never done.

The name of Jesus was given before. When He was to come into the world, an angel messenger said, "Thou shalt call His name JESUS; for it is He that shall save His people from their sins." It was then a prophetic name. The mother was to utter it as expressing the hope of her own heart and all the human race which she represented. "Thou shalt call His name Jesus." It marked a purpose. It uttered a prophecy. It sang of a hope, as Mary first, with the Babe on her bosom, bending over Him in sweet maternal love, in obedience to the angel command, called Him Joshua, Jesus.

He went His way, and lived His life; and He went His way and died His death; and He went His way and brake the bars of death asunder; and He went His shining way back to the everlasting spaces; and then He was invested forevermore with the same sweet name that His mother had uttered in obedience to the angelic message as a prophecy. Now the prophecy of the name is fulfilled. Let Heaven recognize it. Let earth know it. Let hell tremble at it. Joshua, Jesus, human Saviour, is the Divine Lord of all life forever and forevermore! God gave Him the same sweet name to make the infinite music of all the coming ages when He exalted Him to His right hand. And do you wonder that Paul said that it is above every name?

Jesus, the name above every name, above every name in preciousness. No name so dear to the ear of God as the name of the One Who did His will, accomplished His purpose, wrought out His infinite plan of salvation. No name so dear to man as that. There are other names very dear to us, and names that become dear according to the persons for whom they stand. I could name human names that some of you find no music in that thrill with music for me. But bring me the sweetest of them all, and the dearest, and utter it, and then say this one word, Jesus, and all the earthly music becomes dim, and dies away, and the earthly glow is cold.

> Jesus, Thou joy of loving hearts,
> Thou Fount of life, Thou Light of men,
> From the best bliss that earth imparts,
> We turn unfilled to Thee again.

Oh, men and women, there is no name in all the world so sweet as this to the world. Away on the lonely sea to-night some soul will sing it, and it will be a haven of refuge. In the midst of the awful loneliness of the crowded city some tired heart will utter it, and it will be a pillow of rest. Out yonder, on the veldt in Africa, some young man, tempted and tried, will hear it and will win. There is no name like it. You know it, you do not want me to argue it. It is above every name in preciousness to God and man, and it is above every name because it is the name that stands for manifestation of such love as men have never dreamed of. Stronger His love than death or hell. Love that reaches to the lowest, love that lifts to the highest, love that lasts forever. Shakespeare sang of earthly loves, and said:

> Love is not love
> That alters when it alteration finds.

Did you ever find any earthly love that quite rose to that level? If you want me to find you a love that alters not when it alteration finds, I bring you back to Jesus. He loved me. He loved me—I cannot tell why, but He loved me. And in my heart of hearts I know it, and, in spite of all that I have been, He loves me still. There is no one else like this in love—"above every name."

And what is the purpose of God? I have touched the fringe only. You will follow it out. That is a part of the sermon that never could be finished. You will finish it when you are tempted to-morrow. You will finish it when you are in sorrow the next day. You will finish it when you are in perplexity the day after. You will finish it all the way through the week, and if you will only trust Him you will find there is no name like it in Heaven above or in earth beneath.

By now, finally, God exalted Him, and gave Him this name for a purpose. What is it? That every knee should bow, that every tongue should confess that He is Lord. I am not now going to discuss the principle and deal with the general purpose of God, I am going, rather, to ask you what relation exists between you and this crowned Man at God's right hand. Have you bowed the knee? Have you confessed Him Lord? Oh, if I could shut you up to this question! Have I bowed the knee to Him? Have I crowned Him? Have I confessed Him Lord? A great many will have to say, if they ask this question honestly, No, I have done none of these things. I have admired Him, read about Him, loved to listen to anybody who talked about Him. I have faced my Lord, but I have never bent the knee, I have never cast my crown, the crown of my manhood, my womanhood, at His feet. Then, so far, you have violated the purpose of God concerning this Man. There must be the bending in His presence. There must be at last the confession that He is Lord. To-day that confession brings salvation. I do not know how long it will. I find no warrant in my Bible for telling you that if you confess Him Lord in the age to come you will thereby be saved. Here and now confess Him Lord. Crown Him resolutely, submit to the Man at the center of God's universe, accept His pattern as the ideal of your life, the mystery of His passion as your way of salvation, the assurance of His presence as the guarantee of your victory. Trust Him and you shall be saved. "If thou shalt believe in thy heart that God raised Him from the dead"—that is, that He has been exalted and crowned—"thou shalt be saved; for with the heart man believeth unto righteousness, and with the mouth confession is made unto salvation." Now I pray you, in the name of my Master, and for the sake of your own soul's eternal welfare, ask that question, Have I confessed my Lord, and, if not, Shall I? May God in His mercy bring you to the one only true choice.

CHAPTER XVI

LIFE THROUGH DEATH

I am the good Shepherd; the good Shepherd layeth down His life for the sheep.

JOHN 10:11.

IN THIS PARTICULAR STATEMENT OF THE TEXT AND IN THE whole of the passage surrounding it we have an illuminative statement of Christ with regard to His death and its relation to our life. He affirmed that He is the Good Shepherd, and quoted as supreme qualification for the fulfilment of the function of the Shepherd the fact that He laid down His life for the sheep.

It is very important that we should clearly understand that this declaration means infinitely more than that He died for the sheep. When Jesus said in the words of my text, "I lay down My life for the sheep," He did mean that He would die, but He meant more. He meant to say, "I lay down My life for the sheep" that they may have the life I lay down. "I have come," He said, "that they may have life, and that they may have it more abundantly." What life is it that He had come that we might have? His own life, as His words, "I lay down My life for the sheep," make plain. So that the great statement of my text includes the fact of His death, and that profounder fact, that by the way of His death His life is at the disposal of men.

I ask you, then—and may God help us all to approach such a subject reverently—to consider the death of Christ in relation to the impartation of life to believing souls.

We all know in art the importance of background to any picture. I shall take a little time to put in the background of my theme by considering the death of Christ in relation to Himself alone, and this in order that I may proceed to put in the foreground of the picture the death of Christ in its relation to sinful and sinning men.

With regard to this subject of background, let me ask you to think with me carefully of that death of Christ in relation to His life, and apart from its great connection with our salvation. It is a somewhat difficult thing to do, I grant you. We have become so familiar with the story of His death as related to His mission and to our salvation. We have so constantly and almost unconsciously—and thank God that it is so—thought of that death as being intimately related with our profoundest need. But shall we attempt for a moment to look at that death simply in its relation to His life?

Let me say at once, in order that I may arrest your attention and aid you in following me along this line, that if the death of Christ stand alone in relation to the life of Christ, and be not seen to have immediate connection with the sin of man, then the death of Christ will make me an infidel immediately. That is a superlative statement. I desired that it should be so, for by such superlative sentences I am attempting to put in this dark background.

There is no problem so terrible and so impossible of solution in all the realm of evil and all the fact of pain as the death of Christ, until we catch its profounder meaning and accept the great evangel concerning it, which He declares.

The death of Christ creates the greatest moral mystery that the mind of man can ever attempt to solve. The death of Christ at the age of thirty-three or thereabouts was the eclipse of light, the extinction of love, the ending of the one life that is by all men—whatever their views of the Person of Christ may be—conceded to be the perfect Pattern and highest Ideal of human life that the world has ever seen.

I say, first of all, that the death of Christ was the eclipse of light. Form what opinion you will of His Person, the fact remains that "never man spake like this Man." My brethren, I pause because a sentence like that lures a man on to exposition and defense of it. I repeat it. "Never man spake like this Man." No other teacher that the world has ever had has pressed into so few and brief sentences so much wisdom which has been productive of such tremendous result in the history of the race as the teaching of Jesus.

The teaching of Jesus was clear, authoritative, rational. He never speculated. There was nothing hesitating about the teaching of Jesus. He said things that had any other man said the world would have ceased to listen to him long ago on account of pride and arrogance. And yet men listen to Him. One illustration will suffice me at this point. There was a day when, standing in the midst of the crowds, He said this: "I do always the things that are pleasing to God." Can you find me another teacher who dare say such a thing and be believed? If I came and faced my congregation on some Sabbath and said to them, I always please God—when the newspapers, religious or irreligious, noticed it, they would say, "From that moment people ceased to believe in him." And quite right that they should. But I find in my Gospel of John this fact: after He had said, "I do always the things that are pleasing to God," from that time "many believed on Him." That is the marvelous mystery of Jesus Christ. His teaching was clear and authoritative and rational and final, and He said such things concerning God, and the soul, and eternity as man had never said and never thought, but which the human conscience knew at once to be true. And He had not said half men wanted Him to say when He was arrested, condemned by the most iniquitous mock trial that ever disgraced the pages of human history, and murdered in cold blood. The Light was eclipsed. Men were groping after it. The world had had other teachers, and the most honest and remarkable of them had said they could not speak of certain subjects with authority. Both Socrates and Plato, among the Greek philosophers, announced that they could teach men only to ask questions concerning God, the soul, and destiny; that another teacher must come who could answer these questions. And He came and answered the questions concerning God, and the soul, and destiny; and yet before His teaching seemed to be well nigh begun He was put to death.

But I go further, and say that in the death of Jesus I see the extinction of love. Among all the love stories that have charmed the hearts of men there never was such a love story as the story of Jesus, and every man knows it if he will stop and think. Jesus' was a love absolutely and utterly self-forgetful. His was a love equal to intense severity and devoid of fear. His was a love patient enough to discover good where no one else could discover it, and to wait for its development. His was a love strong enough to denounce wrong in the heart and life of His best beloved. His was a love strong enough to look Peter in the face, and say to him, "Get thee behind me, Satan." I know you better than you know yourself. You have the making of the common blasphemer in you, Peter. His love was strong enough to say to that same man: You will deny Me, but trust Me, and I will realize the good. "Let not your heart be troubled."

His was a love that flamed out strongest in death. I am not now referring to the essential values of the death, but to the simple human story. Oh, man and woman, Christian or un-Christian, did you ever hear such language, "Father, forgive them, for they know not what they do"? Yet a Man

Whose life was all love was arrested at thirty-three years of age, and murdered, and God did not interfere.

Or take one other point. The death of Jesus was the ending of the one life that was a perfect pattern according to our human ideals. His was the one life which revealed the meaning of life eternal, in which the intellect was illumined by the spiritual, the emotion impulsed by the eternal, and the will dominated by Deity. Yet that perfect life was permitted by God to be arrested and ended in bloody brutality.

In the presence of the death of Christ I find myself confronted by the most superlative manifestation of the problem of evil that the world has ever seen. And I ask this question, and I do not hesitate to ask it: Is the moral Governor of the universe good? There is nothing in that death to show it, until you have the evangelical explanation of it. These are the questions we ask in the presence of the Cross, if we think at all. There is nothing else that compares with this. A life, perfect in light, perfect in love, perfect in essential life, and yet priests in malicious hatred inspired the brutal government of the Roman power to lay foul hands on the fair life and murder it. Where is God? When I stand in the presence of the Cross, I ask, Is God good, and is He powerful? These are the questions that come to me.

Now let me again put this thing superlatively. It is on my heart as a burden. Unless what the New Testament teaches about the death of Christ be true, that there was more value in it than ever can be associated with the moral personality of Jesus, that there was some infinite mystery lying behind that death that awaited the revelation of God, then that Cross makes me an unbeliever. That is all background, dark and mysterious background. I have emphasized it only that we may now turn to the great foreground of revelation.

Christ has answered our problem. I ask you simply to listen to this one word of Jesus about His own dying. The first factor contributing to the solution of the problem is the fact that Christ knew of His death, and distinctly foretold it, and went quietly and resolutely toward it, knowing its manner and method before He came to it. That helps me to a solution, though not to the final one. In the unclouded intelligence of eternal life He foretold His dying. In the overwhelming love of eternal life He chose that method of dying. In the overcoming power of eternal life He accomplished His dying.

I say, in the first place, that in the unclouded intelligence of eternal life He foretold His dying. All through the Gospel story this is evident. I recommend to young men and women interested in this to obtain a book, the most luminous and valuable I have ever read on the New Testament teaching on this subject. I refer to Dr. Denney's *Death of Christ*, more valuable as a treatise on the Atonement than anything I have ever read, because in that book Dr. Denney does not attempt any philosophic account, but simply interprets the New Testament teaching. Among other things that Christ taught about His death, I find this word at the beginning of His public ministry. I see Him engaged in one of those first activities when He cleansed the temple, and men came to him and said, "What sign showest Thou unto us, seeing that Thou doest these things?" and He said, "Destroy this temple, and in three days I will raise it up." The men who listened to Him did not understand Him. The materialists round about Him did not understand Him. They laughed at Him. They thought He spoke of the material temple; but the inspired exposition goes on, "He spake of the temple of His body." So that, in effect, when men said to Him at the beginning, What is your authority? He said, The authority of My death and resurrection. That was the final thing. Not the ethical teaching, not the social order, but the dying and resurrection.

Or, if we go on a little further into the public ministry,

we find Him sitting one night, not among the crowds, but with a lonely inquirer on the housetop. It was a great mystery to Nicodemus, that necessity for new birth; and he asked Jesus two questions. First, "How can a man . . . ?" That is the question of critical unbelief. Then, "How can these things be?" That was the question of inquiring honesty. And when he asked Him the second question, How can a man have this life, or by what process is it communicated to him, Jesus said to him, "As Moses lifted up the serpent in the wilderness, even so must the Son of man be lifted up; that whosoever believeth may in Him have eternal life." In effect, Jesus Christ said to the inquiring soul who asked the way of life, The only way of life is by My death. Through that, the new life of which I speak will be placed at the disposal of men.

So that whether He cleansed the temple, or talked to an inquiring soul, underneath His act and His teaching, His right, His authority in His own consciousness, was the right, the authority of that very Cross which fills us with the sense of problem, and almost of pain.

Then, again, not only did He foretell it, but in the overwhelming love of His life He chose it. How often it was suggested to Him that He should omit the Cross from His program. I think, perhaps, the suggestion came first at the beginning of public ministry in the wilderness, when the devil, making to pass before Him in splendid array the kingdoms of the world, and the glory of them, said to Him, "All these will I give Thee if Thou wilt fall down and worship me." It was subtle, insidious—yes, I must use the word—devilish. What did he mean? Here is a short cut to these kingdoms. Thou hast come for them, and according to all the foreshadowing of the past, and the purpose of Thy heart, Thou art going to death. For remember, Jesus, being baptized in Jordan's waters, typified His consent to die with the transgressors. Take this short and easy method. One moment's homage, and I will give Thee all the kingdoms. Christ turned His back on that short and easy method, choosing the Cross, God's way of suffering and dying, in order to gain possession of the kingdoms.

Again the temptation came when He turned from the ministry to the nation and began that to His own disciples, and Peter said to Him, "That be far from Thee, Lord," pity Thyself, Jesus in stern words said to him, "Get thee behind Me, Satan . . . thou mindest not the things of God, but the things of men." The things of men are the things that save life from pain, the things of pure selfishness, that make men choose the easy path. The things of God for the salvation of men demand the Cross, and suffering, and pain; and thus He turned His back again upon the suggestion that He should miss the Cross.

In the gospel according to John it is recorded that certain Greeks wanted to see Him, and when His disciples came running and said, Master, some Greeks are here, and want to see Thee, He said the very strangest thing in all the world, "Except a grain of wheat fall into the earth and die, it abideth by itself alone; but if it die, it beareth much fruit. . . . If any man serve Me, let him follow Me."

What was His meaning? Most evidently this: The Greeks desire to see Me. They cannot see Me. No man can see Me now. They must wait for My dying and its issue to see Me. The way of the Cross is the only way by which a man can see Me. Thus He anticipated and deliberately chose the Cross. And we have but to read His prayer to see how the Cross burdened Him, overshadowed Him. He said, "Now is My soul troubled; and what shall I say? Father, save Me from this hour. But for this cause came I unto this hour"—and He did not say, Father, save Me from this hour, but "Father, glorify Thy name." The supreme passion of His life was not to be saved from anything, but that God's name should be glorified. And the answer came, "I have both glorified it, and will glorify it again." And then the word of Jesus rang out about His Cross: "Now is the judgment of this world; now shall the prince of this world be cast out. And I, if I be lifted up from the earth, will draw all men unto Myself." He deliberately chose the Cross, as well as foretold it.

And once again, in the overcoming power of that eternal life; the Cross which He knew and chose, He accomplished. Those were the very remarkable words that Jesus spoke in connection with the declaration of our text: "Therefore doth the Father love Me, because I lay down My life, that I may take it again. No one taketh it away from Me, but I lay it down of Myself. I have power to lay it down, and I have power to take it again." Have we not been a little inclined to say that Jesus died because men murdered Him? There are some senses in which that is correct. But here is the profounder truth. Jesus said, "No one taketh it [My life] away from Me, but I lay it down of Myself." Did you say that is poetic, a mere figure of speech? But listen, He said something else. "I . . . take it again." Now, if He took it again I will believe that He laid it down, and no man took it from Him. Did He take it again? Yes, thank God for the answer. If somebody says no, then you will question the authority of the statement that He laid it down. In secondary senses—in the sense in which man was an instrument of a Divine purpose—men took His life away; but in the underlying profundities, God gave Him commandment, authority to lay down His life Himself, and He did what none other has ever done, He laid it down and took it again. To me death is a fact, but to Him it was an act. He is lonely and sublime and majestic in the mystery of His dying, and I see Him laying down His life through the secondary process of human murder, but in the underlying fundamental authority of a Divine counsel. And that, my brethren, is what Peter meant when preaching on the Day of Pentecost, he said of Jesus, "Him . . . by the hands of lawless men did crucify and slay." But Peter also said He was "delivered by the determinate counsel and foreknowledge of God." So that I see in this dying that appalls me, this great Cross that shocks me, first, that Jesus knew and foretold it; second, that He went toward it, choosing it; and third, that He died of His own will, and authority, and power. And in that death of Christ, which He—to use the word used in connection with the Holy Mount—accomplished, I have at last touched some secret spring of life. This death is not the ordinary death of other men. It is different, removed, supreme, and marvelous beyond all dying. So that the dying of Christ at the end of His life has in it qualities, quantities, virtues, values, that can be in no other dying.

And now let us go a little further. What did Christ say concerning His death? I confine myself now to the simple statement of this text. He said, "I am the Good Shepherd." The Good Shepherd and the wolf are favorite figures of Jesus. If you go back to Matthew, you will read that He saw the multitudes of the cities and villages and was moved with compassion because they were as sheep scattered, having no shepherd. And that word "scattered" means flung to the ground, torn and mangled by wolves—harassed. The wolf is the one that destroys the sheep. The Good Shepherd is the One Who loves the sheep, and Who will enter into conflict with the wolf that destroys the sheep. How will He do it? The Good Shepherd laid down His life when He took hold on sin and entered into mortal and final conflict with it. There was only one way to overcome it, and that was by dying. The Good Shepherd did not hesitate at dying, in order that by His dying He might make dead the thing that spoiled the sheep. The Good Shepherd entered into conflict with the wolf, and therein laid down His life for the sheep.

Let us go still further. The Good Shepherd laid down His life for the sheep. There is a greater truth contained in this than the figure that Jesus used here can possibly contain. Here is a supreme truth that submerges the figure. No truth of God can finally and fully be contained in figures, even those which Jesus used. This is not to question Jesus, but it is to say that figures always faint and fail before infinite facts; and whatever figure Jesus used, you find it was full and overflowing.

I take the figure of the Eastern shepherd. I see Him going into conflict with the wolf. I see Him die as the wolf dies, that the sheep may be delivered and die no more. But here the figure fails. Jesus said, "I take it again," and I take it again for the sheep. Now, suppose the Eastern shepherd dying slew the wolf, and then, taking hold of his own life again, gave it to the sheep, so that the sheep that were not strong enough to enter into conflict and have victory over the wolf should take the very nature of the shepherd and become able to enter into conflict and overcome. That is the figure of the dying of Jesus and the liberation of His life. He died for the destruction of the destroyer, but He rose again, and in His rising He took back His life, not to hold it, but to give it; not to possess it, but to pass it on to others. And to-day I believe in Him, and have His very life, so that I, who could not have victory over the wolf in my own strength, but in His strength, have received the very nature that triumphs over the wolf; and I am made master of the things that mastered me by the thrill and the throb of the very life of the Shepherd Who died and rose again.

"I am the Good Shepherd, the Good Shepherd layeth down His life for the sheep." And out of this comes the great evangel. The wolf which snatcheth and scattereth is overcome. The Shepherd life which overcame him is communicated, and in its power I also may overcome. Eternal life is now at the disposal of men who put their trust in Jesus; and in that gift there are two values, the value of the death for the putting away of sin, and the value of the life, that men may go and sin no more. The Good Shepherd giveth His life to the sheep.

The contemplation of the life eternal in Jesus is the most overwhelming and disheartening exercise possible to man, and if I have nothing in Christ other than the revelation of what eternal life means, that revelation serves only to reveal my degradation. Unless in some way the life revealed can be communicated to me, unless, somehow, the great ethical beauty manifested can become the dynamic virtue operating in me, then the revelation does nothing for me. No man has ever yet been lifted out of degradation by the contemplation of an ideal. No man has ever yet been saved—and I use the word of set purpose—by looking at the glory of Jesus Christ.

Think of it a little more carefully with me. You tell me of the light of His intelligence operating in the realm of eternal love, and I tell you that the light blinds me. You tell me of the love that impulsed all His doing, and I tell you that the love makes me ashamed of my lovelessness and utter selfishness. You tell me that the exercise of His will was sufficient to resist all temptation, and I am amazed, but I am not helped. I am not helped by looking at the light, or hearing of the love, or watching the great life principle, because it is all outside me. In my ignorance I stand in the presence of the light, and in my darkness I stand in the presence of the love, and in my base unworthiness I stand in the presence of the life that operates to perfect volition; and I say with the Apostle, "To me who would do good, evil is present." There is a paralysis in my veins and blood, and though I admire the ideal, I cannot translate it into the real. Such light reveals darkness. Such love makes one blush for very shame. Such strength of will makes me afraid; and by all this I mean that the incarnation alone never did, and never can, save a single soul.

What, then, must be done? That life must be given up in and through death. Had there been no sin to atone for, perchance there might have been the communication of a life that should have made me undying without the death of the Cross. But because sin is there, the death of the Cross must be the harvest of sin; and in that lone and awful moment, when in His dying He cried, "My God, My God, why hast Thou forsaken Me?" He spoke the words that I ought to speak. Then He was at the utmost issue of sin. Then He was in the deepest depth of sorrow. Then He touched the unfathomable and unutterable mystery of silence. He was God-forsaken.

> I see the crowd in Pilate's hall,
> I mark their wrathful mien,
> Their shouts of "Crucify" appall
> With blasphemy between.
> But of that shouting multitude
> I know that I am one.

Ask me the meaning of this death, and I stand in the presence of it intellectually, and assert that it is a mystery. But, ah, me, when there lies before me His thought of it, His estimate of it, His declared purpose in it, then I bow my head in the presence of the Cross and say, "He loved me, and gave Himself for me"; and out of the mystery of that dying, that substitutionary, vicarious, atoning dying—and if you take those words from me you make me an infidel at once—there comes to me the great gift of life.

And now in the communicated life of Christ, liberated through the mystery of His death, I see, for the intelligence is illumined; I love, for the emotion is enkindled; I obey and serve, for the will is brought under its proper impulse and motive. And all this in the eternal sense. The present becomes part of the future, and death becomes the gate of life, because the Good Shepherd gave His life for the sheep.

Have we that life? It is at our disposal. He tasted death for every man, and unless we have it, then we have no intelligence that takes in the infinite, no love that fastens on God and man and fulfils all the law, no power equal to the obedience that blossoms into righteousness.

And if we have not the life, let us take it. It is God's gift to us. "He that believeth on the Son hath life, eternal life."

CHAPTER XVII

FOLLOW ME

Follow Me.

JOHN 1:43.

I HAVE SELECTED THESE TWO WORDS FOR OUR PRESENT MEDItation because they seem to have been the favorite form of invitation on the lips of our Master, and I have selected them from this particular verse because it gives us the earliest recorded use of them.

Other occasions of their use we read as lesson. A little later on one of his disciples expressed a desire to remain with his father, saying, "Lord, suffer me first to go and bury my father," which, by the way, did not at all mean that his father was then dead; in the Eastern idiom he was expressing the fact that he was devoted to his father, and desired to abide with him until the hour of his death. To such a one Jesus said, "Follow Me . . . leave the dead to bury their own dead." A little further on, passing on His way, He saw Levi (Matthew) sitting at the receipt of custom; looking at him, He said, "Follow Me," and immediately Matthew left the seat of custom and went after Christ. The words next occur, so far as we are able to arrange them chronologically, in that memorable scene at Cæsarea Philippi, when Peter came to the hour of his great and glorious confession concerning Christ and thus made possible the great and glorious confession of the Christ concerning His Church, which was immediately followed by the Master's declaration of His coming suffering and triumph as He spoke of going to Jerusalem to be buffetted and bruised, and killed, and on the third day to be raised from the dead. Against that word as to His coming suffering, blind but intense affection made this protest, "Be it far from Thee, Lord: this shall never be unto Thee," and was sternly rebuked by Jesus, "Get thee behind Me, Satan; thou art a stumblingblock unto Me; for thou mindest not the things of God, but the things of men." Immediately, in that atmosphere and in those circumstances, Jesus uttered these words again, making them most emphatic in application to His own disciples, "If any man would come after Me, let him deny himself, and take up his cross, and follow Me." Yet a little later in that period of public ministry when the Lord was even nearer to His Cross, there came the young ruler, clean, upright, straightforward, yet conscious of a lack in life, as his question gives evidence, "What shall I do to inherit eternal life?" To him the Lord ultimately replied, "Follow Me." Then again, beyond the Cross and the resurrection, in the flush of that wonderful morning by the shore of the lake as He restored Peter after his deflection from faith, the Lord's last word to him in that connection was, "Follow Me"; and again beyond it, Peter, still the same in temperament, inquired what John was to do, and in words that have in them an ultimate rebuke thrilling with tenderness Jesus said to him, "If I will that he tarry till I come, what is that to thee? Follow thou Me." There is a most illuminative sequence in our Lord's use of this particular term, "Follow Me."

Let us first inquire the simplest meaning of this call which Jesus uttered in so many different circumstances, and with such varied application, "Follow Me." Let us first carefully observe that there is a marked difference between this word and another which our Lord made use of in other circumstances. Subsequently to the initial call of Peter and Andrew, James and John, Jesus found them fishing and He called them, no longer to Himself as disciples, but to definite co-operation in service. Our old version reads thus, "He saith unto them, Follow Me, and I will make you fishers of men"; the Revised Version has drawn attention to the difference as it translates, "Come ye after Me, and I will make you fishers of men." In one of the passages which we have read the two ideas are present, the one containing the word spoken by our Lord at Cæsarea Philippi, "If any man would come after Me, let him deny himself, and take up his cross, and follow Me"; there are two ideas, *to come after*, and *to follow*. If we were dealing simply with English words, this might be spoken of as a distinction without a difference; to come after is to follow, to follow is to come after; but we are dealing with the words which our Lord used, and in them there is a very distinct difference. He did not say, Come after Me, to Philip when He first found him. He did not say, Come after Me, to Peter when He last left him. What, then, did He say? The word He employed is one, but it is constituted of two parts, the first of which I shall speak of as a particle of union, and the second as a simple word which means a way. What, then, did Jesus say? Come in the way with Me. This is My way; I am walking this way, Come after Me. The thought involved in following is included, but there is more in it than that. I shall make no attempt to minimize the imperial call of Christ, I will attempt to emphasize it presently; but let us at first emphasize the sweetness and tenderness and grace of it. I shall attempt to interpret it thus— this is not translation, this is interpretation—"He findeth Philip: and Jesus saith unto him, Join Me in the way." He said to Peter by the shore of the Sea of Galilee; "When thou wast young, thou girdest thyself, and walkedst whither thou wouldest: but when thou shalt be old, thou shalt stretch forth thy hands, and another shall gird thee, and carry thee, whither thou wouldest not. . . . Join Me in the way." Presently, when Peter said "Lord, what shall this man do?" Jesus answered, "If I will that he tarry till I come, what is that to thee? Join Me in the way."

I go back to the ancient prophecy of Isaiah and I read this, "We have turned every one to *his own way*," and in the same prophecy, "Let the wicked forsake *his way*, and the unrighteous man his thoughts: and let him return unto the Lord, and He will have mercy upon him; and to our God, for He will abundantly pardon. For My thoughts are not your thoughts, neither are *your ways My ways*, saith the Lord. For as the heavens are higher than the earth, so are *My ways* higher than *your ways*, and My thoughts than your thoughts." It is that One Who spoke to Philip and said, This is My way, join Me in this way. It is an imperial call, an unequivocal demand for surrender, but thrilling with infinite grace, calling men at once to subjection to Him, and to comradeship with Him, in the way.

This is perhaps the simplest and the sublimest formula of the Christian life to be found in the pages of the New Testament.

It is the simplest. It is Christ's word at the wicket, and it is simple enough for the tiniest child. It presupposes nothing as necessary but need and trust, and trust acting itself out. Do not forget that, I pray you, when you are dealing with children. Do not ask your child to accept a doctrine in order to be a Christian. Do not demand of your child some experience through which you have passed. Say what Jesus would have said to the little one, and try to say it, so far as you can, in our Anglo-Saxon speech, with the same thought there was in His speech. Jesus says to the little one, Come along with Me, walk My way, come with Me.

But if it is the simplest, it is also the sublimest. If it is the King's word at the wicket gate, so simple that every child can hear and understand it, it is the King's perpetual demand. He never changes it from the wicket to the homeland. If it is so wooing and winsome that the little one can hear it and obey it, it is severe enough for the most highly developed man, demanding renunciation of all that hinders, surrender of all that a man is, and absolute, unquestioning loyalty to the Lord. If it presupposes nothing other than trust and need as necessary on the part of the one to whom it is addressed, it assumes the wisdom, power, and right of the One Who utters the word; for we must interpret this word of Jesus in the atmosphere of His ministry and revelation. We must remember that He came to reveal, and to reveal God; that He claimed it as His supreme business to speak to men in the realm of the spiritual and eternal. When He said to Philip, "Join Me in the way," He was not thinking merely of a journey from Galilee to Judæa, He was thinking of that pathway that a pilgrim must take ere he find his way to the everlasting habitations. Consequently, when He said, "Follow Me," there was on His part the assumption of infinite wisdom, absolute right, and perfect power. So that whether I think of the little child unable to appreciate high doctrines of grace or of the man fully intellectually equipped for facing the final problems of life, the King has the same thing to say and He says it with wooing winsomeness to the little one, "Follow Me," Join Me in the way; and He says it with superlative, unequivocal authority to the proudest intellect that has ever faced life's problems, "Follow Me," I will solve the mystery and fulfil thy life.

Let us turn now to examine some of our Lord's uses of the words. As hurriedly as we may we will glance at the passages I have read to you, and see what He meant when He said, "Follow Me."

The first occurrence of the word arrested and guided

the slow man. Some of you will remember that three years and nine months ago I preached on the same text dealing wholly with Philip and tracing his story. He was always the slow man, the quiet, unobtrusive man. As Mr. Elvet Lewis beautifully says, he was the man who was always on the fringe of the crowd, and was therefore able to help people whom others might have missed. He was a man who did not seek Christ, not I think because there was no longing in his heart for the things that are high and holy; but because of his slowness. He was the man whom Christ went and found, knowing perfectly the secret in his heart though no one else knew it. He was the man, the slow man, who made no impression on his fellow disciples, or so little that Matthew, Mark, and Luke tell us nothing about him except that he was one of the twelve. It was only John who could appreciate all the silent, subtle forces that did not impress others in that man on the fringe of the crowd. All the stories about Philip are in John. To that slow man Jesus came and said, "Follow Me," Join Me in the way. Philip was arrested, and from that moment found his Guide.

The next incident in chronological order is of a strange and startling nature, a contrast to the first. As I have already said, a disciple of Jesus asked to be permitted to return to his father and take care of him. It may be interesting—I say this especially for young people—that I should remind you again of the light on this passage that came to me from a conversation with Dr. George Adam Smith. He told me how on one occasion he was in the byways of Syria and was anxious to secure a certain young Arab to be his guide. The young man sat in the door of his tent, and there by his side sat his father, hale, hearty, patriarchal. Dr. George Adam Smith was trying to persuade the young man to accompany him on a somewhat perilous adventure, and he refused, saying: "Suffer me first to bury my father," thus using the actual words we have in the gospel story. Here, then, was a man who asked to be permitted to bury his father, to stay by him and care for him until his earthly life was run. Jesus said to him, "Follow Me.... Leave the dead to bury their own dead." Mark this, I pray you, this call of Jesus brooks no burying of the dead if that interferes with loyalty to the Lord. If the first illustration shows us the infinite tenderness of this call, the second arrests us and shows the absolute severity of this word of Jesus.

Take the next in order. Matthew was sitting at the receipt of custom. We must be Hebrews to understand this picture, or at least we must get back into the Hebrew atmosphere. What was he doing? Matthew's calling was the degradation of a high ideal. Matthew had bent to the Roman yoke, in order to collect from his brethren the taxes of the oppressor. You say, Why do you call that the degradation of a high ideal? Read his gospel. Mark his quotations of the ancient prophetic writings. Watch very carefully the whole method of the gospel of Matthew. Matthew's ideal was that of kingship, empire, authority. He was a man molded on imperial lines. I believe that was the reason why he had hired himself to Rome. The glamor of Rome had possessed his soul, and he had lent himself to Rome—a Levite to collect taxes from his brethren. It was the degradation of a high ideal. It was an attempt to come into touch with the great conception of authority and empire. Jesus Christ, passing, saw him, knew him, understood him; knew his devotion to this high ideal of empire, knew that the prophecies which had charmed him in his youth were such as foretold the coming of a great King Messiah; and He said to him, "Follow Me." He took him with Him, led him through the years and revealed to him the Kingdom and the King, and fitted him for the writing of the gospel which stands out in the Bible as the gospel of the Kingdom of God and of God's anointed

King. If the ideal was a high and noble one, and if it had been degraded in an attempt to realize it, when this Christ passed by the man He took hold of him, redeemed his ideal, and enabled him to fulfil it on the highest possible level.

Take the next illustration, that at Cæsarea Philippi. I go back to the distinction I made at the beginning. In this verse I find the two ideas. "If any man will *come after Me*," that literally means, If any man will come behind Me, follow Me, in our usual sense of the word, then let him *join Me in the way*. The text from which we have preached over and over again in order to emphasize the supremacy of Jesus does emphasize His supremacy, but it thrills with His grace. Peter had just said, "Thou art the Messiah," and Jesus had said, "I will build My Church. . . . I will give unto thee the keys of the Kingdom of heaven." Christ had said to him, In order to enter into that Kingdom and build that Church I must go to Jerusalem and suffer and die and rise again; and Peter had said, That be far from Thee; God have mercy on Thee, not that. That word of Peter was almost profanity. Now the Lord said, "If any man will come after Me"; if you really mean to follow Me, if you, My disciples, desire to come with Me, your coming must be thorough, your coming must be complete, you must come by the way of the Cross, the way of resurrection, the way by which I am going. But if any man would come after Me, let him join Me in the way; he must come My way, but let him come with Me. You cannot shun the Cross; but share it with Me. You cannot escape the severity of My terms, but let Me be your Comrade as you tramp the *via dolorosa*. This formula of Jesus in this application insisted on the closest association with Himself in the pathway of obedience; therefore it was a word of severity, yet a word of infinite grace.

I go a little further and see the rich young ruler. Notice in what sense He used the word in speaking to that young man. He asked, "Good Master, what shall I do to inherit eternal life?" Jesus replied to him, "Thou knowest the commandments"; and in brief form He repeated the six of the second table of the decalogue, the six which condition human interrelationships. The man looked back into the eyes of incarnate Purity and said—and it was no empty boast but an actual fact—"All these things have I observed from my youth up." What did the King say to this man? "One thing thou lackest yet." What was the one thing? Hear the Lord through before you decide. "Sell all that thou hast, and distribute unto the poor, and thou shalt have treasure in heaven: and come join Me in the way." What did this man lack? Poverty? Nay verily. The element of control, mastership! When Jesus said, "Follow Me," to that man, it was necessary that He should first point out to him that which, though not evil in itself, was nevertheless destroying all the forces of his humanity, in that while ministering to the self-life, it was shutting him out from all high heroisms and noble motives. Christ would sweep away the forces that destroy in order to realize the heroic dignity of human life. *"Follow Me"* was the supreme word of command, and it revealed the secret of victory over the forces that destroy. How is this man, nursed in the lap of luxury, of fine temperament, of clean record, but being destroyed for lack of fine heroism, how is he to be saved? He must follow the Christ, and in order to do it in his case there must be the parting with all that which ministers to the self-life. But even here the call was of grace, as He invited this man to comradeship, by saying, "Join Me in the way."

Take the next illustration, "Follow Me," spoken at the seashore to Peter. What did the word do then? It transfigured the Cross. It was to make clear Christ's intention that I omitted the parenthesis in reading this evening. I want you to ponder that passage again at your leisure. I have not suggested that John's parenthesis is out of place or unnecessary; I believe it was inspired by the Spirit of God, and must remain. In order to make impossible any doubt as to what Christ meant when He said to Peter, "When thou wast young, thou girdest thyself, and walkedst whither thou wouldest: but when thou shalt be old, thou shalt stretch forth thy hands, and another shall gird thee, and carry thee whither thou wouldest not," John said, "This He spake, signifying by what manner of death he should glorify God."

Let us, however, forget for a moment that interpolation of John, and remember that without any break Christ added to that foretelling of the Cross, this word, "Follow Me." What did that mean to Peter? The word was spoken by the side of the lake on a memorable morning. What relation did that morning bear to the past? It was the risen Lord Who spoke. At Cæsarea Philippi Peter had shunned the Cross, and had been rebuked. By the side of the lake, Jesus brought him back to the Cross, to his own personal cross, and said to him, if reverently I may change the words of the Lord, Peter, you shunned the Cross for Me, you were afraid of it when you first saw it; you have been afraid of it through all the intervening months; but you must come to it, actually come to it, stretch out your hands and be crucified, die by the cross; follow Me, join Me in the way. And immediately Peter would say to himself, He went to the Cross, but He passed beyond the Cross and is risen from the dead. When Jesus, in that connection, said, "Follow Me," to Peter, it transfigured the coming Cross by revealing to him the fact that whatever man shall follow Jesus by the way of the Cross also shall follow Him beyond the Cross into the light and glory of the Easter morning that lies on the other side.

The last illustration seems almost commonplace by the side of some of the others, yet it is wondrously placed. "What shall this man do?" asked Peter concerning John, and

Jesus replied, "What is that to thee? Follow thou Me." It revealed in a flash, in which there was light, humor, satire, tenderness, the awful dignity of one man's life, and the fact that in this following every man must follow for himself, and that is enough for a man to do. If I were given to announcing sensational subjects, I think I should take this for a text, and announce as my subject, *"Mind your own business."* If the phrase sounds commonplace, think it well out. Mind your own business; in this respect it will take thee all thy time and eternity to realize My purpose for thee: "Follow thou Me." It was the individualizing of the man as to his personal relationship to Christ; and at the same time it was a word that declared to Peter that if the Lord demanded all his loyalty, He was not unmindful of John. Leave him to Me, I can care for him also. "Follow *thou* Me," the emphasis is there.

This hurried survey will enable us to see something of the breadth and glory of this word of Christ.

Hear it again, "Follow Me," Join Me, Come My way. What was His way? How shall I answer my own inquiry. Let me do it for a moment by mentioning certain names which will carry a congregation such as this to associations, which are revelations concerning the Lord. It was the way of Nazareth; long years of the daily round, the common task. It was the way of the wilderness, the short, sharp, fearful struggle of a naked soul with wickedness stripped. It was the way of the crowds and human sorrow, perpetual ministry and virtue going forth. It was the way of Gethsemane. It was the way of Calvary. It was the way of the high places and the outpoured Spirit. "Follow Me," join Me in the way. Set thy soul in the direction of My soul, and relate thy spirit to God, as My spirit is related to God.

Is that it? Then in the name of God I am helpless, I cannot do it. But in the strange, wonderful economy of Christ's dealings with men we begin where He ended, and work backward through the processes of His life. You will find that all through your Bible. I will give you one illustration, without turning to it. Take Exodus and read again the story of the pattern which God gave to Moses in the mount; then read the story of how Moses made the tabernacle, and you will find that it moves in the opposite direction. The pattern given begins at the center and moves outward to the finish; the work done begins where the pattern ended and works in to where the pattern began. It is always so.

Where am I to begin this following? I begin where He ended. I begin with Pentecost. That is the fulfilment of the great word. There were senses in which this word was never fulfilled in the experience of these men until Pentecost. We begin when we receive the Spirit of God, "He hath poured forth this which ye see and hear." When that Spirit comes to me I begin my following. That immediately admits me to the resurrection life which is life indeed, and it is by the way of that resurrection life that I come to personal experience of the Cross, "that I may know Him and the power of His resurrection and the fellowship of His sufferings." By that identification with Him in the Cross I enter into fellowship with Him in the agony of the garden. Through that and through that alone I pass into fellowship with His ministry amid the crowds of men. It is then the temptation becomes hardest in the normal Christian life; not to the man who never has yielded to Jesus has ever come temptation of the fiercest fury which appalls the trusting soul. Take it as a demonstration of nearness to your Master if the enemy is assailing your soul with fervor. Remember, tried, tempted heart, that temptation is not sin. It is the saint most closely associated with his Lord who knows the power of temptation most keenly. Then what? The most difficult thing of all Christian life, Nazareth and the commonplace.

I do not wish this to be divided into compartments as

though I would teach that to those who have been called to public service there will presently come the lonely pathway. There is always a lonely pathway to the Christian soul. There is always a Nazareth for all of us. The teacher who regularly faces a congregation on the Sunday, whose work is largely in the glare of publicity, has a Nazareth, a home, and that is the place where it is most difficult to be true, true in the commonplaces.

Yet that Master says one thing, "Follow Me," join Me in the way. You can never enter it save as you crown Him Lord, and no man can call Him Lord but by the Holy Ghost. Pentecost is the first thing. I cannot be in the resurrection life save as I come there with Him. He says, Follow Me, walk with Me in the way. This intolerable agony of sin mastering humanity, and demanding sacrifice in order that men may be delivered, who can deal with it? The Lord says, You shall indeed drink My cup and be baptized with My baptism; come with Me, join Me in the way.

Leave out these things and come to the last. Oh, you business men who say the preacher has no temptations, do not believe it! To the man who preaches is granted the freedom from observation which is of the essence of opportunity to sin, for indolence, and for incipient blasphemies. How can I be true when my door is locked and I am alone? There comes into the room, though the door be never unlocked, One Who says, "Join Me in the way," "Follow Me! That is the answer.

What is the secret to the great call of Christ? A vision of the Lord Himself. That vision will create the enthusiasm to follow. That enthusiasm constitutes the secret of abandoning all that hinders.

In this evening hour Christ is saying this selfsame thing, "Follow Me." What that means to me to-day I cannot tell you. What it means to you I do not ask you to tell me. We know, each man, woman, youth, maiden, for himself and for herself, what this means now. Shall we not obey? Shall we not say, Lord Christ, we will follow Thee, only let it be with Thee. Take us by the hand and lead us; we would come after Thee, but it will be easier if, sweet paradox of Thine own words, we may come after Thee by walking with Thee!

CHAPTER XVIII

GODLINESS AND GAIN

Supposing that godliness is a way of gain. But godliness with contentment is great gain.
I TIMOTHY 6:5, 6.

THE ARRESTING WORD OF THE TEXT IS "GODLINESS," FOR IT IS twice repeated. The word becomes more arresting when this letter is read through in close relation and connection, and it is discovered that it occurs therein no less than ten times.

What is godliness? is a question preliminary to our meditation. The word "godliness" in my text and throughout the whole of the letter to Timothy is not really a translation of the Greek word, but it is a fine interpretation of the value of that word. Yet I think we cannot rightly understand its value save as we take a little time to consider the word of which it is a translation. The Greek word, literally translated into our common speech, would be *good reverence.* One is immediately conscious of the insufficiency of that translation to convey any particularly illuminative idea to our minds. It comes from a word meaning well reverent, and that again comes from a root which means to revere, to worship. In our word *godliness* the first syllable is our supreme word for the Almighty, God. That particular word is not suggested by any part of the Greek word, but it is suggested by the whole fact of the Greek word, for it describes that attitude of reverence which is born of the consciousness of God. The godly man is the reverent man, the revering man, the worshiping man. Godliness is that poise of the spirit, that attitude of the soul which is the true outcome of a perpetual recognition of God, and realization of His presence.

There are those, then, who suppose that the attitude of reverence toward God is a way of gain. That it not so, it is a heresy, it is a false conception. Nevertheless, reverence toward God in the true, deep sense of the word is in itself a gain that makes man independent of all other gain or loss. We brought nothing into the world, and it is certain we can carry nothing out. Having food and raiment, let us therewith be content. So much for the word itself, and the general thought it conveys.

The letter to Timothy was written to him during the period in which, in obedience to apostolic instruction, he was exercising the oversight of the church in Ephesus. We have to remember the condition of Ephesus at this time; it was the center of abounding commerce; its citizens were mastered by a passion for wealth. The supreme ambition in the activities of the city was that of getting gain. There was, moreover, a strange religious aspect of all this, using the word religious in its lowest sense, speaking not of the Christian fact within the city, but of the pagan fact. It was the place where the temple of Diana stood, and that temple had become to the merchantmen of the city both sanctuary and bank; it was the place of their worship, and it was the place where they deposited their gains. Thus, the worship of Diana not merely permitted, but had become in itself the very essence of devotion to the getting of gain. Ephesus was in the grip of what to-day we would describe as the lust for gold. In that city of Ephesus there was a church of Christ. You will remember how, in Paul's letter to the Ephesians, a letter written some time before this one to Timothy, a letter written during his first imprisonment, as this was written during the period of his last imprisonment, he charged the Christian people in Ephesus that they should buy up the opportunities, seeing that the days were evil, and in that description of the days he revealed the fact that the spirit of Ephesus was a peril to the church of God in the city. We find constantly in these apostolic writings that Christian men and women in the Greek cities were affected by the spirit of the age, and were therefore in peril. The church of God is always in peril when it allows itself to be affected by the spirit of the age. There is no heresy more subtle and dangerous than the somewhat widespread one which charges us that the church of God should catch the spirit of the age. The business of the church is not to catch the spirit of the age; but to correct the spirit of the age, and bring the spirit of the age into harmony with the mind and will of God. It is quite evident as we read carefully this letter written to Timothy exercising the oversight of this church that the peril to which I have referred had affected certain teachers of the Christian religion as well as members of the church. It is with this fact that Paul was dealing in this particular paragraph. "If any man teacheth a different doctrine, and consenteth not to sound words, even the words of our Lord Jesus Christ, and to the doctrine which is according to godliness; he is puffed up, knowing nothing, but doting about questionings and disputes of words, whereof cometh envy, strife, railings, evil surmisings, wranglings of men corrupted in mind and bereft of the truth." He then touched on the inspiration of such false teaching in the case of the men of Ephesus, "supposing that godliness is a way of gain." It is a very severe paragraph, a terrible indictment, an awful condemnation of the men who were in the mind of the Apostle as he wrote to Timothy. They were teaching some other doctrine than the form of sound words, the words of Jesus Christ, and there was biting satire as he described them as "doting about questionings and disputes of words"; he then described the effect produced, disputations, "wranglings of men corrupted in mind and bereft of the truth"; finally, he touched the inner secret of the whole thing, "supposing that godliness is a way of gain," and immediately proceeded to correct their heresy by enunciating the truth that godliness in itself with contentment is great gain. So much for the word, and so much for its setting.

Now I leave the context and the peculiar application which Paul made to the Christian teacher, in order that we may consider together the proposition involved in our text, and make the broader application which it warrants.

First of all, I shall ask you to think with me of the atmosphere in which a warning such as this and a declaration such as this became necessary. Our text presupposes that the main passion characterizing the age was a desire for gain. I shall ask you, in the second place, to consider with me the heresy which is suggested by my text, "Godliness is a way of gain." Finally, we shall observe the truth declared in my text, that godliness in itself with contentment is great gain.

In my introductory words I have referred to Ephesus, and by so doing I believe have brought this congregation face to face with the fact that the conditions in the midst of which we live are very similar to those that obtained at Ephesus. While there is a very remarkable contrast between all that was merely local and incidental in Ephesus and in our own cities and our own age, the essential matters, the attitudes of mind, and the master inspirations of human life are identical. I think that the man must be wilfully and blindly optimistic who will deny that the master passion of our own age, in this our own land, is a passion for possession. I am prepared to admit every exception that may suggest itself to your minds at the moment, and yet admitting all the exceptions, I affirm that the great inspiration of activity in our age is not that of conquest, is not that of discovery, is not that of learning, but that of gain. We can look back in the history of our own land, to hours in which the master passion of the people was conquest. I am not discussing its worthiness or unworthiness. But that is not so to-day. There was a time when the spirit of the age, expressing itself, not in the voice of the multitude, but in the sympathy of the multitude with certain outstanding men, was a passion for discovery. There was a wonderful period, short though perhaps it was, in the history of our own people in the last century, when a consuming passion for learning took possession of the nation. But I very much fear that in the day in which we live these things master men only as they may contribute to that more subtle passion for gain. I find that policies and governments are inspired by markets. I discover that even until this hour we are still as a nation in the presence of great national and international complications because of revenue. You hardly need that I illustrate. If I do, I shall give you the old illustration which has passed my lips so often in this place: we are still dallying with opium because of revenue. If I read that there is some kind of threatened international crisis which I do not profess to understand, and the interpretation of which I decline to take from yellow journalism, I nevertheless find, whatever paper I read, that the main thing involved is the protection of interests, and when I analyze the revealing words I find that the interests are those of markets, methods of getting gain. We are appallingly mastered to-day by the passion for gain. I should not mention these things if I had not higher business on hand, that of reminding you that subtly, yet surely, this master passion has commandeered religion, and that to-day there are many people

—I will not say teachers, I am not dealing with teachers, I am making the broader application—living and acting under the impulse suggested by these apostolic words, "supposing that godliness is a way of gain."

I pass from that attempt to speak of the atmosphere which makes the warning necessary, to the warning itself. What is this mental attitude which the Apostle describes in the words, "Supposing that godliness is a way of gain"? Here, let me say in parenthesis, is one of the supreme cases in which the Revised Version has delivered us from one of the most serious blunders. I pray you, mark carefully this translation and the way in which the word is put. "Supposing that gain is godliness" is the old form. No man ever imagined that gain is godliness; that is not the trouble, the peril, the heresy, but something far subtler. "Supposing that godliness is a way of gain." I sometimes think an idea like this is best illustrated by a concrete case. You will at this point understand my reason for taking you back to Genesis, and reading that very brief paragraph in the history of the dealing of Laban with Jacob, in which, in passionate protest, Jacob referred to the methods of Laban for twenty years. I am not going back to the paragraph. In returning to the story I am trusting to your perfect familiarity with it, for, so far as the Old Testament is concerned, Laban stands out as a man who looked on godliness as a way of gain. Laban was perfectly willing to use Jacob because of Jacob's godliness, to make use of him because of his belief in the God of Abraham and of Isaac, to squeeze out of him everything to his own advantage and then to fling him away. That is the supreme concrete illustration I find in the Old Testament. I am not going to deal with Laban, but I ask you to consider this type of character as it exists in our midst to-day. This is not the man who despises religion, and sets himself in opposition to religion. This man will never try to undermine the faith of another man. This is the man who appreciates to the full the social values of Christianity, who is perfectly well aware that the Christian, the truly godly man, is a true man, a temperate man, faithful in all his duties and in the fulfilment of his obligations. The man to whom I am referring is the man who will carefully select those with whom transactions are to be had upon the basis of their religion. He will be very eager to know that the man he appoints to a place of trust in his office is a godly man. He is not himself a godly man, in any sense of the word, sees no good in prayer, worships never, in his inner soul he may even scoff at the thought of godliness, but he knows the moral, social, commercial value of godliness, and he will be very careful, so far as possible, to realize on the godliness of others.

Let me be concrete; he will let his house to godly people rather than to ungodly people. Why? Because he knows they are far more likely to care for his property than ungodly people. A man who looks on godliness as a way of gain is, in municipal and parliamentary matters, Christian in sentiment, he will take his stand on the side of everything that is in the nature of truth and righteousness; but when you touch the personal note, when you come to deal with the man himself, when you come to see the man under the awful searchlight of the Divine thought of him, or see him weighed in the infinitely just balances of the sanctuary, you will find that his godliness is nothing more than something which he practices in the hope of gain. This apostolic description is the most searching and the most appalling to be found in the whole revelation of the New Testament. The peril described is at once the most subtle and the most blighting and blasting of any. That man is almost beyond hope who will maintain external rites, and traffic with the principles and practices of godliness while the motive is gain. That is the heresy of all heresies the most terrible. A man who will employ the language of the sanctuary, wear the livery of the temple, pronounce the creeds of the church, to maintain a position in society and commercial life that will enable him to satisfy his lust for gain is of all men most hopeless.

I turn from that consideration to the corrective truth, for after all is said and done, there is an element of truth in the idea that godliness is a way of gain. There is an element of truth in it, while it is a heresy. Just as there is an element of truth in that phrase that some of us remember having seen at the head of our copybooks when we were learning to write, "Honesty is the best policy." The man, however, who is honest only because it is the best policy is a rogue. That is the very heart and center of this business. The man who is godly only because godliness is a way of gain is ungodly at his heart, and is rejected of heaven.

Yet, in order that we may understand the subtlety of this peril it is necessary that we should dwell for a few moments on the truth. We notice with what immediateness the apostle proceeded from graphic description of the peril to enunciation of positive truth, "godliness with contentment is great gain."

Now, the ultimate definition of godliness is found in the first great chant or anthem of the Christian Church, which the Apostle either wrote for the first time, or which he quoted.

"Without controversy great is the mystery of godliness; He Who was manifested in the flesh, justified in the spirit, seen of angels, preached among the nations, believed on in the world, received up in glory."

According to that revelation, godliness with contentment is indeed great gain. "Great is the mystery of godliness," which I understand to mean: Great is the mystery which is the final inspiration of godliness. Then that mystery is described: "He Who was manifested in the flesh, justified in the spirit, seen of angels, preached among the nations, believed on in the world, received up in glory." We are at once conscious that the Apostle had in his mind the Son of God, the Lord Jesus Christ. Leaving the descriptive phrases, and speaking only of the Person Who was described by the Apostle, let us put the statement thus: Great is the mystery of Him, Who in Himself was the incarnation of godliness, and Who in the fulfilment of His mission is the inspiration of true godliness in others. We immediately see the reason for another passage, which we read as lesson, the one in Colossians, that great passage in which this same Apostle deals with the mystery. There he first spoke of the mystery of the Church, further on of the mystery which lies within the mystery of the Church, "Christ in you the hope of glory," and still a little further on, of the final mystery, which is Christ Himself. As in that Colossian epistle he traced the secret back into its innermost marvel, let us take it in the other order: the first mystery is Christ; the consequent mystery is Christ formed, fashioned, in the life of a man; the final mystery is the whole Church, consisting of all such as are indwelt by this Christ. Great is the mystery of that Christ and all those in whom He is formed, and ultimately of that Church in which the glory of the revelation shall be included and revealed.

This seems to wander a great way from the text! Not a hairsbreadth. In this light the unworthiness of the former conception is immediately seen, "supposing that godliness," the attitude and externality of reverence, "is a way of gain." "But *godliness*"—and we must still think of the spaciousness of godliness—let it be understood according to the interpretation of the sacred writings, let it be recognized in its marvel, in its light, love, life, liberty, glory; *godliness*, as revealed in the incarnation of the Son, as realized in the soul, of a man who has been brought into relationship with Christ;

that godliness which is infinitely more than a pose or attitude of external reverence; that godliness which is the perpetual attitude of external life, after the pattern of spiritual worship, that godliness is great gain.

Mark carefully the juxtaposition of the terms, "Godliness with contentment." Contentment is an essential concomitant of godliness. Where there is real godliness, the attitude of the life well reverent, there is perpetual contentment. I venture with reverence, and may I say with some reticence, to appeal again to the supreme example of godliness received in the revelation of Jesus Christ. According to the New Testament revelation of Him, do you know of a more radiant revelation of perfect contentment than that of Jesus Christ, perfectly at peace, perfectly quiet and at rest, never disturbed, always calm and dignified? Why? Because His spirit was adjusted to the will of God, the poise of His life was well reverent toward God, meeting the stress and strain, even of the last darkling hours of the final tragedy, in a calm, contented manner.

The man who makes godliness an appearance of his life in order to gain, is forevermore characterized by lack of peace and by unrest. The man who has seen the vision, and whose soul has answered it; the man who has found God, and who has forevermore a sense of His glory, and is submissive to the call of His will, that man is quiet. "He that believeth shall not make haste."

I find in this same letter another statement: "Godliness is profitable for all things, having promise of the life which now is, and of that which is to come." I pray you do not minimize that, do not attempt to qualify it. Let it sing its own song in your heart, "Godliness is profitable for all things." Godliness is profitable for physical life. It is enough to say that surely, now; I need not argue it. Godliness is profitable for mental life; true godliness never blunts the intellect or stifles the voice of reason; it creates the atmosphere in which it is possible for a man to prosecute investigation; it gives him the right to ask questions, says to him in infinite wisdom, Secret things belong unto God, but revealed things are for you and your children; admits the right of inquiry, quickens the intellect, makes keen, alert, alive the mental powers. When I pass beyond the physical which I do not argue, and the mental on which I have uttered some few sentences, to the spiritual, again, argument is unnecessary.

Godliness is profitable in every human obligation, in social life, in political life, in all human interrelationships. Let two godly men deal with each other in business, it is a profitable transaction. Let a godly man stand by his godliness six days a week in the market place, it is a profitable thing. I am not so sure, you say. I have a business man listening to me who says, I am not so sure. I have attempted during the past week to live the life of godliness, and if I could have sacrificed it I would have been a wealthier man tonight! Would you? Would you change the wealth of a clear conscience for the gain of gold? You know you would not. Godliness is profitable for all commercial transactions.

Godliness is gain in wealth, for the man whose wealth has been gained in a godly fashion, and who is living a godly life, will always understand that he is but a steward of the God Who has prospered him, and he will make to himself friends by means of the mammon of unrighteousness, that when it shall fail they will receive him into the everlasting habitations.

Godliness is gain in poverty. I am not defending poverty. It is a very long time since I have been guilty of declaring that poverty is a blessing. God overrules it, and makes it a blessing; but poverty is outside the economy of God. It is not His will that a man or woman should feel in the rush of human life the grind of poverty. Let us understand that

God in His provision for humanity has provided for humanity; if man has lost the key to the situation, and does not know how to manage the gifts of God, the blame is on man. While that is so, and while the conditions in which men live to-day are conditions which bring poverty to some, I still bring you to the poor man or woman in this city, fine in character, godly in poise of spirit, who is struggling for bread; and I will let you talk to that man or woman, and you will find that he or she knows the gain of godliness: all the sackcloth is transfigured, and loneliness is canceled, and the bare and frugal meal becomes a sacrament of heaven when the soul is truly godly.

"Godliness is profitable for all things, having promise of the life which now is, and of that which is to come." I need not argue Paul's final words, the life which is to come, all the afterward of revelation, explanation, compensation; that richer life we are sure of if we are godly.

Make the comparison between these two things. One man says that godliness is a way of gain, and one man knows that godliness in itself is great gain. They use identical words when they are talking, they recite similar creeds, they are not like the people in the Old Testament, one party saying shibboleth and the other saying sibboleth. They both say shibboleth. You cannot tell the difference between these two men by looking at them or listening to them. How shall we find it? It is in one quantity; contentment, rest, quietness, peace. Are you making godliness a way of gain? It is revealed by the feverish unrest of your life that you are. Are you finding godliness gain? It is revealed by the quiet dignity of your life that you are.

Let us try to feel our way into the heart of this. What is the supreme heresy in the first case? That this man puts gain first. What is the essential truth in the second case? That this other man puts godliness first. The master passion in the one case is gain, and godliness is looked on as a means to an end. That is heresy. The master passion in the other case is godliness at all costs, and that godliness is gain in itself. That is the way of God. Remember that to say that godliness is a way of gain is essential godlessness. Christ will not allow us to crown Him, because He feeds us with material bread. The multitudes would fain make Him King. Why? Because He had fed them. He would not take the crown on those conditions. Godliness is in itself essential wealth. Here were other men, who crowned Him, not because of gain, but because of the supreme necessity of the case, because He had captured them; then He became to them all they needed in things material and moral, and spiritual and eternal. That is infinite wealth!

Which is your conception? May I urge the question? Are you simply religious because it is respectable so to be, because by observing the externalities of religion you gain some advantage in society? That is, of all blasphemies, the worst. On the other hand, do you desire to be godly as the deepest passion of your life? Knowing, as you do, that you are full of failure, do you desire that you may be well reverent, submitted to this God, under His will? Then you are already possessed of undying wealth.

Let the last note of this message be that of the gain of godliness. Be right with God, and you will be right with every other personality in the universe, right with every other relationship of human life. Be right with God, and you will be right with the devil, you will master him, and be safe in the hour of temptation! Be right with God, and you will be right with your fellow man, loving him, and expressing your love in integrity, justice, honesty, mercy, benevolence. Be right with God, and you will be right with your possessions, you will not say that anything you have is your own, but that it is His, and you are His steward. Be right with

God, and you will be right with the powers of your being; be they what they may, they will be realized, fulfilled. Be right with God, and you will be right with death, enabled to face the hour of dissolution with a song and a shout of triumph, "O death, where is thy victory? O death, where is thy sting? The sting of death is sin; and the power of sin is the law: but thanks be to God, which giveth us the victory."

Godliness is indeed great gain.

CHAPTER XIX

THE SECRETS OF REST

Rest in the Lord, and wait patiently for Him.

PSALM 37:7.

WHATEVER PLACE MENDELSSOHN REALLY OCCUPIES IN THE firmament of composers, it is certain that no single number of the great oratorios has made profounder or more lasting appeal to the heart of humanity than the poised and perfect air, "O rest in the Lord, and wait patiently for Him." This is due, not only to the perfection of the music, but to the fact that Mendelssohn understood the theme.

The place of the writing of the air in his own life is full of interest, although not now to be dealt with at any length. Those of you who are familiar with the story of his life, a wonderful life of only eight and thirty years, will remember that it was in 1838, when he was twenty-seven years of age, that the subject of Elijah was suggested to him for an oratorio, and that it gradually took shape through years of stress and strain. You will also remember that in 1846 it was produced in Birmingham, and that he went back home again, broken in health, to die in a little more than a year. There can be little doubt that when the music of Elijah was written by Mendelssohn he was himself passing through stress and strain, yet living in the secret place of the Most High, knowing what it was indeed to "rest in the Lord."

Those of you most familiar with that oratorio will know the place this air occupies therein. It is in the second part. We have listened to the angry clamor of Jezebel in that strange hour when it seemed as though unrighteousness must inevitably triumph again over righteousness in Israel, in spite of the victory on Carmel. We have seen the prophet descending from the altitude of his triumph to the lowliness of the juniper tree. Under the juniper tree we have seen the angels come and minister to him. Mendelssohn, in his arrangement of the oratorio, has gathered some of the strains of the perpetual music which had comforted the heart of man, and has treated them as though the angel sang them to Elijah. Among the rest are the words of our text, "Rest in the Lord, and wait patiently for Him." That placing of the air in the great oratorio is in perfect harmony with the spirit of the psalm, the introductory part of which we read as lesson. It opens in an atmosphere electric with trouble:

Fret not thyself because of evil-doers,
Neither be thou envious against them that work unrighteousness,

and moves in its earliest verses through stages of experience until at last the ultimate note is reached in my text,

Rest in the Lord, and wait patiently for Him

Let me attempt this morning to lead you first in meditation on the attitude described: "Rest in the Lord," interpreted by "wait patiently for Him." In the second place, let us inquire quite honestly, Is this possible? Finally, and briefly, let us attempt some personal application.

First, then, the attitude described in this passage: "Rest in the Lord, and wait patiently for Him." I have already reminded you of that to which I now return for a moment. The text occurs in the first seven verses of the Thirty-seventh Psalm. The rest of the psalm is but exposition, explanation, application of the theme of these verses. All its fundamental verities are in these seven verses. Will you note the boundaries of them: the first phrase is,

> Fret not thyself because of evil-doers."

The last word is,

> Fret not thyself because of him who prospereth in his way,
> Because of the man who bringeth wicked devices to pass.

It is immediately evident that this opening movement in the great psalm is in the nature of a protest against panic. Whether the Psalmist was speaking to his own soul, or was writing to comfort and help a comrade, we cannot tell; the fact of importance is that behind the psalm we become conscious of strange conflict; it was composed in an atmosphere perplexing to the man of faith; in the background we see evil-doers, men who work unrighteousness, and we see these men prospering in their way, bringing their wicked devices to pass. Wickedness is triumphant. That is the picture in the background. The psalm is addressed to a troubled soul, troubled by this vision of the apparent victory of evil, and I repeat that these opening and closing words, so far as the introductory movement is concerned, are those of protest against panic, "Fret not thyself," literally, Make not thy heart hot in the presence of the apparent victory of iniquity.

Between that opening word, "Fret not," and that final word, "Fret not," we find an ascending scale: "Trust in the Lord. . . . Delight thyself in the Lord. . . . Commit thy way unto the Lord. . . . Rest in the Lord, and wait patiently for Him." Rest, that is the eighth note in the octave. The fundamental note, and the first, is trust. Trust, delight, commit, rest, and wait patiently! As I was preparing my sermon I wished that I could take this congregation and divide it into sections, and make them sing the notes. I would like those occupying the section on my left hand to sing on one note, "Trust in the Lord." I would like those sitting in the central section to sing on another note, "Delight in the Lord." Then I would like those sitting on my right hand to sing, "Commit thy way unto the Lord." Finally, I would like those in the gallery to sing on yet another note, "Rest in the Lord." Then we would have a fine harmony, a perfect chord, the fundamental note, "Trust in the Lord," and the eighth note completing the music, "Rest in the Lord, and wait patiently for Him." All around, the victory of iniquity, the clash of arms, the sound of war, the triumph of unrighteousness, and in the midst of it the music, "Trust . . . delight . . . commit . . . rest in the Lord, and wait patiently for Him." Such is the musical motive, theme, method of the great psalm.

For a brief moment longer let me detain you on one matter to which I have already twice referred. The theme of the psalm was that of the energy and prosperity of evil men, causing perplexity and fretfulness to the man of faith. That is the situation. The men of faith, men who have endured on many a hard-fought field as seeing Him Who is invisible, men who have made great ventures on the basis of their conviction that the spiritual is true, men who have made sacrifices in the interests of the ultimate conquest of the world in righteousness for God, are conscious that things do not seem to be going that way; the drift is against righteousness: Jezebel, in spite of the victory, on Carmel. That is the background. War in spite of arbitration. New rebellions everywhere in spite of revival of spiritual interest. How is it that iniquity prospers? What is the meaning of the fact that these evil men are bringing their wicked devices to pass? The heart is hot, restless. Panic seizes the soul. To that condition the psalm appeals: "Fret not thyself because of evildoers"; and the ultimate word is, "Rest in the Lord, and wait patiently for Him."

What is this word "rest"? You notice in the margin of the Revised Version a suggested alternative reading: "Be still before the Lord," or even more directly and literally, "Be silent to Jehovah." The word "rest" is one which literally means dumbness: be dumb, be silent, be quiet. You recognize immediately that this is not fatalism, but faith. If I take out of my text the phrases "in the Lord" and "in Him," it has no meaning and no value. If I take out those words, what have I left? "Rest . . . and wait patiently." That would be the uttermost word of fatalism, and absolutely impossible of realization by intelligent men. "Rest," but "in the Lord"; be dumb, be silent, but in the consciousness of Him. We are to be still in the consciousness of the fact that whatever the appearances of the hour may be, men and affairs are still within the grip of His government.

Yet, as I have pondered these words, I have come to the deliberate conclusion that the only interpretation of the opening injunction to "rest in the Lord" is to be found in the closing injunction to "wait patiently for Him." These are not two things which can be separated; rather, they constitute one great inclusive charge to rest, to be still, to be silent, to be dumb before God, and all that interpreted by that strange word, the meaning of which we are so apt to miss, "wait patiently for Him."

When, for myself, I really began carefully to ponder this great and final word in the music of the psalm, I confess I was almost startled to discover the meaning of this particular word which we translate *wait patiently*, for there are not two words in the Hebrew, but one. I was startled, I say, when I looked at this word carefully. Take the word as to its real meaning, and it seems entirely to contradict our popular conception of what it is to wait, and to wait patiently. The root meaning of the word is to whirl incessantly; it suggests incessant movement instead of quiet passivity. One was driven therefore from the word to its use. That it would be entirely false to the spirit of the psalm to interpret the meaning of the Psalmist by the root significance of the word is apparent, therefore we must discover the use of this Hebrew word. One found that it was occasionally used exactly as it is used in the psalm to indicate an attitude of soul in the presence of God; but it is far more often used to indicate strenuous agony, proceeding through processes, toward ultimate triumph. It is a word that has within it a sense of pain. It is a word which is persistently used for the travail which issues in birth. In the choice of the word there is a fine recognition of the fact that the hardest thing the man of faith can do is to wait. There is agony in the waiting, but it is the agony that moves toward realization. There is a pang in the waiting, but it is a birth pang. There is travail in the waiting, but it is travail that is co-operative with forces which are moving to victory. Consequently, one discovers in the use of this word, strangely startling in its root significance, that to wait patiently recognizes two things, sensitiveness of the wrong and sensitiveness to the issue.

When thinking of these things I heard outside my study window the sigh of the wind, and became conscious that autumn was upon us, and I confess that sorrow and sadness crept into my heart, sadness that dimmed the brightness of the vision. When I put down my work I took up the *Westminster Gazette*, and the first thing that met my eye was a little poem written over the signature of S. Gertrude Ford. I want to give you that poem. I will read it without interpretation, save to say that if you listen to the two views of autumn you will see the two viewpoints of the soul that waits, sensitiveness to the darkness and the tragedy around, but also sensitiveness to the issue, the larger fact that lies beyond.

Two Visions of Autumn

    Leaves flaming and then fading; pomp of mists
        That wreathe, at dusk and dawn, the mountain's brow
    With pride of opals and of amethysts;
        The nest bare on the bough;
    The swallow on the wing; the reign of flowers
        Whose beauty breathes a wail of "Ichabod,"
    Chrysanthemums that crown autumnal hours,
        Asters and golden-rod;
    The last crops garnered and the last-ripe fruits
        Gathered; a sound of sighing in the air—
    A sigh, too, in the tune the robin flutes,
        And Autumn everywhere!

    Autumn! the sleep that brings the waking nigh;
        The scattering of the seed, not sown in vain,
    That needs must fall into the ground and die
        If it would live again;
    The building of the throne where spring shall sit,
        Girt round with all her lovely pageantry;
    Such death, and only such, as holds in it
        The birth that is to be—
    This now and Winter later; then, O then,
        The violet's breath, the cuckoo's call, the fair
    New life that leaps in birds and beasts and men,
        And Springtime everywhere!

That is waiting patiently. And the singer sang to me out of her consciousness of autumn the profoundest interpretation of my text: to the nest that is empty on the bough there is sensitiveness to the flight of the swallow, to the moaning, sighing of the autumn winds; but there is also the rarer sensitiveness to the issue, the life wrapped in the womb of death that shall burst to life in flowers, and bring the victory that is to be.

"Fret not thyself because of evil-doers" because at the moment it seems as though the darkness were comprehending, apprehending, extinguishing the light, because it seems for the moment as though unrighteousness were winning its victory. "Fret not thyself," but rather "trust . . . delight . . . commit thy way . . . rest and wait patiently," keen and sensitive to the agony of the hour, but more sensitive to the springtime and the summer that are to be.

Is this possible? That depends entirely on our conception of God. What is our doctrine of God? Let me ask the question in another way, using the word with great carefulness and accuracy: What is our theology, our science of God? I want to make this affirmation: a man's conception of God creates his attitude toward the hour in which he lives. Or, to reverse the order of my statement, my attitude toward the hour in which I live is a revelation of my conception of God. Let us be careful in this matter. Our figures may imprison us, may dwarf our thinking, may blight the possibility of true spiritual conception. What is our conception of God? Is He King? What do you mean by king? A king may be a despot. Is He Shepherd? What do you mean by shepherd? What is the ultimate passion of the shepherd, the fleece and the profit from the carcass of a dead sheep? Is He a Father? Be very careful; a father may be one who gives his child an inheritance of death. By all of which I mean to say the highest, inspired figures of the Bible must be very cautiously used. We must always remember, when speaking of God, that we cannot interpret Him by the figure. We must know Him Himself, and so correct the figure to the standard of the infinite fact.

Trust in the Lord, delight in Him, commit thy way unto Him, rest in Him. Who is He? Whether I am able to rest in

Him depends on the answer I give to that inquiry. I have to ask these questions to drive me back to this library. What God is revealed in the Bible? Let me summarize.

He is a God of knowledge. Here I dare not trust myself to stay, and I need not. I am speaking to men and women who know their Bibles, and the music of that fact is singing its way into your hearts, "He knoweth my down-sitting and mine uprising, my going out and my coming in." He putteth my tears into His bottle; He numbereth the hairs of my head. I lift my eyes to the heavens, and look at the marvels there, unknown, unfathomable, and because He is strong in power not one faileth. He knows.

He is a God of wisdom, which is infinitely more than a God of knowledge. Knowledge is consciousness of the facts. Wisdom is knowledge in its application to necessity.

He is a God of holiness. Let me change the word "holiness" to the old Anglo-Saxon word "health"; He is the God of health, spiritual, mental, physical, and therefore the enemy of disease in spirit, mind, and body. His passion is a passion for completeness, holiness, perfection, and therefore He will make no truce with sin, and will sign no contract with imperfection. He is a God of holiness.

He is a God of might, able to do all His wisdom suggests, and His knowledge proves necessary.

He is a God of justice, judging not by the seeing of the eyes or the hearing of the ears, but by His perfect knowledge of the underlying motive. For that justice the heart of man cries out almost more than for mercy: to be judged ultimately by One Who will take into account the passion that burned and yet always seemed to be defeated. The God of infinite justice.

He is a God of patience, content to wait and walk with man; and in all poetry there never was a dream more beautiful than that He walks with men, accommodating the fine majesty of his goings to the feeble, halting frailty of human failure. The God of patience.

To summarize all, He is a God of love. I cannot grasp the idea in its totality, but it is inclusive, exhaustive, final.

These are all characteristics which merge in the fact of being, and I want some revelation that will help me to condense, to focus the glory that cannot be seen. The answer to that demand came when He appeared in human flesh and tabernacled among men and they beheld Him full of grace and truth. That is the revelation of God. The measure of our rest is the measure of our knowledge of God as He has been revealed to us in Christ. Restlessness is the revelation of lack of familiarity with God as He has been revealed in Christ. To know Him is to know that beyond the autumn is the gracious winter, and beyond it the glorious spring and triumphant summer, the endless cycle of operation that produces the results on which the heart of love is set and makes the very wrath of man to praise Him while the rest He girds upon Himself and restrains.

There are inevitable questions that a man must ask if he meditate on such a theme as this. Am I at rest? Have I learned to wait patiently? The problems are patent enough, God knows, and we know! Only the callous and hardhearted are unconcerned in the presence of the problems. This waiting patiently is not waiting callously, indifferently; it is not lazing in an armchair while the world drifts on in its agony. It is keen, sensitive, agonizing, consciousness of pain; but underneath is ever heard the anthem of the glory of God assured. The problems are patent enough; we need only merely interpret what I say by the last and most immediate manifestation. I was reading that little poem of Blake, the "Anguish of the Innocents." I am not going to read the poem; I remind you of certain phrases:

> A robin redbreast in a cage
> Puts all heaven in a rage;

and again,

> A dog starved at his master's gate
> Predicts the ruin of the state;

and yet again,

> A skylark wounded on the wing
> Doth make a cherub cease to sing.

Dear old Blake, father of nature poetry, he was very near the heart of God; he knew. If you are insensitive in the presence of the problem of the hour you are not waiting patiently; if there is no whirling agony there is no true waiting. Yet there is a great difference between this whirling motion of the sensitive soul in the presence of agony and the fretfulness of the unbelieving heart.

Wait patiently. How can I do it? I take you back again to the thing I tried to say at the beginning: "Rest in the Lord" is the final note in an ascending scale. What are the things preceding? Trust in Him; that is the first venture of faith. Delight in Him; that is the discovery of His way and His law, and falling into His line. "Commit thy way unto Him"; that is, see to it that He has the governance of your life. Then rest in Him.

This, of course, is not the whole, or else we are but idle and noneffective, and that were to deny the persistent Bible teaching that man is called to fellowship with all the enterprises of God. Is He the God of knowledge? Then it is ours to know. Is He the God of Wisdom? It is ours to enter into fellowship with Him, to act wisely. Is He the God of holiness? Then we must be holy. Is He the God of might? Then we must be strong. Is He the God of justice? Then we are called to do justly. Is He the God of patience? Then we must be patient. Is He the God of love? Then love must master us.

But in order to give true effective service it is necessary that we should learn to rest and to wait patiently for Him. So may He bring our hearts into patient waiting through Christ.

CHAPTER XX

WATCHING FOR SOULS

They watch in behalf of your souls.

HEBREWS 13:17.

"WATCHING FOR SOULS" WAS A COMMON PHRASE IN THE speech of our fathers. It has largely fallen out of use in the Christian Church in the present day, or it is carelessly used, with sad ignorance of its Biblical sanctions and its proper values. It is, nevertheless, an illuminative and forceful phrase warranted by the whole Biblical revelation, and remarkably focused in my text, "They watch in behalf of your souls."

While, incidentally, the statement constitutes an argument giving urgency to an appeal, essentially I find in it a revelation of the responsibility of spiritual leaders. I propose, therefore, to come to the consideration of the text, not in its incidental relation to the context, but in its essential revelation of the responsibilities of Christian men and women.

We shall consider, first, the Biblical sanctions of this word of the writer of the letter, and, second, some of its immediate applications.

Commencing with the Biblical sanctions, we are, first, quite simply and necessarily arrested by the central word, the word that gives thought and meaning and direction to the whole conception, "They *watch*." What is it to watch? If I take the word translated "watch," and feel my way into its heart I find that it suggests sleeplessness. Thayer says that the word has in it "an image drawn from shepherds," and at once, if we recognize that fact, the ampler atmosphere into which we are introduced is suggested. As a sprig of heather suggests the Highlands, or a spray of edelweiss suggests Alpine heights, so this word admits us into the atmosphere of the Divine conception and method.

What, then, is that conception, and what that method? The Biblical relations I endeavored to indicate in measure by the readings of the evening, that majestic word of the Twenty-third Psalm with which we started, "Jehovah is my Shepherd; I shall not want," the graphic picture which Ezekiel drew of the failure of the shepherds and the scattering of the sheep, that tender passage revealing the compassion of the Master's heart in the presence of the scattered sheep; that superb language in which He claimed for Himself the function of shepherdhood, "I am the good Shepherd," and yet again the tender light of the Galilean shore, when He commissioned Peter and through him all disciples to feed the lambs and shepherd the sheep, until we reached the focused light of our text; and I believe that in the reading there broke on us a true conception of what it is to watch for souls.

The fundamental thought is full of august majesty and broad with the beneficence of Deity. "Jehovah is my Shepherd," said one lonely singer millenniums ago; and down the millenniums and through the centuries his song has been taken up and repeated in lonely hours, in the midst of the rush of life, and as men have crossed the desert where no water is. It is the profoundest word concerning God in His attitude toward the sons of men in their sorrow and in their sin. It is a word which has within it all the other great facts concerning Him. It is the synonym for His Kingship. It is the revelation of the meaning of His Fatherhood. So we start with that fundamental truth that Kingship in the Divine economy is Shepherdhood, that God is King because He is Shepherd, and that His activity of sovereignty is forever the activity of His Shepherd heart. That is fundamental.

We turn from that fundamental word of the psalm and go through the prophetic writings, selecting one only from the mass of material—that in Ezekiel, perhaps the most graphic of them all, in which we have the picture of the sheep scattered, and hear the thunder of the Divine denunciation, not of the sheep but of the shepherds. Those who should have bound up their wounds and healed the sick and sought the lost, and folded the flock and fed them, all these, said Ezekiel, had fed themselves instead of the sheep, had clothed themselves with the wool while the sheep were left to starve and to be scattered on the heights. Therein lay the supreme condemnation of the false shepherds.

I pass from these Old Testament Scriptures with the fundamental song of the Shepherdhood of Jehovah, through that stern denunciation of the men who had failed to fulfil their function as shepherds of the people, and I come to the New Testament. I read that when Jesus saw the multitudes He was moved with compassion, and the reason was that He saw them as sheep having no shepherd. I go a little further on in the days of His public ministry, and hear Him in that wonderful discourse which John alone has chronicled, describing His mission in this selfsame figure, "I am the good Shepherd." The hireling—mark the infinite scorn of it, the satire of Jesus—the hireling "fleeth because he is a hireling." The good Shepherd Whose own the sheep are enters into conflict with the wolf, grapples with the evil beast that spoils the sheep, and dies in the conflict. In that infinite mystery which is the heart of Christianity, exhausting all figures, He declares, "I lay down My life for the sheep. . . . I lay down My life that I may take it again," thus prophesying the resurrection whereby He is able not merely to slay the wolf, but to communicate to the sheep the virtue and force of His own life that they themselves may be made strong against the marauding wolf. Finally, interpreting the word of Jesus to Peter by all the symbolism of the ancient economy and the attitude of the heart of Christ, I hear Him charge the Christian man that it is his work to be a shepherd, to watch for souls. Such are the Biblical relations.

From these let us attempt to deduce the Biblical conceptions that are suggested in my text. "They watch in behalf of your souls." The first conception is that of the Kingdom of God under the figure of the flock. There is one verse in the New Testament to which we have often drawn attention, and doubtless you have often noticed its peculiar beauty. Speaking on one occasion to His own disciples, Jesus said, "Fear not, little flock, it is the Father's good pleasure to give you the Kingdom." In the economy of God the Kingdom of God will be the family of God; the family of God will be the whole flock of scattered sheep folded under the one Shepherd, Jesus; or, as He Himself did say, at last, when He has found the other sheep, there shall be one flock and one Shepherd. So that beneath this phrase, which seems to us so simple, we discover the ultimate purpose, the folding of the sheep into one flock, the gathering of the children into one family, the building of men into one ultimate, glorious Kingdom of God. That is the underlying conception.

Glancing again at these Biblical quotations, I find another truth, an immediate and present one—that the Kingdom is not established, that the children are not yet at home, or, to return to the line of our thinking, the sheep are still scattered. Jesus went through all the cities and villages preaching, teaching, healing, and He saw the multitudes, the multitudes of the cities, villages and hamlets, rich and poor, high and low, learned and illiterate, massed humanity. In some senses it would be a most inaccurate thing to say that Jesus never saw whether a man was rich or poor; in some senses it would not be true to say that He was unconscious of the phylacteries that were on the garments of the Pharisees or of the rags of the beggar; but in a profound and deep sense I do affirm He was unconscious of all these things. He was not attracted by wealth, He was not attracted by poverty. Let me change the tense to the present. Christ cannot be the Head of a labor church, He cannot be the Head of a capitalist club; but He is in the club where wealth gathers, He is present when poverty is arguing its necessity and grappling with its problem. He is attracted by humanity, indifferent to the false divisions in His passion for humanity and His determination ultimately to destroy the divisions that separate, and to create one flock and one Shepherd, the very Kingdom of God. He was conscious, and He is conscious today, of the scattered sheep, the fleeced, wounded sheep, the harried, worried souls of men. That is the condition that Ezekiel saw, the condition that Christ apprehended, and which exists until this moment. This London of ours teems and throbs with agony and unrest, sheep having no shepherd, the prey of wolves that raven, marauding by night and prowling by day, and stripping men of the things most precious to them. This is Christ's outlook: the Kingdom is not yet, the children are not home, the sheep are not folded. That vision of the condition of humanity is part of the light focused in my text, "They watch in behalf of your souls."

Tarrying yet a moment longer with these Biblical conceptions, I find the revelation of responsibility involved in the meaning of our text. What is it to watch for souls? Let us go back to Ezekiel and remind ourselves of the things that the shepherds did not do. Ye did not feed My flock, ye did not strengthen them, ye did not heal them, ye did not bind them up, ye did not restore them, ye did not seek the lost! Watching for souls is doing these things. Or I turn from the message of Ezekiel and come to the final, inclusive word of the incarnate Son of God, and I ask, in the light of that great passage in John, What is it to watch for souls? First, it is to enter into conflict with the wolf, and then, at personal cost and suffering and sacrifice, to be patient with the sheep as we lead them back to the fold and to the one great, only Shepherd of souls. Watching for souls demands sacrifice, expresses itself in sleepless vigils, in untiring activity, in going out after those that are lost, and bearing them, in the virtue of expended strength, back to the fold and back to the Shepherd.

So far, I have attempted merely the interpretation of the Biblical sanctions that lie behind this great text. Now, in the second place, I desire to turn to the practical, immediate application of the truth. In this letter occur the great words, "Jesus Christ is the same yesterday and to-day, yea and for ever," and I want to crave your patience for a moment while I say that thing again, asking you to consider whether you really believe it, "Jesus Christ is the same yesterday and to-day, yea and for ever." I am not at this moment interested in the last stupendous word "for ever." I am intensely interested in "yesterday" and "to-day." What He was He is, what He felt He feels. I ask your patience while I emphasize that. Do we believe it, do we act as though we knew it and believed it? Are we not in awful danger of imagining, somehow, that this crowned Lord of all of Whom we sing is removed far away from the actuality of human pain and suffering and human sin? Have we not some subconscious conception of Him, as in a land of glory where no shadows fall, removed from immediate consciousness of human agony and immediate sympathy with human pain? The proportion in which we are mastered in our thinking of Christ by any such conception is the proportion in which we are misunderstanding Him, and are cutting the nerve of our endeavor in dealing with other men. We have to commence by reminding ourselves that He is the same, His vision of the ultimate is the same, His vision of the present condition is the same, His conception of the responsibility resting upon Himself as the Servant of God in the compulsion of His own nature of infinite love is the same. He has not changed. Did He see the multitudes in the olden days harassed by wolves, fleeced and fainting by the way? So sees He the multitudes of to-day. Was He moved with compassion then? So is He now. May God deliver us from any false and blasphemous idea that God has no sorrow, that He is impassive and unmoved in the midst of His universe, in the presence of human sorrow resulting from human sin. That is a libel, a lie, a contradiction of the whole Biblical revelation. Faber knew the heart of God better. He sang truly when he sang, "There is no place where earth's sorrows are more keenly felt than up in heaven." At this moment all the surging sorrows of London and the world are focused in the heart of the Son of God. We must start there. To fail to believe the great truth that He remains the same is to be so out of sympathy with Him, so out of touch with Him, as never to be able to watch for souls.

Let that be granted, and then I may proceed. The first thing we need if we are to watch for souls is a clear vision of the ultimate. The responsibilities of the immediate result always result from the nature of the ultimate. Watch a builder at his work, at his one small corner of the building! Why that accuracy of eye and the corrective precision of the plummet that every single brick be truly laid? Because, if not to him, at least to the architect under whose inspiration he labors, the ultimate building is in view. That was what Michael Angelo meant when he said that trifles make perfection. That was why he spent so many hours perfecting the curves in the marble. He had seen the angel in the marble, and every movement of the chisel and hammer was directed toward the final, the ultimate. I am more and more convinced that one of the perils of our day in Christian service is that we are so occupied with the immediate that we fail sometimes to lift our eyes and look toward the ultimate, we lose the vision of God's final victory, and so we fail to do the finest work.

The ultimate in the work of Christ is the establishment of the Kingdom of God on earth; the ultimate in the work of Christ is one flock and the one Shepherd. It is when that ultimate glory had broken on the soul and possessed it, when that gleaming splendor of the final day of God has surcharged the life of the shepherd; it is then that the immediate becomes instinct with meaning, and that, to quote the Apostle Paul's great word, we labor "that we may present every man perfect in Christ." I pray there may come to every preacher and teacher, to all Christian men and women occupied in service, a very clear vision of the goal toward which God is moving and toward which He calls us to move in comradeship, fellowship with Himself. Christ's work for this world will never be done until there is one flock and one Shepherd, the end of nationalities in the one nation, the necessary cessation of war in the reign of the Prince of Peace, the last of strife and weariness and sin and sorrow in the final victory of the Shepherd Who laid down His life for the sheep.

The process leading to that ultimate includes a method of judgment as well as a method of mercy. There is a day of vengeance. He will not quench the smoking flax until He send forth judgment unto victory. But that day of judgment is not within our responsibility. We have nothing to do with it. This is the day of His seeking, the day of preparation for the Kingdom, and we are to work consistently in our watching for souls with the vision of the ultimate before us, realizing that every man won back to the Shepherd, every little child fed as a lamb of the one great flock, is a contribution to the dawning of the morning that waxes to noon and never wanes to eventide, when the "kingdom of the world is become the kingdom of our Lord, and of His Christ."

If in order to achieve fulfilment of this ideal of watching for souls a vision of the ultimate is necessary, then also a vision of the immediate is necessary. Here I would speak with great carefulness and with great sympathy, and with strong conviction. What is our view of the men who are without our Christ? Has it ever occurred to you that the word to which I have referred describing Christ's vision of the multitudes is a very strange word, and that it certainly would not have described His disciples' view of the multitudes at that time? It is still more certain that it would not have described the multitudes' conception of their own condition. Remember, it was He Who saw them as sheep not having a shepherd, sheep scattered. They did not so think of themselves. Blindness had fallen on them, hardness of heart, that terrible hardness which is failure to appreciate one's own condition. It was His eye that saw them so. His vision—mark this carefully—of the scattered, fleeced, failing condition of the multitudes was born of this very vision of the purpose of God. What measurement do you put on humanity in order to understand it? If you once see humanity as God intended it to be, then you will understand how far it fails and comes short. Look out over the world to-day, look out over our own city, our own land to-day, and we see multitudes; we meet them every day, pass through their midst on the highways of the city, gaze on them when they are massed for sport or spectacle, or tragedy. How do we see them? Comfortable, respectable, fairly moral? Are we satisfied with the condition of the multitudes? Then we have not Christ's vision, and that because we lack the life that makes the light as we look. There are some men to-day who look out on the multitudes and speak to me only of the magnificence of humanity. There are others who speak only of the depravity of humanity. In each case it is a partial vision. The vision of Christ was one that clearly saw the magnificence and possibility of humanity within the economy and purpose of God, the glory of the race; and that clear vision of the dignity of humanity, of the worth of one soul, of the splendid possibility of human life, created His vision of the ruin and the failure of humanity. You and I will never be watchers for souls of men until we see the glory of God's thoughts for them, and in the light of that see the awfulness of their failure. The Kingdom is unrealized, the family is broken, the sheep are scattered! That vision also is necessary if we are ever to become watchers for souls.

Let these things be granted; then the measure in which the life of Christ is our life, the measure in which we have surrendered ourselves to His indwelling, so that His life gives the vision and creates our sensitiveness to the need of humanity, is the measure in which we are prepared for our service.

What, then, is our service? What, then, is our responsibility? If we see that ultimate, if we see this present condition, what is our responsibility? To bring the sheep to the Shepherd. I think perhaps if I stay for exposition I shall rob that statement of some of its power. That is the inclusive declaration of the responsibility of Christian men and women in order to establish the ultimate Kingdom of God, in order to meet the present necessity, to

> Lead them to Thy open side,
> The sheep for whom their Shepherd died.

It should be true of all Christians, "They watch in behalf of souls," and that watching means that they are incessantly laboring at sacrifice to gather the sheep to the Shepherd.

From these general words of application let me pass, in conclusion, to some particular words. We must recognize, in the life and work of this church and of all churches, that this is our business. Our business is to attach men to Christ. Here are the perils which threaten us in Christian work—the peril that we should attach men to ourselves, and the peril that we attach men to our church. The peril is that the preacher should imagine that when he has gathered a crowd about himself he has done Christ's work. No. I know how this thing searches, how it creates the doubt whether there may not be failure in the very fact that men and women gather about a ministry. I must be true to God and my soul. If I do but gather here men and women to hear me, I am of all failures the most terrible; unless through the things I say I can lead you to my Lord, how I fail! Unless I can attach you to Christ, and bring you to the one and only Shepherd of souls, then I also am a "blind mouth," the most terrible of all human failures. It is true of every teacher in the Sunday school. It is true of the whole Church. You tell me that you have erected your buildings, and that they are now being crowded with men and women who come to the socials and attend the clubs, and you are getting on! Are you leading them to Christ? If not, you are failing utterly. It is not enough to throng the building with multitudes, to crowd classrooms and club rooms with interested, patronizing men and women who will take the material things and imagine they are Christians. Unless you are bringing men to Christ, into first-hand relationship with Him, you are failing.

If that is our business we must prepare ourselves to the enterprise. We must partake of the Shepherd nature, have the Shepherd heart. It is through manifestation of the Shepherd that we must lead souls to Him. It is only as Christian souls constitute the media that they can be avenues of approach to the Shepherd. I must be like Him in my passion, in my patience, in my purity, or I cannot do His work.

Our responsibility is also that of availing ourselves of the resources at our disposal. If I am to feed the flock of God I must be familiar with the sustenance of souls. I must be a student of the Word of God, not merely of its technicalities, but of its dynamic. I must be a man of prayer, or, as I prefer now to put it, a man often talking with the Shepherd Himself if I am to help Him in His shepherd work.

Then it is not merely necessary that we recognize this as our business, and not merely necessary that we prepare ourselves for this enterprise; we must actually give ourselves to the business. That is the business of the preacher in his study, in his pulpit, in his social relationships. Woe be to the minister of Jesus Christ who establishes social relationships with his people of such a nature that he is not able to talk to them about their souls! Woe be to any man in the ministry who becomes so friendly with a member of his congregation at the club that he cannot grip him on the matter of God and eternity when occasion arises!

That is true of the teacher in the class. Dear fellow worker in this great enterprise, teacher in the Sunday school, what are the children and young people gathered about you for? They create your opportunity to lead them to Christ. It is true of all office holders in the church. It is true of the men who seat this congregation; it is true of the choir; it is true of those who preside over the finances of the church. The ultimate reason of everything must be to lead men to His open side, the sheep for whom the Shepherd died.

It is true of the church in the neighborhood in which it exists and in its world relationships. The Church has nothing to do with social relationships, apart from its insistence on the necessity that men shall find their way to Christ. If men want me to come out and help in their fight to get better conditions, I will come, provided always they will crown my King. My business is to present men to Christ and Christ to men in individual life, and then, on the basis of regenerate humanity, to reconstruct society.

This is the business of every church member. This is your central responsibility at home. Fathers and mothers, the supreme word of your parenthood is this—watching for souls. If I have fed my bairns, clothed and educated them, and have given them a start in life, and nothing else, God have mercy on me! Unless I have by some form or fashion, principally by example, led them toward my Saviour, then how I have failed!

It is the business of Christian men and women in their business life. You are responsible, my dear Christian lady, for the servant girls in your home. They are not employes merely. You are responsible for the men you pay wages to —at least, that your influence may be Christian, that you show by your character that you are related to the Lord. It is a blasphemy of the worst kind to say you employ a hundred hands. You employ a hundred men, and for each man who is spirit, mind and body, who is coming into contact with you, you are responsible. By your attitude toward him, by the graciousness of your character, you ought to lead him toward Christ.

Watching for souls, a phrase of the days of our fathers, fallen largely into disuse, misinterpreted in a narrow, mechanical method all too often to-day, is yet a great phrase, indicating the responsibility and the enterprise of the Christian Church.

May that God Who is the Shepherd of humanity, and Who has revealed Himself in the One Who is the good, the great, the true Shepherd, lead all those of us who rejoice in His Shepherdhood into such fellowship with Himself that of us also it may be said, "They watch in behalf of souls."

CHAPTER XXI

GOD'S THOUGHT OF THE KING

This is My beloved Son, in Whom I am well pleased.
MATTHEW 3:17.

THESE WORDS CONSTITUTE THE INSCRIPTION STAMPED around the Image imprinted on this gospel according to Matthew. The Image is that of the King. We have the book of His genealogy, the story of His birth, the record of the ministry of His herald. Then we see Him as lawgiver, Administrator of the affairs of a disorganized and chaotic Kingdom, a Warrior proceeding against the foes of the Kingdom and entering into conflict with them. Finally, He appears as the Conqueror of all His enemies, and we listen to words of sublime dignity as standing in the midst of a handful of men He says, "All authority hath been given unto Me in heaven and on earth."

This King impresses us with a sense of mystery. No man can take up this gospel of Matthew and read it naturally as human document, free from all prejudice, without being compelled to say that it presents a Person Who baffles all attempts to understand Him on the human plane. His words are of the simplest and of the sublimest. His deeds touch human life in all its departments, and yet to such effect that human life is seen with a glow of glory on it which we do not detect when others approach it. Who, then, is the King

Whose image is stamped on the page? The inscription round about the mystic majestic head of the King is that of my text, "This is My beloved Son, in Whom I am well pleased." The voice that uttered the words was a voice out of the heavens, the voice of God Himself.

These words therefore constitute both introduction and conclusion to the study of this gospel according to Matthew. In them we hear the voice of God introducing us to the King, challenging our attention; we are invited by this introductory declaration to follow Him in the light of the claim, and to discover whether it is probable that the claim is justified by the life He lived, by the words He uttered, by the work He accomplished. Those who follow the story through will find how fitting is this inscription around the image of the King.

Even if it be a work of imagination then he who wrote wrought well, beating his music out in perfect harmony with the chord of the dominant; for apart from this inscription and revelation there is no explanation of the One Who is revealed in the story.

In this declaration therefore we have the secrets of the Kingly authority of Christ laid bare, and in that sense we approach it. On the declaration flash the lights of the anticipations of the people who stood round about Him on this occasion, of the immediate circumstances in which the words are recorded to have been uttered, and of those subsequent demonstrations to which I have already made reference.

All Old Testament hopes had centered in the coming of One of Whom the prophets, psalmists and seers alike spoke as Messiah, the Servant of God, the Messenger of God. These aspirations of the past are explicit in the Second Psalm, and implicit in all the prophetic writings. In that psalm emerge into clear and definite statement the underlying hope and aspiration of all the singers and seers of the Hebrew economy. There are different opinions about the psalm. It is said that the reference is to David as the anointed King of Israel. It is suggested that the reference is to Hezekiah. While there may be elements of truth in these contentions, it is impossible to read the psalm and imagine that all its values were fulfilled in the case of David or of Hezekiah. If the psalm is of David, it is of David as God's messenger, His Messiah in a limited sense. If the psalm concerns Hezekiah, it concerns Hezekiah as God's messenger, God's servant, God's Messiah in a limited sense. But there are values beyond these. In the case of either of these men, there were local, immediate, incidental applications of value, but shining through are larger meanings than the man understood who wrote the psalm, and fuller harmonies than the singers detected who sang the songs. This psalm has its fulfilment in Christ and in Him alone, so that when we hear this word spoken in the listening ear of the Hebrews, "This is My beloved Son, in whom I am well pleased," we recognize at once that they would understand it to mean that all the hopes implicit in their ancient prophecies, and focused in this declaration,

> I have set my king
> Upon my holy hill of Zion.
> I will tell of the decree:
> The Lord said unto me, Thou art my son;
> This day have I begotten thee.

were fulfilled in the One of Whom this word was spoken.

The light of the immediate circumstances is, in some senses, more wonderful. I pray you look at the scene. John has been baptizing with the baptism of repentance, calling men back from their wanderings toward the reign of God. He has been pre-eminently the prophet of righteousness, stern, hard, ascetic, tremendous in his denunciation of sin and his insistence on righteousness. Suddenly he, a man of fine moral character and of intense spiritual insight, is confronted by another Man, Who asks his baptism. The Man Who asks his baptism is a Man of such apparent moral perfection to the man of spiritual insight as to make this very prophet of righteousness immediately feel convinced that he needs to be baptized of Him. While I listen to this word of John, and understand it and yet am amazed at it, I see a yet more strange and wonderful thing. This Man Jesus, of the high and awful purity, which so impressed the prophet of righteousness that he felt his need of cleansing in His presence, identifies Himself with the baptism of repentance, numbers Himself with sinning men; the One Whose purity had appalled the prophet of purity demands that He shall be plunged beneath the waters of the river with men impure and sinning. It is a strange and arresting picture. Immediately following thereupon that Man emerging from those waters of baptism is anointed by the Spirit of God, and with a visible symbol, for His own eyes and perchance for the eyes of the prophet, such as had never before been employed and never since has been employed for the Spirit of God—the symbol of a dove. It was a symbol that suggested harmlessness and sacrifice.

It was thus, in the midst of such circumstances, that heaven's silence was broken after long centuries, and the voice of God was heard saying, "This is My beloved Son, in Whom I am well pleased."

On this inscription flashes also the light of subsequent demonstration. The ministry of three years, compelling loyalty in certain form and fashion, a ministry in which teaching was uttered, the authority of which men were compelled to acknowledge, even though they did not obey it; a ministry in which His ability to deal with all the limitations and sorrows of humanity was demonstrated so that men at least never questioned His power to work the wonders of His will; a ministry which wrought in the lives of all who dared to follow Him such experience of His supremacy that they yielded themselves to Him, and counted it the highest, holiest honor of life that they were reckoned worthy to suffer shame for His name.

In the terms of this inscription blend the accents of the eternal and the temporal. While they are separated from each other, they nevertheless merge. In separation we have, first, the eternal word concerning this King, "This is My beloved Son"; and second, the temporal word concerning Him, having immediate and local value, "in Whom I am well pleased."

But the temporal and eternal merge in each of these separated parts. This Man was visible to the eyes of the prophet, visible to the eyes of the multitude, a Man of our humanity, a Man of our own flesh, a Man so like the rest of men that none noticed Him save the one man whose purity of soul quickened his spiritual intelligence and enabled him to discover Him. Did not John say to the multitudes, "In the midst of you standeth One Whom ye know not"? They had not seen Him, He was so much one of them. Yet the Divine voice drawing attention to this Man of our common humanity said, "This is My Son"; and in that word, as we shall see, declared the eternal and abiding relation, uttered suggestively the mystery of the Person of Christ in His relation to the undying ages.

Or if you take the other part of the declaration, you will find the same merging of the eternal and the temporal. "In Whom I am well pleased," and the reference was to the One on Whom our attention has been fixed in such a way that we are impressed with the majesty of His Person. The Son of God, "in Whom I am well pleased"; and there was an immediate and temporal meaning in the word, having application and value for that hour, and for the things of our present temporary and present life.

Thus are we introduced by the inscription around the Image, by the first word of God recorded concerning our Master, to the King Who will pass before us as we take our way through this gospel according to Matthew.

Let us, then, consider the inscription in its two parts. First, the eternal, "This is My Son"; second, the temporal, "In Whom I am well pleased."

As we approach this strangely difficult theme, which cannot be exhausted, about which no final word can be spoken, we must bear in mind that the one fact of relationship here declared is that of the Sonship of Jesus.

If we place this word in Matthew against the word in the Second Psalm, we find a distinction and a difference. The word of the psalm says:

> I will tell of the decree:
> The Lord said unto me, Thou art my son;
> This day have I begotten thee.

I listen for the sound of the voice of God on the banks of the River Jordan, and this is what I hear:

> This is My beloved Son, in Whom I am well pleased.

There is not a word in this declaration by the Father about begetting or beginning. We must have that distinction in mind if we are to approach the subject reverently and intelligently. The two facts are not the same; the first is that of sonship, the second is that of a begetting, which indicates beginning. That begetting of the psalm has no reference to beginning of being, but to the initiation of a work. If the psalm be Messianic and its first fulfilment was in the case of David, then the begetting had no reference to the day of David's natural birth, but to the day when he was anointed king. If the psalm is Messianic and its first reference was to Hezekiah, then that which the expositors suggest may be true, that the reference was to that day when, rising from sickness and death, he started on a new life which God had granted to him. Of these things I have no certainty. If I take that psalm and find it in my New Testament I immediately discover what the word means in relation to Jesus. It is four times cited, two of them certainly by Paul, two of them in the letter to the Hebrews, probably by Paul. When Paul was delivering his first great message in Antioch in Pisidia he quoted that psalm and placed it in relation to the resurrection of Jesus, and declared that it was in that resurrection hour that He was begotten. You will find in his letter to the Romans when referring to Jesus as being, according to the flesh of the seed of David, but according to the spirit, Son of God, he declared that He was declared, determined—or as I have ventured to say if we dare to anglicize the Greek word, horizoned—Son of God by the resurrection from the dead. In the letter to the Hebrews it is declared that He was begotten Son of God, brought into the realm of manifested Sonship by the resurrection, and it is certain that the disciples of Jesus never perfectly understood His relationship to God until the morning of the resurrection. The morning of the resurrection was the day of birth for the disciples, because it was to them the day on which He was begotten Son of God to their understanding and to their comprehension. It was Peter himself who declared in his first letter, "We were begotten again unto a living hope by the resurrection of Jesus Christ from the dead."

We may dismiss for the purpose of this meditation all reference to that word in the psalm, "This day have I begotten thee," and take only the declaration of the psalm, "Thou art my Son," and that of God in the hour of the baptism of Jesus concerning His Person, "This is My beloved Son."

In that word we have, first of all, a revelation as to the nature of the King. He was of the very nature of God. All figurative terms must be used with a recognition of limitation. If we speak of a son we implicate a beginning, but that is because we are using our term in the realm of the finite. Finite sonship results from finite fatherhood; but we must cancel our limitations when we reach the heights of the Divine. A word which will again defy our finite analysis is the word "eternal," yet it must be remembered that this word cancels the limitations of time. Eternal fatherhood, eternal sonship, not the beginning of the sonship of this Son of His love. As the proceeding of the Spirit of God from the Father through the Son is eternal so also Sonship is eternal. That which is of supreme importance is the revelation of the fact that the King is of the Divine nature. He shares the very nature of His Father, is of the Divine essence. That is the deepest and profoundest truth about the King. He is not merely bone of our bones, flesh of our flesh, humanity of our humanity. He is all that, but infinitely more.

In speaking at Antioch in Pisidia Paul argued from the Sonship of Jesus which was demonstrated by His resurrection the impossibility of death holding Him ultimately. He passed into death, but He emerged therefrom as none other emerged therefrom or ever will. Death laid no corrupting touch on Him. He did not see corruption. Peter in Pentecostal power declared, "It was not possible that He should be holden of it." The first fact in this identity of nature is that of eternal being. He will bow and bend to death and enter into its profound darkness and know its mystery, but He cannot be held of it. It is not correct to say merely that He triumphed over death by the way of the resurrection. Resurrection was necessary because of His nature. He was not deified by resurrection. He was raised because He was of the nature of God, and could not, holy One as He was, ever ultimately see corruption.

In the passage in Romans the Apostle teaches that His

Sonship connotes His absolute holiness; according to the flesh, He was of the seed of David; according to the spirit of holiness, He is Son of God, and the resurrection did but demonstrate that holiness of character which was part of His essential Deity.

In the opening words of the letter to the Hebrews it is shown that His identity in nature with God by reason of His Sonship proves His absolute sovereignty. "Unto which of the angels said He at any time,

> Thou art My Son;
> This day have I begotten thee?

But of the Son He saith,

> Thy throne, O God, is for ever and ever."

In the fifth chapter of Hebrews the writer declares that because Jesus was Son of God He was moved with compassion and became a great High Priest, bearing our infirmities, providing eternal salvation for the sons of men.

The Son of God is of the very nature of God, therefore eternal, therefore holy, therefore sovereign in authority, therefore saving, even at the cost of sacrifice and of death. All the things of Deity were realized in the Kingship of the One manifested in time in such form and fashion that human nature might gaze on Him and be led to understanding of the hidden and profound secrets of God.

The eternal value also reveals the fact that the King has right to the inheritance of God. Again I go back to this Hebrew psalm, and I notice that in the seventh verse I have these words:

> Thou art my son;
> This day have I begotten thee.

And in the twelfth verse,

> Kiss the Son, lest he be angry, and ye perish in the way.

Those who may be familiar with these psalms in the original language will at once recognize that we have two different words here. The word translated "son" in the seventh verse is not the word translated "son" in the twelfth verse. There is the same value in both words, the suggestiveness, with which we have attempted to deal, of identity of nature. In our reading of the Bible we have been made familiar with both these words in proper names, as for instance in the names Ben-jamin, and Bar-timæus. If I may take these prefixes as being the simplest way of illustrating what I am attempting to say, this is it,

> Thou art My son—Ben.
> Kiss the son—Bar.

There is the same underlying value of identity of nature in each, but there are two applications, two thoughts.

In the first you have the great Hebrew word, peculiarly Eastern, so difficult for us Westerners to understand, the word that speaks of sonship as being that which builds the house and continues it. We know so little of house building in that sense. Ask the man from the East how old he is, and do not be startled if he tells you two thousand years. He is counting all the family, feeling the solidarity of the race, recognizing his responsibility for that which lies behind him; he glories in being Ben-jamin, son of the right hand, builder of the house, continuer of the history.

The second word simply means heir. The first word indicates responsibility, contribution; the second indicates blessing, the thing a man receives.

In that psalm we have the suggestion that Messiah should be the Heir of God,

> Ask of me, and I will give thee the nations for thine inheritance,
> And the uttermost parts of the earth for thy possession.

The anointed King is the House Builder, the One who will accomplish the will of the Father, and therefore He will obtain the inheritance which is His right. The Son Who shares His Father's nature being of that nature and therefore being eternal, holy, sovereign, saving, is Heir of all the wealth of God in this world, all the nations, and all the earth.

This eternal Son of the eternal God not only shares His nature, and has a right to His inheritance, He co-operates in His purpose, He is the House Builder. Moses was servant in the house of God, but the Son is Sovereign over the house, for He is the Builder of the House. So the King is seen as co-operative with God, building His House, realizing His purpose, moving toward the goal on which the heart of God is set.

Read the psalm to the end and discover His method—the rule of justice, the rod of iron, the exercise of mercy:

Kiss the son, lest he be angry, and ye perish in the way,
For his wrath will soon be kindled.
Blessed are all they that put their trust in Him.

We turn, in the second place, and very briefly to the next word, that of the temporal relation: "In Whom I am well pleased." I do not believe that is temporal alone. I think it is the crystallization of all the infinite music of the eighth chapter of Proverbs. The ancient Hebrew wisdom, the Greek Logos, merge and are fulfilled in Jesus, in the Son of God, in that One in Whom God had forever delighted.

Yet the first application was local and temporal. We have no record of the life of Jesus for at least eighteen years. How has He been living, what has He been doing in those strange, mysterious years? That Voice broke the silence. "This is My beloved Son, in Whom I am well pleased." Being now about thirty years of age He had come to baptism, and these words were uttered. It was a declaration of earthly conformity to a heavenly pattern, of temporal harmony with eternal order. It was the word of God setting His seal on the perfection of the human life of Jesus. It was the confirmation of the personal perfection of the human Christ, of His holiness of character, of the fact that He had reigned in life, suffering nothing to have dominion over Him other than the will of His Father, of the fact that He had exercised a saving, beneficent relationship as He had come into contact with men. These are the things of God, this is the Son of God, and for a generation He had lived in human conditions; now it was over, and God sealed the perfection of His Son as He said, "I am well pleased."

But there is another value and a profounder one in that statement. John had said, "I have need to be baptized of Thee, and comest Thou to me?" and the answer of the Son of God to the Hebrew prophet had been, "Suffer it now: for thus it becometh us to fulfil all righteousness." In that baptism He was numbered with the transgressors. The Pure stood side by side with the impure, consented to a whelming that indicated the need for cleansing, entered into personal comradeship with sinning men; and that which bent Him toward that lowliness was His passion for righteousness. "Suffer it now: for *thus*" by this baptism which is the symbol of death and which is the symbol of another baptism which awaits Me in the days to come, "*thus* it becometh us to fulfil all righteousness," not to observe a rite, but to deal with sin at its fountain head, to master it that so righteousness may be established. A passion for righteousness filled His heart as He consented to John's baptism. It was His consent to a method of identification with sinners that must end in awful death. It was as He emerged from these waters which were the symbol of His identification with sinning men that God said, "This is My beloved Son, in Whom I am well pleased."

Is there not yet another note here, another value? Is there not in this declaration the note of His power for dominion. "This is My beloved Son, in Whom I am well pleased." Man can have only one King, and that is God. No man conscious of his own manhood has ever found, or ever can find in man merely, a king to whom he can and will submit the whole mastery of his being without question. If Jesus of Nazareth be none other than a pure and upright man, I cannot crown Him my king, for I also am a man. There can be no King for a man other than God. There can be no final authority for the dignity of human life other than the authority of God Himself. "This is My beloved Son, in Whom I am well pleased," satisfied, at rest, because in Him man will find Me as King, and through coming to this Man, the revelation of Myself, man will be enabled to crown God King of the life and thus realize the territory of his own being.

Thus "God was in Christ reconciling the world unto Himself." Thus at the opening of this great gospel of the King I find the Divinely graven inscription around the image.

Do we agree with God about Jesus? Yonder is a man at prayer beneath the shade of his own fig tree. Disturbed, he follows the disturber, until he stands face to face with this selfsame Man just after this baptism. Nathanael and Jesus are confronting each other. "Behold an Israelite indeed in whom is no guile," said Jesus. This Hebrew looked into the eyes of Jesus and said, "Rabbi, Thou art the Son of God; Thou art the King of Israel." In that word he agreed with God.

Christ is the test and touchstone of our relation to God. King in very deed is He. Put not upon this King the measurements of earthly kings. That was the mistake of the early disciples until the Spirit illuminated them, and they beheld Him as Son of God. He was the Man of the seamless robe, a homeless Man; but that is God's King. There He is, God's Son, of His very nature, having the right to His inheritance, in Himself having all power and eternal dominion. Then be it ours to hasten to "kiss the Son, lest He be angry. . . . Blessed are all they that put their trust in Him."

CHAPTER XXII

THE KING'S THOUGHT OF MAN

Man shall not live by bread alone, but by every word that proceedeth out of the mouth of God.
MATTHEW 4:4.

THE STORY OF THE TEMPTATION OF OUR LORD APPEALS TO men irresistibly by reason of its essential naturalness. In all its central values it is true to our common human experience. As we read it, far removed as we feel ourselves to be from the Eastern conditions, and puzzled intellectually as we sometimes may be, by some of the methods which are described, we nevertheless are conscious of very close and intimate fellowship with the Man Who is being tempted. Those familiar with the New Testament can hardly read the story without other passages from the apostolic writings coming back to their minds: "One that hath been in all points tempted like as we are, yet without sin"; "In that He Himself hath suffered being tempted, He is able to succour them that are tempted."

There are certain arresting facts in the story to which I shall make brief and passing reference by way of introduction. You will observe that the devil is introduced without any explanation, and that God is admitted without any argument. We stand in the presence of a Man Who is most evidently of our nature; all the elemental forces of our manhood are discoverable as we observe Him: intellect, emotion, volition, the physical, the spiritual, the vocational; everything which is essentially human is seen in the Man Whom we watch in that strange hour of temptation.

The particular text which I have chosen from the story consists of the answer of Jesus to the first temptation. Its first application was that of reply to the suggestion that life is dependent on the material. The first attack of the foe was in the realm of the physical—bread. In that connection our text was the affirmation of the fact that while the material is necessary it is not sufficient for the sustenance of life. It is well that we should observe that our Lord did not speak disrespectfully of bread, did not even declare it to be in any sense or in any circumstances unnecessary to the maintenance of life. "Man shall not live by bread *alone*." Do not omit that word "alone" in your thinking. Christ did not say, "Man shall not live by bread." Man does live by bread; but "man shall not live by bread *alone*." While the material is necessary it is not sufficient. Such was the force of the answer to the attack of the first temptation.

But the statement has a much wider application. Every subsequent answer of Jesus was a deduction from the first. When in answer to the next temptation He said, "Thou shalt not tempt the Lord thy God," He was not telling Satan that he was not to tempt God, but that man was not to tempt God. So in His third answer, when for the third time He quoted the words of ancient Scripture, "Thou shalt worship the Lord thy God, and Him only shalt thou serve." He was not telling Satan what he was to do, but was declaring man must worship his God and serve Him alone. The "Thou" in the second answer, "Thou shall not tempt," and the "Thou" of the third answer, "Thou shalt worship," is the "Man" of the first answer, "Man shall not live by bread alone." Therefore in this first answer we have a central declaration giving us the key to the true significance of the whole story.

I am not so much occupied now with the story of the temptation as with that central and first word that passed the lips of our Lord in the hour of darkness, which revealed His conception of humanity and the secrets of life, a conception which constituted the reason for His attitude under temptation and the secret of His victory over temptation.

Two of the words in the text apprehend us; they are perhaps the simplest, "man" and "live." Of these two elemental words, the supreme word is "live"; the limiting, distinguishing word is "man."

The supreme word is "live." It brings us into the realm of the infinite and abiding mystery of life. We are, however, immediately limited by the earlier word "man."

In order that we may pass to the distinguishing, discriminating word "man" we will pause for a few moments with the second word and with the suggestions which it makes. "Man shall not live." It is life with which our Master was dealing. His own life was being attacked. It was His own life of which He was holding the stronghold, as He repulsed the attacks. I go back, then, to the supreme thought for a moment or two, the thought of life. Life is an interesting word. It is a word that you cannot define because you cannot define that for which it stands. There are some words which we have attached to ideas which exactly represent those ideas. We can grope our way through the processes by which they came into existence, or feel our way down to the roots, until we see how exactly the word fits the idea. When we begin that process with this word "life" we are immediately introduced into the realm of mystery. Philologists feeling their way back tell us that this word "life" came from the Gothic word *liban*, simply meaning, to be left, from the same root as the word "leave." Immediately we are face to face with mystery and a sense of indefiniteness. What do you mean by being left? Then the philologists employ another word to explain what is meant by being left: to *survive*. I find now I have a Latin word and I must translate it, and I do so, *to live on;* but I am back to my original word "live," and so I am working in a circle and there is no definition, save the idea that to live is to be left: life is the negation of death. Death carries away, life is that which is not carried away. That is all. That is mysterious, nebulous, insufficient. We turn back to the philologist and ask him to tell us what the word means. I quote from one alone: "that state in which the organs are capable of performing their functions." Can there be anything more gloriously indefinite? That state in which organs continue their functions. What is the secret, mystic, mighty force which makes for continuity, and what happens when it ceases? We are in the presence of the mystery of all mysteries. The mystery of life is indeed a mystery. It is in the flower, in the glowworm at eventide, in the bee passing from flower to flower and fulfilling a great mission in the world of flowers; in the bird, in the beast; and it is in man, a common quantity or quality, a mystery.

What is life? There is no answer; and the nearest we can get to definition is by declaration of what this mystic, mysterious force does. It does exactly the same thing in flower, glowworm, bee, bird, beast, and man. Let every scientist here remember that I am not a scientist, and I am not a poet. I am a plain, blunt man who speaks the things that I do know, not of life, for that I have never seen, but of the operation of life, which I can observe. Life is that which appropriates, assimilates, and ultimately gives back to the whole from which it takes. These are the three functions of life: appropriation, assimilation, giving. That is common to every realm.

I will tell you in one brief statement from the Old Testament all the story about it: "The secret things belong unto the Lord our God: but the things that are revealed belong unto us and to our children for ever, that we may do all the words of this law." The secret of life God holds in His own knowledge and His own power, and He has never unveiled it to the sons of men.

Passing from that word to the word which I have ventured to describe as the distinguishing, discriminating word of my text, "man," we immediately leave the flowers and the glowworm; the bee, the bird, and the beast; and we look at life in man. Jesus uttered the essential truth concerning human life in the words, "Man shall not live by bread alone, but by every word that proceedeth out of the mouth of God." Man must, if he would live, appropriate more than the material, and assimilate other than bread, in order that out of the mystery of his being he may give larger things than material things. That is our theme.

We turn to this story of the temptation because there we have such a wonderful setting and such a wonderful surrounding enabling us to understand the profoundest truths concerning human life. In this story we have a revelation of the elemental facts of human life, a picture of a common experience of human life, that of struggle and of conflict; and a revelation of the secret whereby a man may live in the full sense of the word, and come to the ultimate realization of the meaning of his manhood.

In the first place, in this story we have a revelation of the fundamental facts of human life. I ask you to observe this Man in the wilderness facing the tempter, and let your eyes rest on Him rather than on the enemy. As you do so you will see that in human life there is a threefold demand, to which threefold demand the enemy makes appeal.

There is, first, the demand for the material, hunger for bread. There is, second, the demand for the spiritual, the craving for an actual spiritual grasp on God. There is, finally, the demand made on self, the passion for a kingdom. Man of the material needs the material; the hunger is the evidence. Man of the spiritual craves the spiritual, to which craving the enemy made his appeal when he said, "If Thou art the Son of God cast Thyself down." Man of the regnant faculty—for man is king in the economy of God, as the psalmist saw and sang so long ago—demands a kingdom over which he can reign. Thus I see the Man in the wilderness and discover the threefold demand of his life by observing the method of the tempter; and I have discovered the elemental facts of human life.

There is, first, the demand on the material. Man of the material needs the material. Life must appropriate, assimilate, the material. Man is not a spirit without a body any more than man is a body without a spirit. It is not for us to reason why; we deal with man as he is, as we know him, as God has made him; and we assert that life demands that we should appropriate the material and assimilate it and recognize our relation to the very earth in which for a while we live. It is absolutely necessary that every human being must have of the earth in order to live. Hunger is a sign of health, it is a sign of strong manhood. It is the man who lacks hunger that you become anxious about, not the man who is hungry. God has made man on one side of his individuality of the earth, and of the earth he must have. This Man in the wilderness, forty days fasting, by the health of His perfect manhood, by the splendor of His perfect physical being, was hungry; and that is one side of human nature that we must recognize and reckon with. In this Bible story everything is resolved in this simplest formula, bread. Bread is but an emblem of things material and physical. Man is of the earth the ultimate glory and the ultimate crown, and nothing lies beneath him in all the mysterious scale of uprising life to which he is not related. Consequently, there is demand in every man's life for that which shall feed the material side of his nature as it is represented in everything that lies beneath him. The healthy man loves a dog and demands a dog. The healthy man loves flowers and demands them. The flowers lie within his own material nature. He must have colors, sounds, beauty. When you find a man who turns his back on music and flowers in the name of saintship, understand he is no saint; he does not understand his own humanity, in his own thinking of it he will degrade that which God has made, and I will not trust him out of my sight. Bread is the simple formula of the whole material order, which is not inherently evil, which is a Divine creation, which finds its ultimate glory in man; and man in health hungers for everything that lies beneath him.

Then as to the next revelation, the demand on God. Man is of the spiritual and he needs the spiritual. In the elemental man, that is, in the man who is nearest to that which is natural to humanity, that demand for the spiritual will inevitably make itself heard and known. It may be that the man who feels the hunger for the spiritual will not understand the hunger. It may be that he will not be able to express in correct words the true deep meaning of this hunger. It may take curious methods of expression; but not merely for bread does man hunger, but for space, vision, for something beyond the near, the immediate, the dust; for some demonstration of spirituality that is independent of the near, the immediate, the dust. Get back to the wilderness and listen to the subtle voice of the tempter, "If Thou art the Son of God, cast Thyself down," cut thyself off from all the ordinary laws of physical being and find out whether there is any reality in this spiritual relationship; make a venture on the spiritual in order to find out. Have you never felt that temptation come to you. Remember, the very temptation is directed toward a perfectly right attitude of the soul. In every man there is the possibility of the realization of the spiritual. A man may affirm that he does not believe in the spiritual, yet within his soul there is a crying out after God; it may be mere speculation, it may be some adventure, it may be that which man will designate, in what he is pleased to call his sober moments, fanaticism; but, thank God, humanity cannot get away from this fanaticism, the passion for some consciousness and grasp of some larger thing that cannot be cabined and confined within the tabernacle of this flesh. That is why men climb mountains and travel. That is why men venture forth on great enterprises. It is a sign of health.

I come at last to that which is the ultimate thing in all human life. According to this revelation, not the demand on the material of which every man is conscious, not this demand on the spiritual and on God which every man feels, though he may not understand, but the demand on self is final. Man is regnant in his very being. He needs a kingdom; he asks some territory over which he can reign, having captured it, having mastered it, that he may administer it. Every man is asking for that; every healthy man, every elemental man, every man who approximates in any degree toward the original Divine intention, asks a kingdom. That is the secret impulse of all production, of all commerce, of all healing ministries, of all art, and—forgive me—ultimately, of all true preaching. It is the passion for a kingdom. A man does not ask a kingdom that he inherits from his father. Man asks a garden of Eden, not an Italian garden, but one in which he can walk and touch mother earth brimming with potentialities, and which he can smite and make beautiful with flowers and golden with harvest. That is elemental manhood. You say you have never felt that? That is the sign of your sin. Sin paralyzes the passion for a kingdom, and a man is content to say, "Let us eat and drink, for to-morrow we die." That is the language of a false humanity. Man in the economy of God asks a kingdom that he can win, master, administer, and over which in the allied forces of his material and spiritual being he can reign in life.

In the wilderness I not only have this revelation of elemental humanity, I have also the revelation of that which is common to man, the experience of struggle. Of course this is the central value of this particular story, and again I ask you to observe there is no explanation of it here, no vindication of it. It is a story that accepts facts and reveals the forces.

I pray you also to remember that this is the picture of human life. I wonder whether this fact of struggle obtains through all the universe of God. I cannot say, I do not know. I know only man and something of the angels through the revelation of Scripture, and something of all that life on this earth that lies beneath man in the great creation scale; and, so far as I am able to observe, I find the same principle everywhere. I do not know the history of the angels. It is not perfectly revealed in Holy Scripture. There are gleams in the revelation, and I read, among other things, of angels who left their first estate, and kept not their proper habitation. I cannot read a sentence like that without discovering that behind that event in which angels left their first estate and wandered from their true orbit there was struggle. There was in the mystery of the angelic world some kind of temptation, and the victory over it was the keeping of a first estate, of abiding in an orbit, the ensuring of eternity, and the yielding to it was the loss of estate, absence from the true orbit.

I turn from that imperfect vision, for the revelation is not perfect, and I look at all the life below man. I would rather speak of the life below man in the language of one whose understanding of God and Christ was far beyond mine, who lived in closer relationship with his Lord and through whom the Spirit of God could write things for our profit, "The whole creation groaneth and travaileth in pain."

I leave these regions and return to man, and here in Matthew I have a picture not of a sinful man. If He were a sinful man, then everything breaks down, there is no meaning in this story; it has no revealing value; it is merely a record. But this is a sinless Man, and into clear light for my eyes emerge the facts of struggle, of the force that creates it, and of the way of victory over it. The first thing that I notice in the story is that according to this story the struggle is caused by a personality who is named the devil. Remember, this is Biblical. We do not hear much to-day about the devil; modern views fail to see him—I think that is the kindest way to put it.

I hear to-day about the angel and the beast in man. I am told that there is in every man an angel and a beast. What I object to in that description is that it is rude alike to the angel and to the beast. I am told that in every man the angel is in process of struggling through, and that the beast is being sloughed off. That is a doctrine of original sin far more terrible than the doctrine of the theologians, because it makes sin more original than man, and suggests that man is emerging out of that which is vulgar and low. That is not the Bible doctrine. The Bible doctrine says Satan, the devil, is the beast and that the temptations which come to man come by suggestion from without.

This story also reveals the process. Let me attempt to put that whole process as I see it into one brief sentence. This story reveals the fact that the enemy of mankind approaches man through what man is. He appeals to the things which are essential in human life, he appeals to elemental things, proper things, God-made things. He appeals to material hunger, he appeals to that which asks for spiritual realization, he appeals to that passion for a kingdom, that passion that demands a territory.

Wherein then lies the temptation in every case? In the suggestion that man shall fulfil the elemental demands of his nature on the basis of anarchy or lawlessness, that he shall cease to obey any law in the realm of the material, that he shall cease to realize that there is a law that governs in the spiritual realm, that he shall cease to recognize that there is a law that governs in the vocational realm.

I look at the story again, and I see not merely the personality and the process, I discover also the pain, the agony, the travail. "He Himself hath suffered being tempted." There is always suffering in temptation, and when suffering ceases temptation ceases. If solicitation toward evil causes you no pain, then it is no temptation, and you are in the grip of the evil thing; spiritual mortification has set in, and God help you, for none other can! Watch temptation at work and mark this: the pain of temptation is felt in proportion to the perfection of the person who is tempted.

I begin with the child. When temptation is first presented to a child, when a child is first conscious of temptation to do wrong, that child suffers. Oh, but you say, that is only a qualm of conscience. Only a qualm of conscience! Hell is a qualm of conscience intensified, prolonged, incurable! What more would you have? The little child suffers. It may be that you will offer it false advantages, and deceive it, until it will forget its suffering and yield to the sin. The child, who is nearer the heart of God than any other, save those who are brought back to childhood by grace, suffers in the hour of temptation.

Or take any seeker after the high and holy, that young man who listens to the preacher to-night who has not yielded himself to this Christ but who has seen the vision and who is aspiring after God, who is desiring to climb the heights—he yielded to temptation yesterday, but, ah, me, the agony of it when it first gripped him. He yielded, and in the sin for the moment was a damnable opiate that killed the pain; but the opiate will pass and remorse will be the return of pain. That is hopeful; but, oh, if the day shall come when there is no remorse, when there is no agony in the presence of temptation! That will be demonstration of the most unutterable ruin possible. Temptation coming to the seeker means pain.

Temptation means pain to the saint—I use the word in its true sense, not of those who are already perfected but of those pressing toward the goal. When temptation assails the saint there is agony in it. There may be yielding, there may be sin; but there is agony in it. Let there be no yielding, there is nevertheless an increasing consciousness of pain whenever temptation assails the soul. It is the experience of struggle.

Finally, I have in this story, and this is the supreme thing, the secret of victory over temptation and of the realization of humanity. If life be a mystery what is the supreme necessity? If life judged by its operations is that mystic force that appropriates, assimilates, gives, and yet cannot be truly and perfectly known, what is the supreme necessity for life? A law. Government in appropriation, that life may know what to appropriate. Government in assimilation, that life may fling out the poison and keep only that which shall nourish. Government in giving. This is a sequence, for if there be true appropriation and assimilation the giving will be true. What life needs is government. Flowers need governing, that they may appropriate and assimilate the right things, and so give the right things. That law must be formulated by someone who knows the mystery. I cannot formulate any law for the cultivation of flowers; no horticulturist is able to formulate the law. He discovers the law and by recognizing it is able to make the chrysanthemum infinitely beautiful which but two generations ago was but the homeliest of garden flowers. What is true of the flower, is equally true of the bee, the bird, the beast, and of man.

I am now face to face again with my text, "Man shall not live by bread alone, but by every word that proceedeth out of the mouth of God." Man must live within the law of

God, who knows the mystery of his being. Man must live by obedience to commands coming directly, immediately, to him for the government of his life. Those commands have been given to us in the Scriptures of Truth; those commands have been given to us in the Son Who is the Logos, the Word incarnate; those commands are being given to us every day if we will listen; only the commands of to-day must be tested by the commands of the oracles, and all spiritual illumination must be tested by the Son of His love, the ultimate, final speech of Deity.

What, then, is man's responsibility? I should be inclined to say to my own soul, as the result of this meditation, Man, thy first responsibility is that of recognition of the mystery of thy life. The last word of Greek philosophy was, Man, know thyself, a great word because it brought man face to face with himself. When a man recognizes the mystery of his own life, then the second responsibility is that he consent to the government of Him to Whom his life is no mystery.

> O Lord, Thou hast searched me, and known me,
> Thou knowest my downsitting and my uprising,
> Thou understandest my thought afar off.

So begins the psalm. How does it end?

> Search me, O God, and know my heart:
> Try me, and know my thoughts:
> And see if there be any way of wickedness in me,
> And lead me in the way everlasting.

"Man shall not live by bread alone, but by every word that proceedeth out of the mouth of God." Recognize that. Make it the first, supreme, essential business of thy life to acquaint thyself with Him, and so be at peace.

CHAPTER XXIII

THE RIGHTEOUSNESS WHICH EXCEEDS

Except your righteousness shall exceed the righteousness of the scribes and Pharisees, ye shall in no wise enter into the Kingdom of heaven.

MATTHEW 5:20.

THESE ARE THE CLOSING WORDS OF THE FIRST SECTION OF the Manifesto of the King. As to their first value, they reveal the personal responsibility of all those who are to teach the ethic of Jesus. The arresting notes are two: first, Kingly authority; and, second, ethical severity. Let us take them in their wider meaning and application as revealing the ethical demand which the King makes on His subjects.

A matter of supreme importance—if a man is to speak out of the consciousness of his own age, and I think he must so speak if he teach the word of God to his age—a matter demanding far more attention than has been given to it lately, is the fact that the moral standard of Jesus is an infinitely more severe one than that of any other teacher. No one will imagine that I undervalue the gospel of His Grace. I shall have to return to it ere I have done; I cannot preach in the atmosphere of this Manifesto without ending under the shadow of the Cross. Nevertheless, I fear that sometimes we have preached the gospel of His grace at the expense of the demand of His ethic. To dwell on the severity of His ethical demand and His interpretation of morality is our present purpose. Yet let us immediately recognize that to which we shall return by way of conclusion, that these words of Jesus must be heard in the consciousness of the whole of the mission of the King, in which mission He acted as Saviour as well as Sovereign, as Lover of the souls of men as well as Lawgiver.

The statement as a statement is perfectly clear, even if it is startling. Speaking to His own disciples, men who had already crowned Him, so far as they had received light; men who had already yielded themselves to His Kingship, so far as they were able to comprehend His meaning, He said, "Except your righteousness exceed the righteousness of the scribes and Pharisees, ye shall in no wise enter into the Kingdom of heaven."

When thus set in their true context, these words of Christ become the more startling: they were words spoken, not to the multitudes, although the multitudes listened, but to men who had already crowned Him in the measure of the light which they had received, to men who were to go out and teach His ethic.

Let us attempt to understand this word of Jesus by considering, first, righteousness as the central idea of the declaration; second, the insufficiency of the righteousness of the scribes and Pharisees; and, third, the righteousness which exceeds that of the scribes and Pharisees.

The clear implication of the passage is the importance of righteousness. That is the perpetual Biblical atmosphere. Among the fundamental things of the Bible, so far as human conduct is concerned, is the supreme message, that righteousness is of paramount importance. That, of course, is the Christian conception, or, to come at once to the very heart of the thought, the master passion of Jesus was righteousness. The inspiration of that passion, if we may dare to press so deeply into the mind of Christ, was that of love. The master passion of all His doing was righteousness, not mercy but righteousness, not pity but purity. Mercy, yes, and pity surely; He was infinite in His compassion and in His tenderness, but never at the expense of right, never by making peace with wrong, never by lowering the standard of Divine holiness, or explaining away the awfulness of Divine purity. The master passion of all His teaching, of all the wonders He wrought, of the life He lived, of the very Cross of His dying, was the establishment of righteousness, and the bringing of all things into harmony with the holiness and purity of God. Those who do not agree with these assumptions of the text will be entirely outside the line of argument as we proceed. Only as we realize that, in the last analysis, the supreme matter of all life and conduct is that it should be righteous, shall we really be prepared to listen to these words of Christ, or be able to grasp their meaning and see how searching and wonderful they are.

What, then, is righteousness? If it be possible for me so to do, I want to escape from theological definitions. I want us to get at the simplest idea, at the abstract idea, at that which is true and commonly known as true in the consciousness of thinking men. In its ancient form, as you will remember, our word read right-wise-ness. That is to say, it came from a word "right-wise," which had as its main value the word "right." That is the fundamental word. Instead of righteousness, say righteous; and instead of righteous, say right; and you are touching the very central thought. Yet immediately you discover that this is not definition. So we press the question further. What is right? If we take this actual word of ours we find that its simplest meaning is No crookedness. Do not stay yet to read into that the moral value, but take it in its simplicity. The root word is a word which means to stretch, so that if you will take in your hand a piece of string, looped and twisted, and stretch it, that is righteousness, that which is perfectly straight. The straightest course is the right course. Go back to your school days and remind yourselves of this phrase, a right line, a straight line. What is a straight line? The one that goes most directly from point to point. Right is that in which there is no loop, no crookedness, no doubling, no deviation from the truly straight. Such is the idea in the word.

We immediately see why in that wonderful process of the formation of our language, the building up of words by which to express ideas, that word was made to stand for the supreme idea in the moral realm: no duplicity, no double dealing, nothing in the nature of a lie either in word or in thought, but straightness, truth, the shortest course.

Twice I have said that righteousness means the shortest course, and I am perfectly sure that in the minds of some there has been protest against the declaration. I sympathize with the protest. One of the devil's suggestions was that the King should take the short cut to the Kingdom—I will give thee all the kingdoms of the world for one moment's homage, a short cut to the kingdom, the shortest way! Would it have been the shortest way? Would He ever have gained the kingdoms so? Was not the lie of evil insidious in that it suggested as the shortest way the way that never reached the goal at all? That is the method of evil. It confronts the soul with a lie. I go back to my definition; right is the shortest way. To take an illustration from the life of our Lord makes one pause, and I do it reverently—Christ's shortest way to the kingdoms of this world was the way of the Cross, and the long travail of the millenniums. One brief, short moment of homage to the devil, and He the Son of God could never have gained the kingdoms! It seemed so easy to take the short cut. I pray that God may write the inner value of that on the heart and soul of every one of us. Some of you were thinking of actually yielding to the suggestion made to you, that you should take the short cut of iniquity toward the goal that you ought to reach by tramping and travail. In God's name refuse. The lie lies in the temptation that it is a short cut. Right is the nearest way to every honorable goal. I repeat, the stretched out, straight line, the right line, goes most quickly from point to point.

If that be our word, great as it is in its suggestiveness and its root values, I take up my Bible and ask, What is righteousness as herein revealed? I am still dealing, not with the word in all its great evangelical values as they appear in the New Testament, but with the word itself, as to its abstract idea. I find the old Hebrew word translated "right" has exactly the same significance, "straight." I find the Greek word has another meaning which will help us. The Greek word comes from one which means to show a thing, that is, to be self-evident. The Greek, former of words, the builder up of language, formed a word for moral rectitude from a root which means self-evident. There is wonderful illumination in that fact also.

The Bible idea of righteousness may thus be expressed: God is the absolute and eternal standard of right. Consequently, human conduct is righteous as it conforms to His will and approximates His character. These Bible writers and Bible teachers, of the old dispensation and the new, never stayed to argue whether God is righteous. That is their fundamental assumption. On that all Biblical teaching proceeds. The Bible position is that God is holy, and therefore His doings are righteous. He is the one eternal, final standard of what is right; consequently, righteousness in human life is conformity to His will and approximation to His character.

Those who do not accept this standard are totally unable to follow the argument of Jesus in my text, for the man who does not admit that God is the ultimate, eternal standard of right, whatever his own view of right may be, stands on a lower level than the Pharisees, for the Pharisees started there, as I shall try to show you. That was their fundamental conception. Those who believe that God is the absolute, eternal standard of right, and that man is right in the measure in which he lives in conformity with the will of God and approximates His character, may go forward in this meditation.

All this is fundamental; but there are differences in the apprehension of what the will of God is, and in these distinctions we shall discover what our Lord meant when He said to the men who were entering into His Kingdom that their righteousness must exceed the righteousness of the scribes and Pharisees.

I think we shall be very unfair to the meaning of our Master if we begin in the twenty-third chapter of Matthew, that chapter from which I read one extract in connection with our lesson, that chapter vibrant with the thunder of His awful woes against these very men. I think we must not begin there. I think we very often miss the keen edge of what Jesus said by beginning at the wrong place.

Where, then, shall we begin? Let us ask who these Pharisees were. The answer to the inquiry may thus be stated. The Pharisees were the Puritans of Maccabean period in Jewish history. Their very name means separated ones, and I do no violence to the name "Pharisee" when I say it means Separatist. That is precisely what they were. We have no history of the actual period in our Bible, but we have the history of its beginning in the books of Ezra and Nehemiah, and we have revelations of the conditions in the books of Haggai, Zechariah, and Malachi. God's ancient people, or a remnant of them, were established at Jerusalem, without any king or prophet. There originated the order of the Scribes, for Ezra was the first. As time proceeded these people were threatened with complete absorption by the Greek power that swept over that whole region, and in that period, of which we have no Biblical history, but of which we have a good deal of authentic history, Judas Maccabeus became the deliverer of the people. There was a period of victories, and these Hebrew people suffered as a result, for they were in danger of forming alliances with the surrounding peoples and of being corrupted by that Greek influence which stood in direct opposition to their own conception of God and religion. It was then, when, humanly speaking, the Hebrew people were threatened with that most terrible form of extinction, absorption, that the Pharisees arose. The passion which actuated those who founded the order was one of loyalty to Jehovah. They constituted themselves into a definite order. I think when we read the New Testament we sometimes forget that the Pharisees were members of a very definite order. There were not more than six or seven thousand of them. The order was a close religious corporation. They banded themselves together as men who would be entirely separated from the Gentiles, from those whom they described as the common people, that is, those who did not take those special religious vows, and especially from the Sadducees, who were the rationalists in religion. The movement was born of the highest, holiest, passion. The order of the Pharisees was an order of men who stood for purity in religion in an hour when Hebraism was threatened by contamination by Greek influence, which would have cut the nerve of the religion of Jehovah. There can be no question, and those who are most familiar with the history of those times will agree with me, that they were the saviours of the nation, the men who enabled that remnant to stand against the encroachment of the forces of worldliness that were sweeping down on the people. These were the Pharisees, and these were the men with whom Jesus Christ was brought into immediate contact, when He began His public teaching.

From the commencement of His public ministry to the close we see Him flinging Himself with all the force of His personality against them and against their teaching. How are we to account for this? Let us look at them again. Let us see what had happened to them in the course of the years, not tracing the movement but seeing the result as it is revealed to us in the New Testament. What had their righteousness become? Let us inquire what was the base of it and examine the structure of it in order that we may understand the failure and insufficiency of it.

What was the base of the righteousness which the Pharisees taught? Conformity to the will of God. When you speak of the Pharisees, remember that they were the most religious people of that period, they were the most orthodox, the men who stood by the old theology. No one will imagine I am condemning orthodoxy, or sneering at old theology.

When we come into the Acts of the Apostles we find that the opposition was not Pharisaic, but Saducean. So long as Jesus was teaching morality, the Sadducees had no quarrel with Him; they were indifferent; it was the resurrection doctrine that put the Sadducees into opposition with Christ. The Pharisees were religious, orthodox, and the base of their morality was their belief that man must conform to the will of God. Wherein, then, lay their failure? In order to answer that question, let us observe the structure which they had built on that base. Three things characterized their righteousness: it was, first, external; second, it was exclusive; finally, therefore, it was evasive of essential righteousness.

It was, first, external. It consisted in a most complex and elaborate system of regulations of life by habits. As every man entered the order he took two vows of initiation. The first was to tithe everything eaten, bought, or sold. The second was not to be the guest of the Gentiles, and to observe all ceremonial purifications. These were the fundamental vows of initiation to the order of the Pharisees. Now observe what had happened in the process of the years. In their desire to interpret the law of God and to make it binding they had added tradition to tradition. A little careful study of the Pharisees reveals things that are almost too absurd to be mentioned. Here is one simple illustration of their traditions. If a man should walk through the cornfields on the Sabbath day he must wear the lightest sandals, as if he wore heavy ones and trod on the corn and thus forced it from its husk, he was threshing on the Sabbath! You smile at that, but I know Puritanism to-day which is quite as foolish! They attempted to explain the meaning of the thought of God by their own foolish tradition until they had heaped tradition upon tradition, and the Lord said to them, "They bind heavy burdens and grievous to be borne, and lay them on men's shoulders; but they themselves will not move them with their fingers."

Moreover, their righteousness was exclusive. They held in supreme contempt all who were outside their own order. In the New Testament we become quite familiar with their attitude toward the publican. That phrase, the "common people," in itself full of beauty because it describes, not the people of one class or caste, but all sorts of people, when used by the Pharisee included all those who were not Pharisees, learned and illiterate, rich and poor, bond and free, the common herd outside the Pharisaic order, on all of whom the Pharisee looked with profound contempt. Notice another revelation of the exclusiveness of the Pharisee, and I shall reveal what is in my mind by again quoting from the words of Jesus, "Ye compass sea and land to make one proselyte: and when he is become so, ye make him twofold more a son of hell than yourselves." There is no stronger proof of exclusivism than the passionate desire to proselytize someone else and bring that other person to your view. You reveal your exclusivism in no surer way than when you attempt to take hold of the man you hold in contempt because he is not with you, and compel him to your way of thinking.

Finally, their righteousness was evasive. Accentuation of the letter had destroyed the spirit. The Sabbath was held so sacred that in the observance of it its hallowed sanctions were denied, so that when His disciples passed through the cornfields and plucked the ears of corn the Pharisees complained that they were breaking the Sabbath, and Jesus said, "If ye had known what this meaneth, I desire mercy, and not sacrifice, ye would not have condemned the guiltless." Have you ever really examined that answer of Jesus? These men were insisting on the sanctity of the Sabbath in such a way as to harm humanity, and Christ swept their traditions away, declaring that even the sanctity of the Sabbath must give way to the sanction of caring for humanity. They would not work on the Sabbath, but they would hold their feasts on the Sabbath, provided Gentiles prepared them. Consequently, I repeat, the very accentuation of the value of the letter had destroyed the spirit.

Wherein, then, lay the failure of these men? What was wrong? If the base of their righteousness was the conviction that righteousness is conformity to the will of God, wherein were they wrong? In that they did not know God. Consequently, they were unequal to the interpretation of the will of God. They did not understand the nature of His holiness. They did not understand the nature of His love. Out of that ignorance of God they proceeded to attempt to bring men into conformity to the will of the God Whom they did not know, and Whose will therefore they did not know, with the result that they libeled the God Whom they professed to extol, and degraded the national conception of God by misrepresentations, enforcing a righteousness which was external, exclusive, and evasive.

The result was the degradation of all life; the degradation of their own spirit to the hard, harsh, critical, cynical, self-satisfied temper which they manifested, the degradation of all their disciples, on whom they laid burdens that they themselves would not lift.

As Jesus moved among these men, the most religious and the most orthodox of men, He flung Himself with holy passion and fervor, and strangely biting words of sarcastic denunciation against their righteousness, against their conception of righteousness, against their attempt to establish righteousness. I will defy you to find me a single unkind or harsh word Jesus ever spoke to sinning man or woman; harsh words were all reserved for false religious teachers, men who misinterpreted God to other men, and who cut the nerve of essential righteousness by attempting to substitute for it the righteousness of triviality and tradition, men who did not know God. Against these He hurled the final anathemas, the awful, appalling woes, of the twenty-third chapter of Matthew.

What, then, are the bases of the righteousness that Christ calls for? Knowledge of God. That is first. According to Christ, all righteousness is conformity to the will of God, Who is love, and Who *therefore* is a God of holiness. As we read the Manifesto and follow its teaching concerning life and its value, marriage and its sanctity, truth and its expression, justice and its manifestation, until we come to the last expression of love, love of enemies, we are driven to say, Who is sufficient for these things? And the answer is: None other than the child of God, for he alone knows God and is able to obey Him.

The manifestations of the righteousness which exceeds are suggested by the words, "Ye therefore shall be perfect, as your heavenly Father is perfect." The word "therefore" tells us that we cannot read that command alone, we must go back. What is there before? "Your Father which is in heaven . . . maketh His sun to rise on the evil and the good, and sendeth rain on the just and the unjust." Godlikeness is righteousness according to Jesus Christ. Love active, love so active that the sun shines on the evil as well as on the good, love so active that God does not withhold His rain from the fields of the unjust man. That is righteousness in the economy of heaven. I am perfectly well aware that we have left some of you far behind. We have left the mere moralist out of sight! This is more than mere morality. The manifestation of righteousness according to this ethic is Godlikeness, active love, positive purity, fellowship with God. Presently, the King continued: "Take heed that ye do not your righteousness before men, to be seen of them," and He gave three illustrations, the giving of alms, the offering of prayer, and fasting, all things that are unnecessary! The merely moral man who has no conception of spiritual things, and no knowledge of Jesus Christ, puts all this out as unnecessary. Christ takes these things and says they are to be observed but not to be announced; they are to be secret things. "Let not thy left hand know what thy right hand doeth" in your giving. When you want to pray, do not announce to the crowd that you are going to pray. Some of these things ought to sift us. I think there are some people who never pray unless there is a special convocation and everyone knows they are going to pray. If you want to fast, fast in loneliness, and do not go out wearing the solemn face which plainly says, I have been fasting; but wear a joyful countenance while your hunger is helping you to do things for God.

The victories of the righteousness which exceeds are those of personal tone and relative influence. The supremest proof of righteousness for the other man is your tone, your temper, your spirit; "Love rejoiceth not in unrighteousness, but rejoiceth with the truth; beareth all things, believeth all things, hopeth all things, endureth all things. Love never faileth." I know people who are very careful never to smoke, and never to go to the theater, never to play cards; and I listen to them when they suppose they are talking religiously, and they are saying hard and bitter things against Christian brethren with whom they do not agree. That is the Pharisaism that Christ hates!

Pharisaism became the chief force against Christ because it lifted the incidental things to the level of essential things, and degraded the essential until ultimately it destroyed them. Said Christ, "Ye tithe mint and anise and cummin," to the neglect of judgment and mercy and faith. Christ does not undervalue the observances which express life. He did not say your righteousness is to *supersede* the righteousness of the scribes and Pharisees, but it is to *exceed* it. He went on, and said: "These ye ought to have done," judgment, mercy and faith, "and not to have left the other undone." He is not careless about the expressions of life, but demands that the details of habit shall be expressions of life, and not substitutes for life. Righteousness in the economy of Christ is an inspiration and not a prison. The Pharisees made it a prison and shut men inside it. What did Christ say of the men they shut in? "Ye make him twofold more a son of hell than yourselves." Righteousness must be the inspiration that touches the secret springs of action, purifying everything at the source.

Behold the King Who uttered the words, Himself realizing righteousness in all the fact of His life, Himself manifesting righteousness in all the glory and beauty of His tender compassion and His tremendous loyalty to truth and holiness.

Finally, behold the King enabling men to be righteous according to His pattern as they put their trust in Him.

I never can have the righteousness that exceeds the righteousness of the scribes and Pharisees save only as He will take me, dwell in me, and make me love with His love, and see with His eyes, and be compassionate with His compassion, and angry with His anger, compassionate toward the sinner, but angry with his sin. May we know that righteousness through the Lord Himself.

CHAPTER XXIV

ETHICAL PERFECTION

Ye therefore shall be perfect, as your heavenly Father is perfect.

MATTHEW 5:48.

PERHAPS NO WORDS IN THE TEACHING OF OUR LORD HAVE given more pause to honest hearts than these. With a due sense therefore of their solemnity, combined with a conviction of the reasonableness of our Master, we approach their consideration. In doing so it is of great importance that we should guard ourselves against two perils which threaten us.

First, we must be most careful not to exclude from these words any of the Lord's meaning. We must not say that our Lord did not quite intend what He said. We must not indulge in that most pernicious form of Biblical criticism, the attempt to accommodate some high word of Jesus to the low living of our own experience.

Second, we must not include any more than He intended. It will be healthy for us if we can escape entirely from all merely technical theological ideas as we approach these verses. We have heard much of Christian perfection, a fine and beautiful phrase. I have occasionally been startled by Christian people who have said to me, Do you believe in Christian perfection? My reply to such an inquiry has been to ask, Do you believe in Christian imperfection? or, Do you believe in imperfect Christianity? Every man who is a Christian believes in Christian perfection. That such an answer to the inquiry may be an evasion of the intention of the questioner I know right well. There may be involved in the question certain conceptions, interpretations, doctrines, theological opinions. Now, it is from these that I desire to escape. Let us hear these words of our Lord just as He uttered them, with the simplicity of children.

With regard to the second of these perils, that of including nothing which our Lord did not intend, let us at once recognize that the change which we find in our Revised Version is most important and most accurate. The mood of the verb is future indicative, and not imperative. Our Lord did not say, "Be ye therefore perfect." He said "Ye therefore shall be perfect."

Yet immediately, in the interest of the first warning, let us recognize with equal care that the sense of the indication is imperative in its bearing on our responsibility, for all His declarations involve responsibility, just as all His commands implicate resource.

Comprehensively, this word of Christ is a summarized declaration of what He expects of those who are in His Kingdom, and therefore it is a summarized declaration of what is made possible to them by Himself.

He came unto His own Kingdom, and found it disorganized, degraded; He came to organize, to restore, to uplift, to supply all the forces that were necessary for the remaking of men and the re-establishment of the Kingdom of God in the experience of the race. Confronting His own disciples, and speaking in the hearing of the multitude that had gathered about Him, He said, This is the sum total of My ethic, "Ye shall therefore be perfect, as your heavenly Father is perfect." Speaking to His disciples in the hearing of that larger multitude, He said, You shall be perfect, for I am here to make you perfect; that is the meaning of My mission.

Let us, then, consider, first, the central idea of the text, perfection; second, the perfection of the Father to which our Lord referred when He said "as your heavenly Father is perfect," and, third, the perfection of the sons which He declared to be necessary.

First, then, the general idea of perfection. The arresting word of the text is undoubtedly the word twice repeated, "perfect." This is the word which gives us pause, suprises us, the word which we have been so anxious to undervalue, the word which has made us declare that our Lord did not really mean what He said, but that we were to be as good as we could. It is impossible to consider or apply this statement of our Lord without carefully considering this word, both as to its actual meaning, and as to its use.

What, then, does the word mean? I am referring, of course, in the first place, to the actual word of the Greek New Testament. Let us get behind the actual word to that from which it came. A third remove from the word here translated perfect is a simple word, meaning to set out for a given point, not to go promiscuously, but to go toward a definite place. The suggestion of the word is that of traveling toward a goal. That is the root idea. From that word another was derived, meaning a limit, the conclusion of the journey, the destination of the traveler, the place toward which the journey was taken; and so the word came to mean a termination, a result, and ultimately, a purpose. From that word was derived the word which is translated "perfect" in this passage. The word therefore means realization, arrival at a destination, the state of being at the limit toward which the start was made.

In classic Greek this word was used of adults, as distinguished from infants, or children undergoing discipline. It was also used in the religion of Greece of those who were initiated into the mysteries; those who had passed beyond the novitiate were perfected, that is, they had arrived, they had reached the goal, the limit toward which they set out when they became novices.

In the New Testament this word occurs only in my text, and in one other place in the gospels, where our Lord said to the rich young ruler, "If thou wouldest be perfect, go, sell that thou hast and give to the poor"; if thou wouldest arrive at thy goal, come to fulfilment of that toward which thou hast been moving, crown everything that has preceded; then yield thyself to My control by sweeping out all that hinders, "sell that thou hast . . . and come, follow Me." In the epistles it is found over and over again. It is there used constantly of those who are ethically adult, not complete in the sense of including everything that is intended by the being, and excluding everything that is not of the being; but grown-up, adult, having arrived at a definite goal. Such is the word, "Ye therefore shall be perfect," not babes ethically, not youths and maidens, but full-grown men.

The varying value of the word is illustrated by our word "perfect." We are conscious of the natural ambiguity of that word. We always need to interpret it by the subject of which it is used. It is not a word that always means exactly the same thing; it cannot. Here is a baby in its mother's arms. Is it perfect? Ask the mother. Meet the baby seventeen years hence, a youth. Is he perfect? Ask the youth. Add another four, five, half a dozen years, he is a man. Is he perfect? Ask the woman he considers perfect. Perfect as babe, perfect as boy, perfect as man; but always room for growth, advancement, development.

Perfect, then, means arrival at one particular stage of completeness, not the impossibility of procedure from that stage to another. Perfection is the reaching of a given limit. When that given limit is reached, there may be a new enterprise, a new vision luring to new heights, and so consequently a new process toward a larger perfection.

We are by this consideration brought fact to face with the supreme difficulty, in the presence of which men have halted, have indulged in criticism, and have attempted to escape the force of the word of Christ, that of the consciousness of the necessary difference between the perfection of God and our perfection. All that we need for the moment is a recognition of the fact that in each case we must interpret by the subject of which we use the defining term. There are certain senses in which it would be absurd to imagine we can ever be perfect with the perfection of God. Therefore, all such senses are necessarily and properly excluded from our consideration. Our Lord, in infinite condescension, used this particular word "perfect" of God in order to accommodate to human understanding a great principle of human life and conduct. So much then for the abstract idea.

Before we consider in separation the perfection of the Father and the perfection of the sons, it is of the utmost importance that we remember that the statement of Jesus has as its central value the suggestion of likeness, and that most definitely. As your heavenly Father, that is *just as* your Father, *exactly like* your Father is perfect. That is not unwarranted emphasis. Whereas there are things we shall necessarily have to eliminate from our consideration, in the matter to which Christ was drawing attention He used the strongest word possible as He demanded on the part of His subjects perfection like the perfection of God.

The consideration of the two perfections will emphasize the difference. The perfection of the Father, the perfection of the sons, these terms marking distinction which must be multiplied by the difference between the Divine and the human.

Admitting that fact of difference, it is ours to look for the likeness which our Lord intended, for in the discovery of that likeness is the supreme value of our meditation.

What, then, is the perfection of the Father to which our Lord referred? This word "perfect" is never elsewhere used of God in the whole of the New Testament. It was manifestly an accommodation on the part of Christ. A great subject is suggested at this point, which is quite aside from our theme. I am more and more impressed, however, as I study these gospel narratives, with our Lord's choice of words. I suppose we are all undergoing a very interesting and profitable revolution in regard to the language of the New Testament as the result of the work of Deissman and others. This, however, is helping us to see more clearly with what accuracy and delicacy our Lord made use of words. He never spoke of His Father by this word on any other occasion. No New Testament writer ever dared to use this word of God. It was, I repeat, a manifest accommodation in order to teach some central lesson.

If the word means reaching a goal toward which a man has traveled, then immediately it cannot have any application to God, for essentially God has no goal toward which He travels. In the fact of His essential being God knows nothing of infancy in His own being, nothing of youth, nothing of age. The vision of Daniel, while poetic, is at the same time strangely illuminative, expressed in the figure that always arrests us, "the Ancient of Days." God, if I may use such poor human words, is always adult in the mystery of His own being. He is taking no journey toward a larger perfection. His perfection is absolute and final and eternal. Yet our Lord spoke of Him here by a word which is entirely on the human level, accommodating His word to the necessity of His teaching. Therefore it is evident that the word "perfect," when used of the Father must be interpreted by the limitations of the context. Moreover, Christ's use of the word is so closely associated with something He had said a moment before that we are compelled so to interpret it.

To diligent students of the whole teaching of our Lord —those who to-day are standing in a place of far greater privilege than these men occupied who were listening to Him —the interpretation of Fatherhood may be, for certain purposes, much wider. We have all that He said about the Father, we have all that He revealed concerning the Father, and we may, nay we must, take all into account when we desire to know God.

For the present purpose I confine myself to the Manifesto. In this Manifesto, of which our text is, as we have said, the crystallized declaration of requirement and resource, these are the things He taught about the Father. First, that He is in the heavens. I cannot help feeling that we lose a great deal sometimes by not being more literal in our translation. Our Lord said, Your Father which is *in the heavens;* He taught us to pray, "Our Father which art *in the heavens,*" always in the plural. I should not like to base any very definite doctrine on that, but it is at least suggestive of the omnipresence of God and the immanence of God, that He is as nigh as the very heavens of the atmosphere in which we live, and as far as the ultimate reach of the final heaven. In this Manifesto He also made these simple declarations concerning God: Your Father seeth, Your Father knoweth, Your Father feedeth. Yet all this is but the atmosphere, not finally revealing the perfection of God to which our Lord referred at this point, but helping us toward an understanding thereof.

Let us look back to some earlier words in this paragraph: "That ye may be sons of your Father which is in heaven: for He maketh His sun to rise on the evil and the good, and sendeth rain on the just and the unjust." Now connect these words with our text, "Ye therefore shall be perfect, as, *just as*, your Father in the heavens is perfect." Do not quarrel with that illustration. I did not choose it. It is the Lord's illustration. The particular words of my text rise straight out of it, and must be interpreted by it. It is of the essence and reality of the teaching of this particular passage. "Ye therefore," not "ye shall be perfect," but "Ye *therefore*." Wherefore? On what does the "therefore" depend, and from whence does it derive its strength and urgency? "Your Father . . . maketh His sun to rise on the evil and the good, and sendeth rain on the just and the unjust." That is a revelation of God. First, it is a revelation of beneficence. Make the word "beneficence" as great as it is; do not degrade it by the low level of our common use of it. When we use great words let us think great thoughts. Beneficence is well-doing, doing well to, doing good to. Your Father is beneficent toward man as man, whether he be evil or good, toward the unjust or the just. Behind the beneficence is benevolence, well-wishing.

That is the Divine perfection to which our Lord referred, love desiring the good of all men, love doing good to all men, love set on men irrespective of what they are in themselves, love for the evil as well as for the good, for the unjust as well as for the just. There comes to my mind a story from the earliest days of my preaching. I have often told it. I will tell it again. A boy in a Sunday-school class one day said to his teacher, Does God love naughty boys? Certainly not, said the teacher. What blasphemy! Yes, God does love naughty boys. God loves wicked men, in their wickedness, and out of the arch of His blue heaven makes His glorious sun to shine on them, and out of the secret chambers where the rain is generated sends it forth in beneficent floods on the unjust as well as on the just. Do not quarrel with the illustration, it is not mine. You might criticize this if I were imagining it, but it is Christ's definition of the Divine perfection. "Your Father . . . maketh His sun to rise on the evil and the good, and sendeth rain on the just and the unjust." That is our Lord's description of the perfection of God. It is the ultimate distinction of God, that He makes His sun to shine on the evil as well as on the good. In the Colossian letter we have a great word of Paul's applied to human conduct which is equally applicable here, "Love is the bond of perfectness." What does that word "bond" mean? Ask your medical man to explain it to you; he can do it better than I can, *sundesmos*, the ligaments of perfectness, holding all other things in unity and making them act harmoniously. The love of God is the bond of His perfections. Deny His love, and what, then, of His justice? How hard it will be, like the justice of man! What, then, of His holiness? How impossible for a man as man ever to find His way into it, to climb toward the light of it. Love is the bond of perfectness in God, and our blessed Master and King caught this one song out of the infinite music, and sang it to the ages. This is the Divine perfection, that He "maketh His sun to rise on the evil and the good, and sendeth rain on the just and the unjust."

What, then, is the perfection of the sons to which our Lord is calling us? "Ye shall be perfect" exactly as your Father is perfect. Mark the idea of perfection thus interpreted. Again I pray you remember the necessary distinction between a father and sons multiplied by the difference between God and man. While remembering that, let us emphasize the thought of likeness. Christ said to His subjects, You must be ethically full-grown. To be ethically full-grown is to be men of whom it is true that thoughts and words are mastered by love, men of whom it is true that action is always love-inspired. In our previous meditation we considered the fundamental word of Jesus, "Except your righteousness shall exceed the righteousness of the scribes and Pharisees, ye shall in no wise enter into the kingdom of heaven." The ultimate expression of that righteousness is love-mastered thinking, benevolence; and love-mastered activity, beneficence.

Take this whole Manifesto and see how the Lord interprets His own ideal. This word about love is the climax of our Lord's enunciation of laws as to earthly relationships. I glance back, and I find, first, the law of life as to murder and hatred; second, the law of purity as to the marriage relationship; third, the law of truth, that no man shall take any oath, but say yea, yea; the law of justice, that the man in His Kingdom shall overtake the demand of justice by such living as will make it forevermore unnecessary. The attitude toward human life as He describes it, the sacredness of the family, the preservation of the purity of the state; the attitude toward truth, the simple statement; the attitude toward justice. How are we going to fulfil these ideals? Only in love. Only out of life love-mastered can these things proceed.

This, then, is not a low standard. It is the ultimate, the highest of all ethical conceptions. Love is the secret of all righteousness, personal, social, national. That does not need arguing; it does need thinking about and remembering. Could war last for a single four-and-twenty hours if love mastered the peoples? That never will be until the King of love shall come and establish His Kingdom; but when He comes, that will be the issue. Every social problem that confronts us today would be solved if only we could make men live a life love-mastered. No sentinel is half so severe as love. If love stands sentinel in our lives, watching over our actions, we cannot lie, we cannot hate, we cannot slander. The measure of high and noble life is the measure of love-mastered life. How we admire that man who in company will not allow another man to be ill spoken of.

> Who steals my purse steals trash ...
> But he that filches from me my good name,
> Robs me of that which not enriches him,
> And makes me poor indeed.

Such a man is of all men most despicable, and the man who will not allow it to be done in his company is the man who is love-mastered.

Do not imagine that love is sentimental, sickly, mawkish, anæmic. If it were, then God deliver the world from it! Love is strong, virile, tremendous in its demands. Love makes demands on self. Love thinketh no evil, "rejoiceth not in unrighteousness, but rejoiceth with the truth; beareth all things, believeth all things, hopeth all things, endureth all things."

That is the God-like perfection which Christ demands, the love-mastered life which expresses itself in gifts bestowed on men without respect to what they are in themselves.

As I ponder these words, as I have pondered them in trying to understand our Lord's meaning, everything has at last gathered itself up for my own soul and my own heart into one question. I am not now so much speaking as a preacher, an expositor; I am telling you the things that have been happening in my own soul while I have been preparing for this service. As the light has shone on me, and I have caught His revelation of God in the perfection of His love, and have then heard Him say, You therefore shall be perfect exactly as your Father is perfect, the effect has been that I have been driven to the asking of one plain question: How?

For in the name of God, if that be the ideal it mocks my impotence. I grant its beauty and glory; I grant that if men live love-mastered lives all the problems are solved and righteousness is established. But how am I going to be perfect with that perfection, how am I to arrive at that ethically adult condition of life when I shall be mastered by love in my thinkings, in my wishings, in my judgments, in my actions? How?

The answer is in the text and in the context. I venture to suggest that our Lord might have used other figures of speech here. In some senses other figures of speech would have been as illuminative as this is, but they would have lacked exactly that thing which I am now feeling after. He might have said, "Ye shall therefore be perfect, as your King is perfect." Would not that have done? Yes, as the revelation of an ethic, but it would have lacked dynamic, it would have lacked the essential Christian secret. Your King makes His sun to shine on the evil and the good, and His rain to fall on the just and the unjust. Would not that have done? Quite perfectly for the revelation of an ethic, for the King is a King of love, but a King cannot give life to His subjects.

But our Lord did not use that figure, He used the figure of the Father, "that ye may be sons of your Father. Now the arresting word is not the word "perfect" but the word "Father." That is a word of hope, a word that woos me, a word that suggests dynamic as well as ethic! I go back to the beginning of the Manifesto and I find that the word first appears when our Lord was telling these very men the purpose for which they are called to high character, "Let your light shine before men, that they may see your good works, and glorify your Father which is in heaven." He never used that figure of speech again till He came to the climax, the love-mastered life, "That ye may be sons of your Father . . . ye therefore shall be perfect, as your heavenly Father is perfect." Then everything that followed thrilled with it. Take the sixth chapter at your leisure, and do what I did when I was reading just before coming to this service, put a red line under the word "Father." Life is to be lived before "your Father" and not before men to be seen of them. Your alms are to be given so that "your Father" may see them.

When you pray, get alone and pray to your Father, and your Father will reward you. When you pray, say, "Our Father." When you forgive men, remember your Father will forgive you if you forgive them. When you fast do it alone with your Father. Do not be anxious about the necessities of this life. Your Father feedeth the birds, and your "Father knoweth that ye have need of all these things."

So the music runs. The King is Father; the subjects are sons. And therein is suggested the central verity of the gospel of the Lord Jesus Christ, that He comes to give men not an ethic alone, but dynamic; not light on a pathway merely, but life enabling them to walk therein.

Such love of our fellow men must proceed out of life, and the Manifesto is not all the mission of the King. There was not merely the Mount of Light, whereon He enunciated the ethic that burns us:

> There is a green hill far away,
>   Outside a city wall,
> Where the dear Lord was crucified,
>   Who died to save us all.
>
> We may not know, we cannot tell
>   What pains He had to bear,
> But we believe it was for us
>   He hung and suffered there.
>
> He died that we might be forgiven,
>   He died to make us good,
> That we might go at last to heaven,
>   Saved by His precious blood.
>
> Oh dearly, dearly has He loved,
>   And we must love Him too,
> And trust in His redeeming blood,
>   And try His works to do.

CHAPTER XXV

THE SANCTIONS OF ORDINANCES

Is it lawful on the sabbath day to do good, or to do harm? to save a life, or to kill?

MARK 3:4.

THE STORY OF THE HEALING OF THE MAN WITH THE withered hand is part of a larger whole. Matthew, Mark, and Luke tell the story, and each places it in relation to the cornfield dispute about the Sabbath. Mathew and Mark read as though both events took place on the same Sabbath; Luke, however, distinctly says that the healing of the man with the withered hand was on another Sabbath. The difficulty in the mind of the enemies of Jesus, both in the cornfield and in the synagogue, was that of His apparent violation of the Sabbath. Moreover, there can be no escape from the conviction that this attitude on the part of Christ which caused their criticism and aroused their hostility, was definite and intended. In all the incidental wonders which He wrought He was moving quite definitely along the line of an illuminative and corrective mission. Whereas there can be no doubt that every incidental putting forth of His power was an expression of the compassion of His heart for needy men, the way in which he selected the hours and the occasions proves the larger purpose of His will. Not only did he heal this man on the Sabbath day, He also cast out an unclean spirit; probably on two separate occasions He healed Peter's wife's mother of a fever, He loosed the woman who had been bound in infirmity for many years, He healed the man with the dropsy, He gave sight to the man born blind, and He healed the man who had lain in the grip of infirmity for eight-and-thirty years, as He found Him in the porches of the Bethesda pool, all on the Sabbath. These workings of wonders on the Sabbath day were all wrought in the atmosphere of conflict concerning the Sabbath. We find not merely the story of the deed recorded and the declaration made that it took place on the Sabbath; we also find, side by side with these statements, the account of how He challenged them or they challenged Him. I repeat that He definitely violated the Sabbath according to their conceptions of the Sabbath.

The meaning of this maintained and definite attitude on the part of our Lord is revealed very clearly in these two stories: the story of the disciples in the cornfields on the Sabbath plucking the ears of corn and Christ answering the criticism of the Pharisees, and the story of how, on coming into this synagogue, He entered into discussion with them and then healed the man with the withered hand.

I propose asking you to fasten your attention with me on this story of the healing of the man with the withered hand, not so much in order that we may observe its wonderful teaching concerning the method of Jesus with individual cases, but in order that we may consider this attitude of Jesus, and endeavor to understand His meaning, and apply the values to ourselves.

First, I am going to trespass on your patience as I attempt very rapidly to reconstruct the story from the three accounts that we have; I read them of set purpose. I maintain that here as elsewhere in the gospels these stories are not contradictory but complementary. Each man told the story from his own standpoint quite simply, not necessarily giving all the details. The careful comparison of the three will enable us to see what happened, and so prepare us for the study of this particular word of Christ.

Matthew, Mark, and Luke tell of His entry into the synagogue, and of the fact that there, in the synagogue, was the man with the withered hand.

Mark and Luke tell us that when He went in, the Pharisees watched to see whether He would heal, that they might accuse Him. Yet in their watching they paid Him an unconscious compliment: they expected that He would heal. They already knew enough of Him to know that the one man of all the crowd of worshipers most likely to appeal to Him was the most needy man in the crowd, the man with the withered hand.

Matthew alone tells us that they not only watched Him, but challenged Him, "Is it lawful to heal on the sabbath day?"

Mark and Luke declare that then Jesus first called the man to stand out, called Him from the place that he occupied in the synagogue, and that the man came forward, and standing in the midst where he might be observed, became the center of observation.

Matthew tells us—and I believe it was at this point that it happened—that when the man stood forth in the midst, Jesus asked two preliminary questions, "What man shall there be of you that shall have one sheep, and if this fall into a pit on the sabbath day, will he not lay hold on it, and lift it out? How much then is a man of more value than a sheep?"

Mark and Luke tell us that He answered their question by asking a question. They had said, "Is it lawful to heal on the sabbath day?" He asked "Is it lawful on the sabbath day to do good, or to do harm? to save a life, or to kill?"

Matthew alone tells us that He added to that this word, "It is lawful to do good on the sabbath day."

Continuing to follow the course of events, we find that Mark and Luke declare that He "looked round about on them." Mark alone interprets the look in the words, "being grieved at the hardening of their heart."

The three evangelists then declare that Jesus addressed Himself to the man in the terms of an impossible command, "Stretch forth thy hand." Immediately the man obeyed and was healed, Matthew adding that beautiful touch of comparison, that the hand "was restored whole, as the other."

Luke tells us of the madness of His enemies, and of the fact that they communed as to what course to pursue.

Matthew and Mark declare that they went out and took counsel to destroy Him.

From that narrative let us now take three central words. First, their question, "Is it lawful to heal on the sabbath day?" Second, His argument, "Is it lawful on the sabbath day to do good, or to do harm? to save a life, or to kill?" Finally, His answer, "It is lawful to do good on the sabbath day." Once again, narrowing our outlook, our text is the argument of Jesus in that atmosphere.

If as the result of that grouping of the records, we see that crowd of hostile souls, that man with the withered hand standing in the midst, and that lonely and imperial figure of the Lord; if we understand that the mental mood of the rulers was that of questioning his attitude toward the Sabbath, and if we see Him violating the Sabbath according to their view, we shall be a little nearer the heart of the theme.

I now leave their question and His final answer, and confine myself to His argument, "Is it lawful on the sabbath day to do good, or to do harm? to save a life, or to kill?" Listening to that argument there are three things I desire to impress on your attention. Therein I discover, first, a remarkable revelation of our responsibility in the presence of all human need. Second, in that argument I discover an equally remarkable revelation of the true value of ordinances, especially Divine ordinances, the Sabbath being the illustration. Finally, in that argument, I find the ultimate test of religion.

First, then, as to the revelation of responsibility in the presence of human need. Let us go back to the synagogue. Taking the case of the man as typical, we see him disabled, incompetent, and suffering. All students of the New Testament, and of the method of the Master's ministry, are familiar with the constant merging of matters material and spiritual in His actions. The physical was always both sign and symbol of spiritual condition. We see in this man with the withered hand, a type of humanity disabled, incompetent, suffering. We shall miss the whole value of our study unless we fasten our eyes resolutely upon that man in this way. We need not travel back to the synagogue, he is in this house; we meet him every day in office, store, shop, professional walk. The children of the King, the disciples of Christ, the servants of God, are constantly face to face with the man with the withered hand, the withered heart, the withered soul, spiritually disabled, spiritually incompetent, spiritually suffering; and over and over again spiritual disability, incompetence, suffering, reveal themselves in physical disability, incompetence, suffering. All human need was focused, suggested, symbolized, by the man in the synagogue whose right hand was withered. What, then, is our responsibility in the presence of that man?

I pray you listen to that which to me is the most arresting, startling, marvelous thing in my text. Said Jesus, with that man standing there: "Is it lawful on the sabbath day to do good or to do harm? to save a life or to kill?" Mark most carefully the startling alternative that Christ suggested: "To do good, or to do harm? To save a life, or to kill?" That is the most disturbing of revelations to the complacent negativism which so often passes to-day for vital Christianity.

There is the man with the withered hand, the incompetent man, on the highway, or in the synagogue; if you see him, you either do him good or do him harm, you either stretch out a hand to save him, or you help to kill him.

The average Christian man, to say nothing of the man of the world, is in revolt against this alternative of Christ. He says: I am doing nothing to help, but I am not harming. I have not stretched out a hand to save the man, but I have done nothing to kill him. That is not Christ's outlook. It may be that refined paganism imagines it can be neutral in the presence of human incompetence, but Christ says not to help is to harm, to fail to stretch out the hand of love is to have complicity with the forces that destroy. That is the heart of the argument. It is the revelation of Christ's attitude toward humanity, of God's attitude in the presence of human incompetence and sorrow. God is such that in the presence of human sorrow He must either help or harm, and harm He cannot; He must either save or kill, and kill He cannot; and therefore we have Calvary, the Cross of His blood, the breaking of His heart, the sacrifice by which He lifts crushed, bruised, broken humanity and remakes it. Let no man name the Christian name and claim relationship to the Christian fact who in the presence of the incompetent man passes by and because he has not added another blow imagines he has fulfilled his Christian duty. To do harm or to do good, to save or to kill, are the graphic, drastic, startling alternatives of Jesus.

Of course, all this must be interpreted by the measure of our ability to do good or to save life. In the strict economy of Divine justice we shall be judged by that measure. I do not say that unless I can save a man I kill him. I do say that when I stand in the presence of need, unless I put forth what power I have to help toward salvation, then in the measure of the help withheld I harm and hinder. To leave the man stranded on the highway when my hand stretched out to him would have helped him but one yard toward home and health and God is to be guilty of his further sinning and further failing. This is the startling alternative of the text, revealing in a most remarkable way our responsibility in the presence of human need. If the man with the withered hand lives with us, lives in our neighborhood, and if we who bear the Christian name and wear the Christian sign pass him, and merely look and pass on, upon us lies part of the guilt of his ultimate undoing. It is that conception of responsibility which was the inspiration of Christ's perpetual violation of the false view of the Sabbath, and we naturally turn therefore to our second consideration.

We have in this text, then, second, the revelation of the true value of ordinances. Take the sabbath as the type, for that was the matter at issue in this story. I go back for one moment to the story preceding this, for in that story our Lord uttered words concerning these men which are vital to our consideration. When the Pharisees criticized His disciples for plucking the ears of corn, among other things Jesus said to them, "The sabbath was made for man, and not man for the sabbath." Those familiar with the Greek New Testament will remember that in that particular phrase we have the Greek preposition *dia*, which I think we have somewhat loosely translated by our preposition *for*: "the sabbath was made *for* man." *Dia* used with the accusative always has one significance, therefore I make no apology for reading the text in another way, "The sabbath was brought into being as the result of man and not man as the result of the sabbath"; or perhaps I might take another slightly different method of translation and read the text thus, "The sabbath was brought into being on account of man, and not man on account of the sabbath." That is the fundamental word.

There are certain things of interest in this statement to which I refer only in passing. You will notice that our Lord said, The Sabbath was made for man, not just for the Jew. Much controversy to-day about the Sabbath is due to the fact that we look on it as a Hebrew institution. According to the Bible, the Sabbath is older than the Hebrew institution. The Sabbath was made for man, it was made as the result of man; man first, the Sabbath second, not the Sabbath first and man consequently.

Here we are at the root of the whole question as to the place and value of ordinance. If, indeed, the Sabbath was made on account of man, as a result of man, for man in that sense, it must never be desecrated by being made an instrument of harm to men, by being made a reason for helping to kill a man. There is the incompetent, disabled, suffering man! What is my duty to him? To help him, to heal him, to save him. But it is the Sabbath! Is he therefore for twelve or four-and-twenty hours to suffer his agony? That is the blasphemy of all blasphemies. The Sabbath was called into being on account of man, and not man on account of the Sabbath. If I may attempt to gather up what seems to me to be the intense and remarkable light of this word of Jesus and express it in a brief way, I would do it thus: *the sanctity of the Sabbath must not destroy its sanctions.*

What are the sanctions of the Sabbath? The well-being of man. If you take the Sabbath and make it so sacred and separate that you allow a man to continue to bear his burden alone without attempting to help him, you are making the sanctity of the day destroy the sanctions on which it rests.

So with every ordinance. I need not say human ordinances, for I have little care concerning them. I would break them all with pleasure. I care nothing for human ordinances. I am speaking of higher things, I am speaking of Divine ordinances. There are not very many, according to the New Testament; but there are some. There is the ordinance of preaching; I do not hesitate to call it an ordinance. There are the ordinances of prayer, and of worship; there are the ordinances of Christian baptism, and of the supper of the Lord. Over all these New Testament ordinances, so finely independent of the trivialities of ritualism and so instinct with abounding life and spirituality, high and sacred as they are, we must write this dictum of Jesus: These were called into being on account of man and not man on account of them.

What is the meaning of preaching? Preaching is not an institution to which man shall be compelled to attend in order to live; preaching is an institution for the proclamation of the living word of God that men may live and thrive and grow thereby. It is made for man, not man for it.

What is the institution of prayer? Why is the Church called on to be a priesthood? What is the meaning of intercession? It is not something ordained, which man must use in order that *it* may continue. Prayer is ordained for man, for his healing, for his helping, that he may come nearer God. For these purposes the ordinance of prayer has been established.

For what end is worship ordained? Now we are getting back very near to our story, to the synagogue, the temple, and so very near to this hour, and this building. What is the place of worship for? Worship is ordained for man and not man for it. The ultimate purpose of our worship and our gathering together for worship is the healing and helping of humanity by bringing humanity into living, vital, relationship with God. God is not demanding that man shall conform simply in order to fulfil an institution that He has created. He made the institution that men in it and through it may find their way to Him. So also with baptism and the supper of the Lord. All ordinances are made for man, and if we are making any Christian ordinance an excuse for leaving some man half-dead on the highway while we observe it, we are blaspheming the sanctions of the ordinance, and so are sinning against God.

Take the Sabbath again as test. In the economy of God the Sabbath is the true test of our understanding of the Sabbath. God's Sabbath is the day for rest and worship. But there in the synagogue is a man with a withered hand. What am I going to do with that man because it is the hour of rest and worship? Let him suffer? Therein is proof that I do not understand the Sabbath. In the presence of that man it is my duty to break the Sabbath, give up my rest, turn from the holy shrine of worship to the holier shrine of service to help him. By so doing I keep Sabbath according to the Divine purpose.

I go further and declare that the Sabbath is the test of our conception of God. Let us return to the cornfield once more, to listen to something that Jesus then said to these men on the question of the sabbath. The words are recorded in Matthew, "If ye had known what this meaneth, I desire mercy and not sacrifice, ye would not have condemned the guiltless." In that word Christ declared that the very method they adopted for defense of the Sabbath was demonstration of their ignorance of God. They did not understand mercy. If you had understood God and the passion of His heart, said Jesus, in effect, you would not have blamed the guiltless.

In the light of this great word of Jesus it becomes our bounden duty to test all our ordinances and arrangements. The test of the church is the man with the withered hand. If to the church no such man comes it is for one reason and one only, that Christ is not there. To the church Christocentric, gathered about the living Lord, the man with the withered hand will surely come. If he be not in the midst, it is because Christ is not there. Let it be known that the loving, tender, strong, mighty, saving Christ is in the midst, and the incompetent, disabled, palsied, spiritually defeated will come. They become the test of the church. If the ordinances and organizations are so perfect that there is no time for them, or if to deal with them would violate the regularity of the sanctuary, then the sanctuary is a sepulcher and of no use to God or man. That is the supreme test of the church's life and the church's work, and of all ordinances.

So I come finally to notice that this text offers the final test of religion. We fix our attention no longer on the man with the withered hand, but on the rulers. Look on these rulers, only let us look at them as Jesus saw them. There is nothing more remarkable in these stories than the emphasis laid on the fact that He looked at them before He healed the man. I draw your attention to the fact that Mark interpreted the look in the words "being grieved at the hardening of their hearts." So remarkable is that declaration, so full of awful light, that one almost trembles to make any attempt at exposition. He looked at them with anger. Do not minimize the word, I pray you. Let us have done with all this soft sentimentality that imagines that Christ was incapable of anger. The word "anger" here suggests the sudden stretching out of the hand in a passion that is active and moves toward punishment.

But just as I am arrested by the flaming fire that flashes from the eyes of the looking Christ, fire that is evidently the fire of actual anger with these rulers, Mark leads me behind the anger in the mind of Christ and writes for me the strange and startling word, "*being grieved.*" The Greek word there is a striking word, and this is the only place in the New Testament where it occurs. We find it again and again in Classical Greek, but nowhere else in the New Testament. Expositors and scholars have come to the conclusion that the only word by which you can convey its meaning is our word *condolence*. What is condolence? Just *grief with*. Condolence is in its truest sense that which I feel with you when you are in the midst of grief. The mystery deepens. He was grieved with whom? They were not grieved. They had no sense of shame. He was in sympathy with all that must inevitably come in the moment of their awaking to the unutterable folly and failure of their own attitudes. *Grief with* them was His fathoming of their sin to its deadly depth and its unutterable darkness. It was the Cross of Calvary, the passion of God manifesting itself in the midst of human failure.

Now observe the reason of that anger and that grief. Because of the hardening of their heart, not because of the hardness of their heart as the Authorized Version renders it, but, far more accurately, because of the hardening of their heart. It was not merely grief over a condition, it was grief over a process. The word "hardening" there is a word that describes a process, the process by which the extremities of a fractured bone are united by a callus. Not the hardness, but the hardening. They were hardening their own heart. If we see these men set in this light we see that they were allowing a false religious conviction to dry up the springs of emotion in the presence of the man with the withered hand; they were allowing prejudice in favor of a false conviction to stifle the conviction that He came to bring them, the conviction of what their attitude ought to be in the presence of all human need. That is the picture of the rulers.

How far are we guilty of their sin? We are verily guilty if for us the Sabbath stifles compassion, if we are so eager to fulfil the obligations of worship that we have no time to stretch out a hand to help the man who needs our help. If we feel that it is more important that we should pray than that we suffer to serve and save, then verily are we guilty. We are guilty of awful sin when worship fails to inspire service. If in coming to this house we have observed the duty of a day, and entered into the realm of rest, and there shall abide with us on the morrow no driving, inspiring impulse to rescue the perishing and care for the dying, then this hour of worship is the most disastrous instrument for hardening the human heart, deadening its emotion, destroying its spirituality. When slavery to the letter denies the spirit, when loyalty to the sanctity undermines the sanctions, then are we guilty of the very sin of these rulers.

In the measure in which we are guilty, Christ's attitude toward us is the same as was His attitude toward these rulers. He is grieved, He is angry, He is already on the threshold, leaving the synagogue; and we can recall Him only as we consent to violate professional regularity in the interest of the compassion of the Kingdom of God.

I pray that this great truth, burning, scorching, arresting the soul, may flame before us in the midst of all our worship. Not to minister, even to our own highest spiritual need, does this building exist; or, if it do, then verily it is a sepulcher; but for the sake of the man with the withered hand, for the sake of the man with the withered heart, for the sake of the man with the withered soul, paralyzed, incompetent, undone, that we may help, heal, remake; and to that end and that end alone Christ abides in the midst.

CHAPTER XXVI

PEACE AMONG MEN OF GOD'S PLEASURE

> *Glory to God in the highest,*
> *And on earth peace among men in whom*
> *He is well pleased.*
>
> LUKE 2:14.

THESE WORDS CONSTITUTED THE ANGELIC ANTHEM OF WELcome to the New Race. The angel messenger had told the shepherds of "a babe wrapped in swaddling clothes, and lying in a manger." In this chorus the angels expressed their understanding of the significance of the event, "Glory to God in the highest." The term "in the highest" does not signify degree but location; "the highest" in the text stands in contrast to the earth, not necessarily separated from it, but suggesting the fact of the two spheres, earth and heaven.

> Glory to God in the *highest,*
> And *on earth* peace among men in whom
> He is well pleased.

This was more than the song that celebrated the birth of the Babe; it was the song that celebrated the race which was to result from the birth of the Babe. The terms are quite explicit: peace, not toward men, but among men. However much we may differ about the translation and interpretation of that which remains of the passage, about this there is no doubt, that it is not peace or good will *toward* men, but *among* men—peace among men in whom He is well pleased. That is at once the limitation of the thought and the indication of the true region of peace.

The significance of the song which the angels sang will be discovered in recognition of the Biblical teaching concerning the interest which angels have taken in this world of ours. Their first song about the world, according to Biblical revelation, is recorded in the book of Job, in that wonderful passage of the Theophany or unveiling of God before the astonished vision of His servant, tried, buffeted and bruised by temptation. In the course of that great unveiling it is declared that when God laid the cornerstone of the earth,

> The Morning stars sang together
> And all the sons of God shouted for joy.

You will remember that Milton couples these songs—the song of creation and the song of the Advent of the Saviour—in the great hymn of the Nativity, when he sings:

> Such music (as 'tis said),
> Before was never made.
>   But when of old the sons of morning sang
> While the Creator great
> His constellations set,
>   And the well-balanced word on hinges hung
> And cast the dark foundations deep
> And bid the welt'ring waves their oozy channel keep.

Such is the first Scripture suggestion about angel interest. They sang in creation.

If Faber was right when he sang that

> There is no place where earth's sorrows
> Are more felt than up in heaven,

then angel sons had surely merged from the major shoutings of creation's dawn into minor wailings in view of the miseries of men resulting from their sin. I immediately say to you that I think Faber was quite right, that there is no place where earth's sorrows are more felt than up in heaven. All sorrow there is transfigured by the light that we know not yet; all sorrow there is modified, and experienced within its relationship to the infinite movements; but sorrow is surely there, for it is in the heart of God Himself in the presence of human suffering and misery. I repeat, I verily believe that often the angels had sung in minor wailing over the miseries of men.

Now at last, as the angel said to the shepherds, "there is born . . . in the city of David a Saviour, which is Christ the Lord." To those angel singers the One born was "a second man," "the last Adam." In the view of the angels his birth was a new commencement in human history. From that child lying in the manger they saw a new race springing, and in celebration of the new race they raised their anthem:

> Glory to God in the highest,
> And on earth peace among men in whom
> He is well pleased.

The first note of the anthem was a recognition of the Source of the New Movement, "Glory to God in the highest." The central note celebrated the issue which had happened that day, "on earth peace." The final note revealed the condition of realization, "among men in whom He is well pleased."

If thus, in this anthem, we discover the note of limitation, and surely it is here, let us remember that the limitation is but declared in order to reveal the condition on which the ultimate purpose may be realized. There can be no question that at last the men of His good pleasure, the men in whom He is well pleased, will be men of all kindreds and races, that, at last, "though a wide compass first be fetched," His victory is secure; that, although the process may be one of conflict and long and painful struggle in the history of the world, yet finally the note of the angel anthem will be found to be the chord of the dominant, and all the music of human conditions will be true to its suggestion.

Let us briefly consider these three things in a slightly different order: first, the issue described, "on earth peace"; second, the condition revealed, "among men in whom He is well pleased"; and, finally, in a closing and brief word, the source suggested, "Glory to God in the highest."

First, then, "on earth peace." Is it not difficult to understand that word? Probably not, in our own hearts and personal experiences as Christian men and women; for already all such as have reposed their trust in this Lord Christ know something of that peace of God which passeth all understanding. But if we look away from these personal experiences, and endeavor to enter into the consciousness of our own times and of the conditions in the midst of which we live, is it not almost impossible to understand this phrase, "on earth peace"? That is to say, the ideal seems far from realization. If we contrast all that is suggested by this phrase with all that we find in history, how startling is the difference between peace and the perpetual conflict and unrest, the pain and suffering of the world. I do not desire to dwell particularly on matters that are wholly immediate and local, and yet we are all painfully conscious of the actual condition of the world. We are all conscious, for instance, of the fact that the world's national peace is a mockery and a sham, that it is merely an armed neutrality based on suspicion. We are all terribly, and more acutely, conscious of the fact that the very peace of our own life is often rudely broken in on by the shock of strife and catastrophe. Where is peace?

Without staying to deal with other of the evidences of immediate unrest, let us take a broader outlook, and I think a deeper inlook, and inquire what are the underlying reasons of the restlessness of the world? I should be inclined to summarize them thus. First of all—this would not be put first by many, but Christian men must put it first—a moral malady without remedy, that is the profoundest reason of human restlessness. Consequent on that there is the fact of suffering without succor, and often without sympathy. And finally we have the fact of death without hope. Of course, in Christian experience death is not without hope, but neither is suffering without succor, for moral malady is not without remedy. But death without hope is the world outlook; I am not for the moment referring to the larger and more terrible fact of death merging into some experience beyond yet more awful; but to the hard fact of death with its severance, its breaking of ties, and ending of companionship, with no certainty of anything beyond; for there is no certainty apart from Christ. These are the reasons for unrest.

Moral malady without remedy, conflict everywhere between good and evil, between principle and passion. Man is in the midst of conflict, plunged into it at his birth. Whatever theory he may have of the universe, and whatever his philosophy may be, he is face to face with this conflict in his own nature, in his city, in his nation, in the world from the beginning; with this most appalling fact, that victory seems to be forever on the side of evil, "wrong forever on the throne." The outcome is perpetual unrest.

Suffering without succor. Without any attempt now to account for suffering, we recognize that it is here. There is the suffering of poverty—and never believe any man who tells you that poverty is a blessing in the economy of God. It is not so. It would be as untrue as to say that disease comes from God. These things may be overruled by God in the great economy of His grace, and be made instruments by which He perfects character; but poverty has no place in the economy of God for man. But its pain is here. There are also the sufferings of sickness and of persecution. And in Nature there is no proof of the Divine sympathy. Lift out of human history this Christ-child Whose birth we celebrate to-day, take this Christian fact out of the world, and we cannot prove that God has any sympathy with humanity. The sun will shine as brightly on your dead child as on your living, loving one. Nature will shed no tears for your agony. Poets talk about nature weeping; but in the day of heartbreak nature will prove nothing to you of the tenderness and compassion of God. There are multitudes of souls to-day suffering without any consciousness of sympathy, and without any immediate succor.

Death without hope. Philosophy has no proof of immortality. In the submerging of the soul in unuttterable agony a man will cry out, "If a man die, shall he live again?" That is an inquiry, but, as in the case of Job, it constantly merges into the wail of unutterable despair, without hope or a gleam of light. We have no proof of immortality if this Christ-child was not born. If all this story is myth, then the world has no sure evidence of a life beyond. These are the things that create the unrest of humanity.

But let us turn to the other side of the matter, and inquire what is peace. Peace is, first, moral rectitude, a perfect ethic combined with a sufficient dynamic, and resulting in a conscience void of offense. That is peace.

Or, again, peace is joy without alloy, the result of an inclusive outlook, the measurement of the part by the whole, the ability to sing "Light after darkness"; and, consequently, a heart full and strong, firm and steady, in the midst of problems which are not yet solved.

Or inclusively, what is peace? Eternal life is peace, the secret of the ages, the transfiguration of death, a spirit homed in God. Such is the experience of peace.

The angels sang "on earth peace." Peace can come only

as there shall come to men who are conscious of moral malady without remedy the remedy for that malady. Peace can come only to men who are conscious of suffering without succor or sympathy that is more than sentiment, as there comes to them the succor that takes hold of suffering and transmutes the sorrow into joy, and gives them the assurance that not here and now is all of that which is here and now, but that the ultimate meanings lie beyond, and that in the economy of God they are meanings of perfect realization. Peace can come only to a world where death confronts men, when, somehow, death can be transfigured, and men cease to speak of death, and talk, instead of decease, of exodus, going out. Peace can come only when death is no longer looked on as a harbor of refuge into which the ship all battered escapes, but rather as the harbor from which the ship puts out to sea and finds the ultimate fulfilment of all being. These are Christian ideals, and can be realized by men only when they enter into Christian experience.

We now turn to that which is central to this meditation, the suggestion of the angels concerning the condition of peace, "peace among men in whom He is well pleased."

This song was sung, first, because of the birth of the Babe. I take up this gospel in which alone the song is recorded, which is peculiarly the gospel portraying the perfection of Jesus of Nazareth, and I trace the story through a little way in order that we may catch the fuller meaning of the angel song, "Glory to God in the highest, and on earth peace among men in whom He is well pleased."

I turn to the fortieth verse of the first chapter, and I read:

> And the child grew, and waxed strong, filled with wisdom: and the grace of God was upon him.

That was twelve years afterwards, measuring the life by human measurements.

I run on down the same chapter to the fifty-second verse; eighteen more years have passed, thirty years from the hour of the angel song, and now I read:

> Jesus advanced in wisdom and stature, and in favour with God and man.

I go a little further in this wonderful story of His life and I read in the third chapter, verse twenty-two:

> A voice came out of heaven, Thou art My beloved Son; in Thee I am well pleased.

Why, then, was the song sung? Because there in the manger lying was the Babe in Whom God was well pleased, which does not suggest that God is not well pleased in the presence of every child, every babe, but which does suggest a difference. It suggests this initial fact of absolute perfection, a new beginning in human history, a strange wonder never to be finally understood. There was the Child, the first of a new race. There is a sense to-day in which any child that lies in its mother's arms, every little one, is dear to His heart, dearer than to the mother who nurses it. But there were peculiar facts about this Child. As a Boy the grace of God was on Him; as a Man of thirty it is declared that He had grown in favor with God and man. Then Luke tells us that the heavens were opened and a voice declared, Here is the Man in Whom I am well pleased. In Him, then, there is peace, for peace is among men in whom He is well pleased.

And still further we follow the story as Luke tells it, and in the first and second verses of the fourth chapter we read:

> And Jesus, full of the Holy Spirit, returned from the Jordan, and was led by the Spirit in the wilderness during forty days, being tempted of the devil.

There He mastered all temptations.

Still reading on in order to discover the music that follows the angelic anthem, we find in the fourteenth verse of the same chapter:

And Jesus returned in the power of the Spirit.

He went to service and to sacrifice, until, let it be reverently stated, "He offered Himself through the eternal Spirit." All the way from the beginning to the end we see the Man in Whom God is well pleased.

Thus we see peace, focused in one human being, peace in the Man in whom God was well pleased. He was a lowly Man, at first a Babe, then a Boy, then a Man, and through all a Servant. One Who went to death in the fulfilment of His service; and all the way He was a Man of peace.

Now, do not let us be anxious for the moment about the ultimate application of all this, but let us earnestly behold this Man of Nazareth, the Man of peace. If there is one thing more certain than anything else in the revelation of Jesus in these gospels it is that of His peace. In neither of these gospel stories can we find any occasion, any circumstance, any hour, in which He was perturbed. Always He is the Man of peace.

When we come to the final scenes—and I cannot tell you why it is so, but I never come to Christmas now without feeling that the cradle and the Cross are close together—I cannot think of Him Who came and rejoice in His coming without thinking of the ultimate in the mystery of His passion; I say, when we come to those last tragic scenes, we find that the One human being, undisturbed, quiet, and strong, was the Man of peace, not the priests, who were determined to ensure His murder, not the cool, dispassionate Roman Procurator Pilate, who was strangely perturbed; but Jesus only was quiet and at peace.

What was this experience of His peace? A perfect and

perpetual victory over sin, the constant transmutation of suffering in His own life, so that under the very shadow of the Cross in the midst of those paschal discourses He could say to His disciples, "My joy"; and, speaking of the deepest thing in His life, the annihilation of death, long ere He was apprehended and crucified, He had said, "I lay down My life, that I may take it again. No one taketh it away from Me, but I lay it down of Myself." Even on the holy mount, having come to the fulfilment of His humanity in the splendor of the metamorphosis, He spoke, not of the death He should die, but of the exodus He should accomplish. In these three things I find the secrets of His peace.

But is that all the angels meant? Nay verily! They sang not only of the Babe, but also of the race that was to spring from Him; not merely of peace in the Man of His good pleasure, but of "peace among men in whom He is well pleased."

Now let us turn from Luke to John, and in that gospel so brief in many respects, and yet so full of understanding of the deepest things in the life and ministry of our Lord, we find that in the midst of the paschal discourses, with the shadow of the Cross upon Him, and the last things close at hand, talking to a little group of men, He said:

"Peace I leave with you; My peace I give unto you: not as the world giveth give I unto you. Let not your heart be troubled, neither let it be fearful" (John 14:27).

And for these men that was the day when they were more troubled and afraid than they had ever been in their lives; it was the day when all the restlessness of the world seemed to be their portion, the day when hope was dying down and every gleam of light seemed wholly vanishing, the day when high and holy aspirations seemed doomed to utter disappointment in that He persisted in going out to die! Yet on that day He said, "Peace I leave with you; My peace I give unto you."

Then follow the next pages in the gospel of John, telling the story of dark days for them, days in which there came the end of all peace; the moral malady against which He had protested was victorious over Him, and He was murdered, suffering without succor finding its final expression in His untold sorrow, as they watched Him as long as they were able and then fled for very fear; death, which He had seemed to count as a small matter in the whole economy of life mastered Him, and He was put into the grave; and all that after He had said, "Peace I leave with you." I am in sympathy with these men in their sorrow and in their inevitable sense that peace was no more.

Now let us turn to the twentieth chapter. Here we find ourselves in the midst of a little company of terrified souls gathered in an upper room with doors locked. I have no criticism for them. I would have shared their fear. I think I would have been more fearful than they, and hardly been present at all. Suddenly standing in the midst is the same One, the Man of God's good pleasure. What is the first word that passes His lips? "Peace be unto you." It was His answer to their fear. And again in a few moments, "Peace be unto you." It was His preparation for their service. Eight days later, with Thomas the great believer present, again He said, "Peace be unto you." It was the call to faith.

From that moment the number of men of peace in the world was multiplied. Much later John wrote, "As He is, even so are we in this world." Was there ever such a daring word written under inspiration? Yet in this very matter of peace how true it was! The peacefulness of Christ's witnesses under persecution has been one of the world's perpetual wonders.

What created the peace that possessed these men and sent them out in the midst of the world's suffering and conflict and darkness? They shared His peace. What was His peace?

Victory over sin. The transmutation of suffering, so that these men—mark the true and deep mystery of the word in Acts—are seen "rejoicing that they were counted worthy to suffer dishonour for the Name." Finally, the annihilation of death, for when they write their letters these men will not speak of death as other men speak of death; they will take up His words and use them, and Peter will say, After my *exodus*, using the very word that Jesus used on the holy mount; and Paul will say, After my *departure*, that is my going away out into the larger life. These are the secrets of peace, "peace among men in whom He is well pleased."

In a final word, notice the suggestion of the angels concerning the source, "Glory to God in the highest." Salvation must come from God and not from man. Salvation must come out of the heavens to the earth; it cannot arise out of the earth and climb to the heavens. Therefore, glory to God is a necessity as it is a fact.

When the Babe was born a movement began that will issue in a race in which He is well pleased. That was the meaning of Christmas to the angels. Who is this Child? He is the Son of God, the Lord from heaven. He is also the Babe of the new race, Who, not by human will or act, laid hold on humanity and entered thereinto for a new beginning, for the accomplishment of the larger purposes of God. Those angels, then, sang o'er the plains of Bethlehem not of the Babe alone, but of the race.

Take this Christ away and all the conditions of unrest abide: moral malady without remedy, suffering without succor and with no proof of God's sympathy, and death as an appalling darkness out of which no ray of certain light shines and out of which no voice comes, and we still shall have to describe it as "the bourne whence no traveler returns." Take this Christ-child away, then, and peace is impossible.

But the Christ-child is not taken away. We are not

merely celebrating a far-off event, we are gathered around the presence of the living Lord Himself, and around all the great eternal facts focused, and rendered visible, by the mystery of Incarnation and by way of the Cross.

Consequently, if our trust is reposed in Him we are men of peace, we are men in whom God by grace is well pleased. Already in us He finds the forces of His own life and of the Son of His love; and He knows that the deepest facts of our lives are those, and that at last they will bring a perfect and final salvation and an eternal peace. Thus while yet we are in the midst of the clash of battle there is peace.

If you take this Christ away, have you any song to sing worth the singing? I know full well that the tragedy sometimes makes faith falter. I know what it is—and if there are those who do not, then let them be patient with me, for I speak not for myself alone—I know what it is in some hour of calamity to say, Where is God? But my question does not alter the calamity; and if I am allowing my unbelief to silence these angels, to hush these bells, to deny this music, then, God help me, what is life?

Oh, hear the song of the angels over all sighing humanity. We are celebrating to-day the infinite mystery, and mystery it is, of incarnate God. From it all light is streaming, and all songs are coming, all hope is flaming, and we believe that at last there shall be peace.

> Joy to the world! the Lord is come;
>   Let earth receive her King;
> Let every heart prepare Him room,
>   And heaven and nature sing.

www.ingramcontent.com/pod-product-compliance
Lightning Source LLC
Chambersburg PA
CBHW052143300426
44115CB00011B/1494